Analyzing Websites

SCIENCES

Computer Science, Field Directors –
Valérie Berthé and Jean-Charles Pomerol

Digital Documentation, Subject Head – Fabrice Papy

Analyzing Websites

Coordinated by
Luc Massou
Patrick Mpondo-Dicka
Nathalie Pinède

WILEY

First published 2023 in Great Britain and the United States by ISTE Ltd and John Wiley & Sons, Inc.

ISTE Ltd
27-37 St George's Road
London SW19 4EU
UK

www.iste.co.uk

John Wiley & Sons, Inc.
111 River Street
Hoboken, NJ 07030
USA

www.wiley.com

Library of Congress Control Number: 2023930464

British Library Cataloguing-in-Publication Data
A CIP record for this book is available from the British Library
ISBN 978-1-78945-103-0

ERC code:
PE6 Computer Science and Informatics
 PE6_10 Web and information systems, database systems, information retrieval and digital libraries, data fusion
SH3 The Social World, Diversity, Population
 SH3_12 Communication and information, networks, media
 SH3_13 Digital social research

Contents

Chapter 6. Analyzing the Mobilization Against the LPR on Twitter: Theoretical Issues and Methodological Challenges   131

Justine SIMON

Chapter 7. Metaphor and Analysis of Websites: Transformations of a Media Object 167
Pergia GKOUSKOU

Part 3. The Website as a Communication Device 191

Chapter 8. Thematic Analysis of Hyperlinks: A Taxonomic Approach 193
Nathalie PINÈDE

Foreword

Sébastien ROUQUETTE

*Communication et Sociétés, Université Clermont Auvergne,
Clermont-Ferrand, France*

In the age of social media, are websites outdated? To answer this question, all we need to do is look at the communication policies of different organizations. They all have decided to continue building and creating content for their sites. And there are many reasons why they are doing this. A website provides a structured way for an organization to communicate online, starting from an organized home page and a permanent menu. This gives the organization the opportunity to respond reactively to current events. It provides an opportunity to respond to requests from Internet users, who have come to expect that any sufficiently large organization will have at least one website to present itself to the world. It allows more in-depth communication at a lower cost.

In fact, the digitalization of our means of communication has created a new communications axiom: the more social media are created, the more vast and fragmented the digital public space is, the more necessary it is for every organization to have a communications tool that serves as a reference point. From Instagram and Facebook to Snapchat, TikTok, YouTube, Twitter or Pinterest, the constantly expanding number of social media outlets does not just mean that websites are not superfluous, it makes them increasingly necessary!

In this exponentially growing ocean of digital signs, the website acts as a "flagship" in organizations' communications strategies. It acts as a base and primary reference point for the communications strategy of the organization, to which the group's social media accounts and satellite sites will link and refer back. This is just

Analyzing Websites,
coordinated by Luc MASSOU, Patrick MPONDO-DICKA and Nathalie PINÈDE.
© ISTE Ltd 2023.

one of the many reasons that make it critically important to define a website strategy customized to the group's global communication policy, which is visible to and understandable by users. That's why the study of website strategies was analyzed in a previous book produced from a body of collective research: *Site internet : audit et stratégie*[1].

And now, Luc Massou, Patrick Mpondo-Dicka and Nathalie Pinède are expanding on this initial scientific work by coordinating this new book. The analyses of the websites presented here serve to perfect our understanding of websites from both a methodological angle and a pedagogical angle.

Given the rapid and dramatic changes in websites in the 2000s and 2010s, such as the mobile Internet, the development of online service platforms, the explosion of video content, addressing these issues is a difficult task. This requires consideration for the ever-increasing dimensions of websites: technical, graphic, aesthetic and social. Yet, this exercise has now become a necessity, given that the ability to design, analyze, and use a website are now frequently required professional skills.

However, one of the great qualities of this book coordinated by Luc Massou, Patrick Mpondo-Dicka and Nathalie Pinède is that it tackles these issues by following two essential guidelines.

The first is that no approach is to be excluded, whether theoretical or practical; whether semiological examinations, studies of enunciation, social semiotics or whether taking into account the pragmatic acquisition of digital culture or the challenges of data visualization. This collective effort avoids the pitfall of establishing a false dichotomy between operational and theoretical skill sets, as well as between ethical considerations and practical effectiveness, instead seeking to promote an opening for new knowledge. Affirming this fact does not imply that the contribution of *Website analytics* centers on the development of new technologies or techniques for website development. Rather, it implies two things. The first is that it involves the study of websites, as well as other questions developed in communications training: it is impossible to make an in-depth analysis of a practice or a professional problem – such as that of the impact of the widespread commercial exploitation of data as part of the communications strategies of large companies' websites – through dissociating operational and theoretical knowledge. To demonstrate the value created by its insights – whether comparative, historical, economic, pragmatic, etc. – communications research must, among other things, understand and integrate analyses of the daily professional practices and constraints of the communicators whose productions are studied. If this is neglected, essential

---

1 Rouquette, S. (2017). *Site Internet : audit et stratégie*. De Boeck, Louvain-la-Neuve.

explanations may be missed entirely. The second is that deploying methodologies for the ideological, graphical or even technical analysis of Internet sites makes it possible both to raise decision-makers' awareness related to these methods of analysis, and to train communicators in the implementation of such procedures.

The second guideline of this book is educational. By integrating a diversified methodological tool into its analyses and extensive experiences obtained in teaching, this book is a clear demonstration of how research and education complement each other. In this regard, this book responds to the need to train communications students in defining and deploying organizations' online communication strategies, thus satisfying the needs for digital skills expected by companies, communities and associations. By explaining how to evaluate, analyze and produce websites, and by transferring these skills and allowing them to evolve, this book thus contributes to training all these future professionals who will decide on the identity, content, graphics, services, architecture or even the hypertext opening of communicational tools as rich and complex as websites.

Introduction

Luc MASSOU[1], Patrick MPONDO-DICKA[2] and Nathalie PINÈDE[3]

[1] *CREM, Université de Lorraine, Metz, France*
[2] *LERASS, Université Toulouse – Jean Jaurès, France*
[3] *MICA, Université Bordeaux Montaigne, Pessac, France*

I.1. An object that is long-standing and yet still current

From a set of interconnected HTML pages to online service platforms and digital social networks, websites have constantly changed their forms and functions, prompting the humanities and social sciences to renew or invent analytical methodologies on the one hand, and on the other hand to think of praxis, courses of action adapted to non-specialists and future players in digital communication. Additionally, the production of online elements has been on the agenda of communications training since its emergence among the general public and professionals in the early 1990s, according to a different and complementary approach to that implemented for computer scientists. This book seeks to compare these two perspectives – methodological and pedagogical – in information and communication science research by studying Web communication in its technical, discursive, methodological and social dimensions, from the time it is designed to its integration into the digital and communication practices of organizations, whether in the public, non-profit or private sector.

To accomplish this, this book draws on a cycle of scientific study days that began at the end of 2015 at Université Toulouse 2 Jean-Jaurès, based on a deliberately critical question: is website analysis still relevant in information and communication? Six years after its initiation, four more study days were organized between 2017 and 2021 at Université Bordeaux Montaigne, at the Institut national des langues et civilisations orientales (Paris), at the Université Clermont Auvergne, and finally at the Université de Lorraine, to carry out further reflection and expand the extent of the research on this subject, the dynamics of which are always present. On this basis, a first collaborative book was written: *Site internet : audit et stratégie*, under the direction of Rouquette (2017), which includes the participation of some of the authors who had been present during the initial session in 2015. In order to highlight all the researchers who contributed to these sessions between 2015 and 2021, this book, the second in this series, builds on and completes the first part, and will interconnect with a third part released by the same publisher, *Digital presences of organizations*, to be published in 2022, also under our co-direction. This will allow us to offer a detailed overview of the research carried out on an object that is both long-standing and yet still current, whose methods of analysis took some time to come into being, and about which we reviewed only four books expressly devoted to the issue in 2015: *Penser le web-design. Modèles sémiotiques pour les projets multimédias* by Pignier and Drouillat (2004), *Les sites web. Conception, description et évaluation* by Stockinger (2005), *L'analyse des sites internet. Une radiographie du cyberespace* by Rouquette (2009) and *Manuel d'analyse du Web en sciences humaines et sociales,* coordinated by Barats (2013).

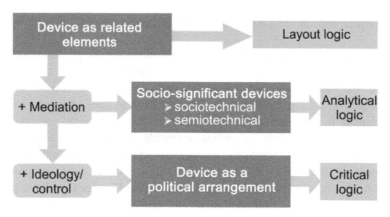

Figure I.1. *Typology of the device in communications research conducted by organizations (Appel and Heller 2010, p. 45)*

For this second volume to be released on the basis of our 5 scientific study days, we have brought together 12 authors to expand on epistemological, methodological and also pedagogical approaches to the analysis of websites, which we have structured into three sections based on the notion of the device, widely used in information and communication sciences (Charlier and Peeters 1999; Leblanc 1999; Appel et al. 2010), and in particular for the communication research of the organizations that interest us here. As noted by Appel and Heller (2010) on the basis of a review of the literature in this specific field, three logical mechanisms of interpreting the device can be distinguished here (see Figure I.1): the logic of arrangement (related elements), analytical logic (mediation) and critical logic (ideology, control).

If it were necessary to position our 10 chapters using this typology broken down along three main axes, and by considering websites as communication devices for organizations[1], we could write them mostly following the analytical logic proposed here. For their part, here is how their authors (Appel and Heller 2010, p. 41) define it:

> A second level of meaning designates the device as a process that the researcher will have highlighted and which takes two orientations: social/technical co-construction and co-construction of meaning. These two different meanings refer to two approaches to research in CIS, and to two epistemologies: on the one hand, communication as a social construction with a connection from research to sociology, and on the other hand, to communication as a construction of meaning with a connection to the sciences of language.

In the three parts of our book, the authors will use this analytical logic in their examination of websites, considering them as processes of mediation comprising social, technical, and semiotic constructs, and which we have grouped into three non-exclusive subsets: the website as a socio-technical, semiodiscursive and communicational device. In each contribution, the authors will develop in greater detail their notional, methodological and/or pedagogical choices and will rely on different examples of analyzed corpus of websites, if necessary.

I.2. The website as a socio-technical device

Considering websites as socio-technical devices involves analyzing the way they bring social actors into interaction with different technological systems on the Web, which have been constantly evolving since its entry into widespread use among the general public in the early 1990s. This is precisely what Camille Alloing proposes in his chapter, where he historicizes five periods of the Web in the communication practices of organizations: the pioneer era of the Web (before 2000), the citation

---

1 Here, we consider these devices as instruments "for capturing and understanding mediation processes and communication situations (or contracts), by identifying the components in play and the way they are connected" (Appel et al. 2010, p. 10).

Web (2000–2005), Web 2.0 (2005–2010), the social Web (2010–2015) and finally the affective Web (2015 to the present). For each of these periods, the author identifies the characteristics of the site as a formal and technical system, describing the nature of interactions and uses made by Internet users, and explaining the digital communications strategies of the organizations involved.

From a more epistemological perspective of the analysis of websites, mixing socio-technical devices and semiodiscursive approaches, Christine Barats and Julia Bonaccorsi will then highlight the points to observe and the difficulties to be faced when interpreting messages transmitted through websites, where the abundance and heterogeneity of digital content and data prompt us to question the way they are produced and how they circulate on the Web, but also the mechanisms and conditions of how they are collected by researchers. Here again, the importance of the socio-technical devices and the place of technical mediation are at the heart of the reasoning, upstream and downstream of the analysis.

Finally, taking a pedagogical perspective, Luc Massou proposes a personal implementation of training experiences in the expertise of websites in Bachelor's and Master's courses in information and communication, for future specialists in digital communication. Whether based on various website analysis grids from the scientific and sometimes professional literature or created ad hoc with Master's students, it is a critical and reflective assessment, both in terms of contributions and limitations, but also methodological constraints and the acquisition of professional skills in the use of these socio-technical devices on the Web.

I.3. The website as a semiodiscursive device

The second part covers the theoretical and methodological approaches that are part of a mainly semiotic perspective, which is based on an analysis of discourses and/or interfaces in websites. Here, Nicole Pignier puts forward a definition of a semiotics of digital design, which involves questioning the way we "make sense" of Web design, in order to create a link between the instances of enunciation – organizations – and co-enunciation – the viewers who use websites. She presents a methodology for a semiotic analysis of multimodality and the interface design of websites, also specifying its limits, and concluding on the enunciative and ethical interrelations of digital design.

Taking a perspective that is once again interconnected through a pedagogical experience at Master's level university courses, Alexandra Saemmer and Nolwenn Tréhondart present a methodology for analyzing websites that is rooted in pragmatic semiotics, but which shifts the focus from the interpretative results to the study of its process of construction. This social semiotics of websites thus compels learners to collectively debate the way their interpretative filters are constructed, so as to make them more aware of this process, and to promote a more reflective posture among future digital communications professionals.

Justine Simon, for her part, explains the theoretical and methodological challenges of the spaces of expression and communication that have been created in the form of social networks such as Twitter. Based on a case study conducted on discursive content spread through this type of online device, she characterizes the diverse forms of online mobilization, between technological dimension, social practice and semiodiscursive practice. The social experience within an online community thus takes shape through choices of interdiscursivity, narrativity and argumentativity, and the variety of this hypertextualized writing thus allows us to grasp the logics of communication according to their authors.

Finally, Pergia Gkouskou studies the relevance of the concept of the metaphor in the epistemological analysis of the "website" object, while positioning it within the evolution of the media landscape. Based on a study of the relevant materials (open data, archives) as well as of institutional websites, the author questions the mechanisms of metaphor (or "visual textualizations") that emerge between designers, users and techno-semiotic devices within a context of hyper-mediated simulation in continuous evolution.

1.4. The website as a communication device

The third and final part brings together chapters based on an analysis of a clearly constituted corpus of reference material to identify the underlying communications issues for the organizations that designed them. In her taxonomic study of 14 institutional websites of universities, Nathalie Pinède bases her methodological approach on the classification of the content found on their home pages from the textual anchors of hypertext links, which she names "hypertext lexical units". By analyzing their dominant classes on this reference group, she reveals informational profiles both in terms of the choices of content published and also in the users primarily targeted by each site.

By choosing a corpus of websites built for international organizations, Marie-Hélène Hermand structures her communication analysis on the tangled web of connections between territories and media devices, and on the concept of intermediate public space (as spaces of proximity and transition into public space), to understand the transitions and/or the transformations rooted in collective imaginations. By studying the semantic universes proposed in their websites, the author thus models the communicational processes of these organizations and the way they redefine the territories on which they depend.

Finally, Camille Rondot gives an analysis of the story websites tell about the new professional skill sets involving "*social data listening*". On the basis of a corpus of websites made for agencies and consultants in the field of digital communications, the author analyzes the mechanisms of a professional rhetoric that implies both a personification and a euphemization of the strategies in play. Her semiodiscursive approach to this body of websites will thus reveal a communicational pretension, that is to say, a project aimed at creating a new profession for a certain conception of communications, from which she will identify the semantic and discursive markers.

I.5. And what comes after this?

As noted earlier, we will complete this first volume published by ISTE Ltd, which was the result of our scientific study days, with a second collective work under our direction. This work will more specifically address the issue of the digital presence of organizations in digital ecosystems (the Web, social networks, the data Internet): communication strategies differentiated according to the types and audiences of organizations, multicultural communication at different scales and construction of online narratives.

1.6. References

Appel, V. and Heller, T. (2010). Dispositif et recherche en communication des organisations. In *Les dispositifs d'information et de communication : concept, usages et objets*, Appel, V., Boulanger, H., Massou, L. (eds). De Boeck, Brussels.

Appel, V., Boulanger, H., Massou, L. (2010). *Les dispositifs d'information et de communication : concept, usages et objets*. De Boeck, Brussels.

Barats, C. (2013). *Manuel d'analyse du web en Sciences Humaines et Sociales*. Armand Colin, Paris.

Charlier, P. and Peeters, H. (1999). Contributions à une théorie du dispositif. *Hermès, La revue*, 25, 15–23.

Leblanc, G. (1999). Du déplacement des modalités de contrôle. *Hermès, La revue*, 25, 233–242.

Pignier, N. and Drouillat, B. (2004). *Penser le webdesign. Modèles sémiotiques pour les projets multimédias*. L'Harmattan, Paris.

Rouquette, S. (2009). *L'analyse des sites internet : une radiographie du cyberespace*. De Boeck, Brussels.

Rouquette, S. (2017). *Site Internet : audit et stratégie*. De Boeck, Brussels.

Stockinger, P. (2005). *Les sites web : conception, description, et évaluation*. Hermès-Lavoisier, Paris.

PART 1

Websites as a
Socio-technical Device

1

Observing the Web through the Lens of Websites

Camille ALLOING

LabFluens, Université du Québec à Montréal, Montreal, Canada

1.1. Introduction

The analysis of websites is a topic that has long interested information and communications scientists, who have addressed it from different angles and with different approaches: semiotics, interface design, public and organizational uses (Proulx 2005) or referencing techniques (Domenget and Michel 2014).

However, defining what a website is remains difficult, as there are many entry keys, but also the object itself: ever since the creation of first HTML pages, though the underlying technologies have evolved little, the forms and purposes of these digital objects have changed according to the trends and expectations of the public or designers (blogs, platforms, showcase sites), their names and their architectures vary. As Pinède points out (2018):

> The current hybridization of forms and genres at the center of the interface, the porosity between websites and social media, the possible interweaving of endogenous (content proposed by the speaker) and exogenous elements [...] blur the picture we have of websites, which can and should be understood as a socio-technical device.

In this chapter, we also want to approach the website as a socio-technical device, and more particularly as an attribute of the digital territory of organizations. We use

Analyzing Websites,
coordinated by Luc MASSOU, Patrick MPONDO-DICKA and Nathalie PINÈDE.
© ISTE Ltd 2023.

the term "attribute" to mean that which qualifies an object, the essential property of a thing. In this case, an organization's website is what qualifies its online presence, serving as a gateway to other spaces where it deploys its content and speeches, that structures its digital territory (Le Béchec and Alloing 2018) and gives it authority and legitimacy to address certain topics:

> Thus, in order to orient themselves within constantly changing digital territories, to focus their attention on the most relevant content, and to ensure that their own information flows in the desired collectives, users seek to identify forms of authority that facilitate the circulation and transposition of signs. These authorities are not governmental, as in the case of "physical" territories, but authorities that have the ability to make sense of the multitude of documents and information that are in circulation.

The websites of organizations, by participating in making sense of this information that is circulating, are at the center of how the Web functions. They are a reflection of its evolutions and the communication practices that are deployed on the Web. They adapt and arrange themselves in order to optimize this digital territory, this authority held by organizations. They are no longer just attributes of the presence of organizations, they are also an attribute of the Web as a whole. Thus, this chapter will not seek to analyze the evolution of organizations' websites to discuss what they are, but rather will attempt to understand what purpose they serve for organizations. In other words: why are websites made?

Since information and communications sciences can be seen as sciences of mediation (Peray 2008) and especially of circulation (of speech, signs, etc.), the problem that will be addressed more specifically here is the following: how is the analysis of websites relevant to observing intercommunal mediations and circulations on the Web? This question is based on two postulates:

– The websites created for organizations as a lens for analyzing developments on the Web make it possible to consider digital communication strategies as a reflection of the conventions of Web professionals, communication trends and technical standards or Web use.

– The website puts information produced by and about organizations into circulation. The website is both the means for and the subject of this circulation.

As for the works that we have been able to carry out on "digital metrics" (Alloing 2020), we therefore propose here a genealogical approach that proposes looking at a website not as an object detached from the environments where it evolves, but to analyze it as being a constituent part of such environments.

1.2. The website as a space and an architecture

Even more specifically, we propose considering websites as spaces within territories, and as an architecture within infrastructures. A space in which we evolve as an audience, and which is based on an architecture, that is to say, principles of organization (coding) and arrangement of signs and content (design). This space is itself located within larger digital territories (delimited by domain names, hypertext links, etc.) where signs and information related to organizations circulate and attach themselves. These territories are found within the Internet, which is an infrastructure – that is, a set of physical and permanent installations, as well as a set of productive forces, ideologies and economies that underlie it all. It is therefore necessary to manage to make constant changes of focus, back and forth between the website within its territory, and the infrastructures into which it is inserted.

In order to structure this navigation, we may rely on four concepts. First, we can question what shapes the website, the statements that perform it (Austin 1975; Denis 2006). Performativity refers to "situations in which the object to which a work relates [...] is not simply noted or described, but modified, or even called to exist" (Muniesa and Callon 2009). Observing the websites of organizations, and their construction of these websites, requires us to consider the following:

– The website *is* the organization. It brings together a set of statements and signs (words, logos, images, etc.) to distinguish the organization, to define it, making it the embodiment of the online organization. This is why it is common to read "check out our website" or "we're online".

– Websites are part of this presence because they are indicated or used as such. Even if the technologies that form this presence are a blog or something of that nature, the fact of referring to it as a website gives it this qualification, this attribute.

The way to name this site, to define whether it is efficient (metrics) or well built (design), is based on a set of conventions that evolve over time. Conventions are understood to mean "collectively established cultural forms that allow for coordinating and evaluating" (Reynaud and Richebé 2007). They reflect what communication practitioners and designers formally or informally establish as being "the right way" to make a site or to use it.

If it is possible to question the way websites are shaped (enunciations and conventions) using these two concepts, it is equally useful to look at what the website itself gives shape to. We can thus think of the website as a device for "qualculation" (Callon and Law 2005), especially when it becomes (or is inserted into) a platform (such as e-commerce). The website thus becomes a space in which entities detached from their original contexts (a photo of an employee, a video, an advertising text, an Internet user comment) are arranged, and which are then reworked, manipulated and transformed in order to be integrated into a single space, like a web page. This arrangement allows the organization to evaluate the value of the site using audience measurement tools (how many visitors on this page that groups heterogeneous elements by creating a new object?), and search engine algorithms to associate this set of qualitative and quantitative elements to position a site or a page in their results.

Finally, we can consider the website as a commensuration device (Espeland and Stevens 1998). Commensuration refers to the process that transforms qualitative elements into quantitative elements to reduce and simplify disparate information to compare it with other information. For example, on the website of an organization, a tool for comparing the prices of products and services between them is made available. This commensuration requires a set of technical standards, the main ones of which we will examine subsequently.

To answer the above problem and its associated hypotheses, this chapter is structured according to five main time periods, for purposes more heuristic than historical, and which will make it possible to follow this evolution of organizations' websites and what they reflect from that of the Web. Table 1.1 provides a summary of this schematic genealogy of the evolution of organizations' websites, and what they reflect of the very evolutions of the Web and digital communication practices, based on three aspects:

– the website: its forms and functions;

– the audience: the observed and expected uses;

– the organization: strategies and integration into communication practices.

This table is thus used to guide our navigation within the chapter. Each of these periods is illustrated using the website www.Allocine.fr, the evolution of which we will follow using elements archived by web.archive.org. AlloCiné is a company that started as a telephone service and then minitel service for booking movie tickets and has since seen its website, created in 1997, evolve into a true web portal (for e-commerce, etc.) and then into a multi-content platform over the course of its acquisitions.

Periods	The website	The audience	The organization
The pioneering Web (before 2000)	Static, a few pages, a landing spot, navigation with three clicks, cultural capitalism	Identified by audience measurements, reads information	A place of experimentation and spreading information, having a (domain) name to appear modern, the advertising economy
The citation Web (2000–2005)	Readable for robots, an arrival and bounce place, produces and receives links, linguistic capitalism	Cites, produces relevance and authority for websites	Natural referencing, become a resource on a topic, being visible, being first, capturing attention
Web 2.0 (2005–2010)	Model of the platform, rich interfaces, affinity marketing logic, informational capitalism	Interacts, provides data, participates in the recommendation, develops profiles	Centralizes content, grabs viewers' attention, provides services, forms a single resource
Social Web (2010–2015)	Attribute in a Web of profiles, showcase site, an object shared with surveillance capitalism	Puts into circulation, creates content, discusses	Promotes the circulation of content, ensures an "information anchor" of their digital territory, diversifies or develops its content
Affective Web (2015 to present)	Experiential space, adapts to audiences, emotional capitalism	Seeks experience, guided by emotions	Causes (re)actions, generates impulses

Table 1.1. *The five periods of the Web*

1.3. The pioneer Web (before 2000)

In 1993, the Internet became "mainstream" (Paloque-Bergès 2015): service providers became more numerous, modems were adopted in homes and it was no longer necessary to have highly advanced technical skills to connect to it. The following year, the W3C[1] (World Wide Web Consortium) was created with the objective to develop recommendations to ensure that Web technologies are compatible between themselves. At the same time, the web page and websites were the spaces through which users created their online presence: "I have my page so I

---

1 Available at: www.w3.org.

exist online, I have my site so I have a presence". The website is a landing site. The first website of AlloCiné is a simple home page that allows users to reach other pages, including a few photos and movie trailers to download (Figure 1.1).

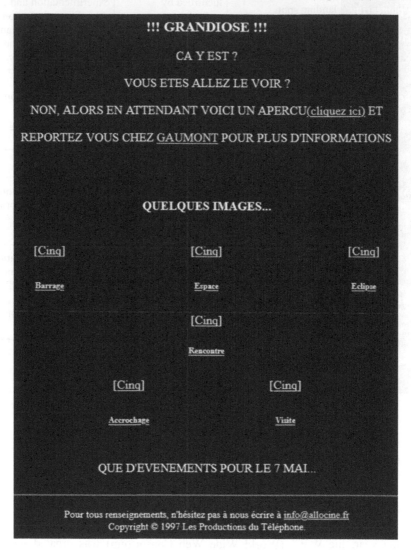

Figure 1.1. *Web page for the film The Fifth Element on the website www.allocine.fr july 22, 1997[2]. For a color version of this figure, see www.iste.co.uk/massou/analyzing.zip*

---

2 Available at: www.web.archive.org.

We arrive at the site through the URL address, for example, and then navigate within it. The first question that organizations then ask themselves is how to bring users to the site and how to make this space better known.

As search engines still operated on the principle of keywords (until the arrival of Google in 1998), and did not offer efficient prioritization, organizations choose to work through classic advertising (TV, radio, etc.): the website became a sign of modernity (Figure 1.2).

Figure 1.2. *Screenshot of a video advertisement for AlloCiné found on a CD-ROM from Studio CinéLive purchased in the late 1990s[3]. For a color version of this figure, see www.iste.co.uk/massou/analyzing.zip*

When audiences come to the site, the question is as follows: how do they navigate between the few existing pages? The initial conventions regarding the ergonomics of sites were formed, such as the "three clicks" principle, which stressed that all pages within the same site must be accessible in less than three clicks. These conventions were built around a postulate that was later questioned – and was even questioned at the time – but which made it possible to formulate good practices and the evaluation of Web design professions in development at the time:

> One of the most essential foundations of the design and development of sites was and still is the imperative to minimize the number of clicks required to complete a task, and to in fact reduce the time required for such task. (Nantel and Berrada 2004)

In this sense, the new version of the AlloCiné site in 1998 provides numerous hypertext links, particularly the latest news, to make them more accessible (Figure 1.3).

---

3 Available at: www.youtube.com/watch?v=0O60LD-vJUE.

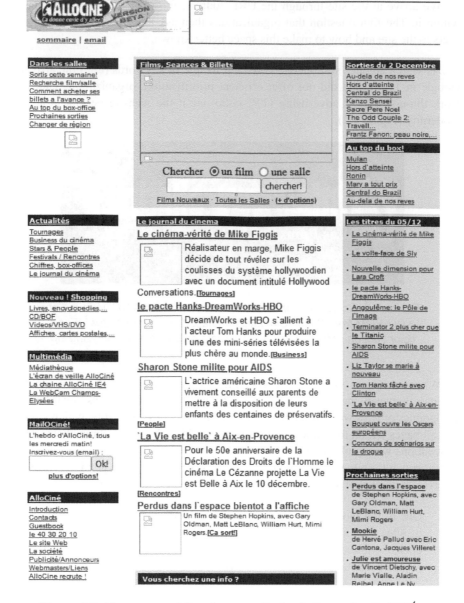

Figure 1.3. *Home page of the site www.allocine.fr, December 5, 1998[4].*
For a color version of this figure, see www.iste.co.uk/massou/analyzing.zip

---

4 Available at: www.web.archive.org.

Relations with the public who browse these sites, including at a minimum the means to identify these sites, to cause them to exist, are done as they still are today, using audience measurements (page views, visits, visitors, geolocation, click-through rates, logs [file transfer, error, repository, agent]) or by the first panels of Internet users created by organizations such as Médiamétrie.

These forms of quantification are performative: they define the contours of a typical audience in order to guide the choices of content design or production (Alloing 2020). These measures also go hand in hand with a nascent advertising economy, in which clicks are perceived as intentional interactions that signal the interest of audiences. Various commensuration processes are set up in order to compare sites and establish the price of advertising space. Internet users are seen as audience members, and their clicks as markers of their navigation, becoming a commodity that can be sold to advertisers and emerging agencies (Jouët 2004):

> The measured Internet user is a product that is sold to advertisers. Of course, this is a property shared with mass media audience measurements, but these are no longer just target groups who are bought on the advertising or e-commerce market; they are also individual consumers. No type of media has ever made it possible to see so much about its audience without them becoming aware.

This advertising economy is part of what can be called a "cultural capitalism" (Rifkin 2001), where the dream of seeing the Internet and the Web as a means of universal access to culture creates tension with the first attempts to appropriate cultural content from a commercial perspective, in order to attract Internet users to advertising.

In Figure 1.3, the AlloCiné site displays advertising banners (not visible in the screenshot) that lead to other sites. Internet users are then potentially attracted to this site at the time to watch trailers, photos of the films and other content not produced by AlloCiné For organizations, beyond building a presence, the primary interest of websites during this period is to be able to inform the public (news, presentation of products and services, etc.) and have a domain name. Indeed, since the end of the 1990s, the first lawsuits involving domain name usurpation or conflicts between brands of the same name were filed (such as the "Alice versus Alice" lawsuit for obtaining the domain name alice.fr[5]).

---

5 Available at: www.lesechos.fr/1999/02/les-conflits-entre-nom-de-domaine-et-denomination-sociale-le-cas-dalice-763354.

To summarize this first period, we can say that:

– websites were a place for advertising experimentation and the spread of corporate information;

– the digital territory of organizations is delimited by the domain name, or also by advertisements on other sites or on portals. Its borders were expanded by the placement of advertising banners on other websites;

– organizations built a reputation using their sites, based on an idea of modernity ("as seen on the Web");

– the first technical conventions were defined by the "pioneers" and the nascent standards: the mastery of technical development of sites, online publication of informative and cultural content;

– the conventions would then be (re)defined by the advertising associations, service providers and the first professionals in the sector (regarding ergonomics).

Intermediaries had already begun to play a central role (advertising agencies, access providers) but would gradually be dethroned by new technological players.

1.4. The citation Web (from 2000 to 2005)

At the beginning of the 2000s, search engines developed and gained importance by establishing a hierarchical order built by the processing of hypertext links and the systematic indexing of large volumes of web pages, following the (hegemonic) model of Google.

At this time, the website became central to structuring a Web where the challenge was to make information visible and available, in response to questions posed by users. The website is no longer exclusively – or almost exclusively – visited by human beings, it is becoming a place that is traversed by many indexing "robots". The architecture of the sites starts to be designed with the search engines in mind: "How do I make sure that my site meets the standards set in order to be visible?" is a question that organizations or their service providers regularly ask themselves. "Map sites", promoting the circulation of "robots" from page to page so that they can be indexed, become more widespread, as well as the selection of keywords and HTML tags, or a specific structuring of web pages.

Therefore, editorial and ergonomic choices are no longer dictated solely by technological standards or the objectives of organizations, but by PageRank (algorithm) used by Google: hypertext citations are presented as a means of an "objective" ranking of web pages based on the subjective considerations of users producing links and clicking on them (Brin and Page 1998). According to this logic, specific to the PageRank designers, the public participates in producing relevance and authority by visiting a site, clicking on the links that lead to it, and by producing links between sites.

Here again, a form of performativity emerges, where websites are relevant and authoritative for the public, since the actions and navigation done by the public are considered as marks of relevance.

The conventions of what a website should be, its usefulness, its performance or its interest, are now defined by a single entity: Google.

Web and communication professionals then develop a set of practices, known as referencing, in order to optimize the visibility of websites on the Google search engine. They apply these standards and conventions to do so. In many cases, they also attempt to poach the system it has created to their benefit.

> Being the first (or among the first) results to be shown to users is to search engine optimization as "being in the right spot" is for fishing, and the analogy does not end there: fishers can fish using a line (having a single indexed web page), or fish using drift nets, a more industrialized style of production: having 300 pages that monopolize the first 300 responses returned to users for a specific query will guarantee capturing the majority of traffic generated by a keyword. (Boutet and Amor 2010)

These actions put websites at the heart of the so-called attention economy, where the objective is to capture the views and clicks of Internet users on websites, to expand its digital territory as well as its referencing with the exchange of hypertext links between sites, for example, which is becoming a common practice.

The digital territory of organizations is thus delimited by all the elements outside of the website that will attract audiences to it. *AdWords* advertisements with Google appear in the results of the engine and on partner sites at the same time to promote this search for attention outside the organization's website.

These contextual ads, built by the processing of keywords entered by Internet users, form part of a linguistic capitalism (Kaplan 2014) by which Google begins to generate profits using the (advertising) redirection it provides to certain sites.

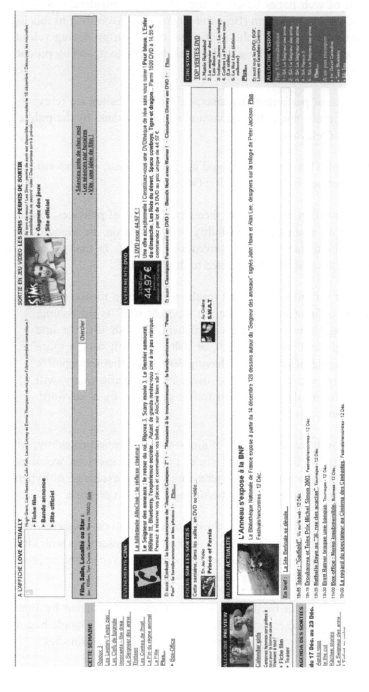

Figure 1.4. *DVD page from the website www.allocine.fr on December 14, 2003 (source: www.web.archive.org). For a color version of this figure, see www.iste.co.uk/massou/analyzing.zip*

For organizations, the goal is to become a resource on a topic related to their activities by being referenced on one or more key terms that lead to a high audience, and to be visible in the results of the engine, that is to say, to be first in line to capture that attention. The website is evaluated according to its authority, which according to Google's standards means its popularity and therefore its visibility: "Your brand is not what you say about it, but what Google says about it" became a frequently referenced quote from journalist Chris Anderson at the time (Alloing 2016). The audience arrives and "bounces" (between pages, between sites, between the site and the search engine). The website is no longer a place of arrival but becomes a place of passage and participates in the global circulation of content and information on the Web.

Organizations try to keep their audience on their pages, at a minimum to direct their attention to their content or information. In this way, the AlloCiné site was built as an information portal that offers many subject-specific sections to navigate, as well as specially produced content (such as broadcasts about cinema), and links to partners and services belonging to the company (phone wallpapers, DVD purchases, ticketing service, etc.). In terms of capturing attention, it is interesting to note that the interface of the site has evolved (Figure 1.4). It has become more colorful, with animated images and menus marked with different colors and tabs.

Then, with what some practitioners would dub "Web 2.0" and the features that came with it, the content presented on the pages would become a driver to make audiences interact and encourage them to express their opinions or provide data.

1.5. The Web known as Web 2.0 (from 2005 to 2010)

"Web 2.0" does not refer so much to major technological evolutions as it does to the development of certain ideologies and socioeconomic configurations (Le Deuff 2007):

> Web 2.0 uses technologies that are pre-existing and accessible to most of the latest versions of browsers. Some have taken a long time to truly emerge, which is not a new occurrence for ICT (Information and Communications Technology) groups. Web 2.0 is thus based on reliable or rather functional technologies [...].

The model of the platform plays a central role. Digital platforms were designed to be self-sufficient: as they evolved, they came to incorporate the conventions of usage and the features included by their competitors in order to encourage Internet users not to go anywhere:

A "platform" refers to a model of organization of the media, made up of a semio-technical architecture, a set of operators for activating and regulating the activities of users, as well as the content offered and a mechanism for its own valorization. (Bullich and Lafon 2019)

Unlike websites, platforms largely cut themselves off from the rest of the Web to maximize their capture of uses and attention by offering services to different actors (content creators, advertisers, Internet users, etc.) whose interactions they regulate. The platform is a space of "qualculation" that adds values to uses and content in order to regulate and sell it, based on the presuppositions of its designers and statistical data. For example, this may include defining the value of a publication by the evaluations that are made of it (stars, ratings), to direct it to other users through algorithms, or associate an advertisement with it. What favored the appropriation and the development of the platform model during this time was as much the production interfaces (*Content Management System* – CMS) offered to users, as well as the deployment of high-speed Internet and the appropriation of Web uses.

Still, in this perspective of data capture, practitioners were developing new *rich interfaces* on websites, with many features (share buttons, comment boxes, etc.). These interfaces are primarily intended to involve users (by commenting, sharing the contents of web pages on platforms, etc.), to entice them to click in order to better target advertising and enhance their databases. The public is no longer seen as merely a source of information that feeds websites, but also as a resource that provides data and produces more elaborate content, as well as an increasingly defined "target" for advertising. Bloggers focus the attention of public relations professionals who seek to diversify the content of websites and offer their audiences more "authentic" visions of the organizations they work for, while making sure to obtain hypertext links to promote SEO. The performance of the sites is evaluated by aggregating the measures of the previous periods (audience, citations, positioning in the results of the search engines). Specific measures appeared for customizing advertising, including the appearance of "display" advertising banners that are intended to be personalized (which insert images and videos, and vary according to users).

The logic of the citation, that of the link, becomes an affinity logic, that of the graph: the personal web page gives way to profiles, navigation from site to site, from platform to platform, is done according to the relationships established by users with each other or with content. The websites of organizations that transform into platforms include, first and foremost, the option to create profiles and blogs, and actively participate in producing content. The AlloCiné site in 2006 was the archetype for these platform sites (Figure 1.5). Its page "Mon AlloCiné" ("My

AlloCiné") offers various features for audiences: creating a profile, a blog, participating in forums and especially criticizing films, which will become its "trademark", while being a way to produce commensuration to compare movies and participate in the recommendation mechanisms. These algorithmic mechanisms, built on this logic of affinity (with other users and/or content) essentially remain at the core of market platforms today (to buy similar products) as well as informational platforms (to access similar content).

Mon AlloCiné

Pas encore inscrit ?
Saisissez simplement votre Email et vous êtes inscrit !

Votre Email :

Vous ne recevrez pas d'emails non sollicités.

Créez votre Compte !

Déjà inscrit ? Connectez-vous !
Votre mot de passe vous a été envoyé par Email.

Pseudo ou email :

Mot de passe :

Valider

▸ Vous avez perdu votre mot de passe ?

Pourquoi créer un compte ?
AlloCiné propose à ses membres **des services exclusifs**, qui vous permettront de naviguer plus efficacement, d'être toujours tenu au courant des nouveautés, ou de partager vos avis avec tous les autres membres !

AlloCiné Alertes
Accédez directement à toutes les nouveautés concernant vos films, séries, stars préférés en recevant chaque jour toute leurs actualités par e-mail !

AlloCiné Blogs
Editez votre propre Blog autour du Cinéma et des Séries grace aux outils exclusifs AlloCiné (banque d'images AlloCiné, citation des articles sur les fiches films, séries, stars ...).

AlloCiné Forums
Participez à tous les débats sur les films, les séries, les stars et l'actualité avec tous les autres membres AlloCiné !

Les Newsletters AlloCiné
AlloCiné Séances : tous les horaires de vos cinéma par email
AlloCiné Mail : l'actualité et les moments forts du cinéma
AlloCiné Séries : toutes les news et les indiscrétions sur les séries du moment

Les critiques ☆☆☆☆
Ecrivez vos propres critiques de films et de séries et soyez publié sur AlloCiné !

Figure 1.5. *"My AlloCiné" page from the website www.allocine.fr, November 16, 2006[6]. For a color version of this figure, see www.iste.co.uk/massou/analyzing.zip*

6 Available at: www.web.archive.org.

These conventions of the so-called Web 2.0, proposed first by marketing players such as Tim O'reilly, would gradually give way (and integrate) with those of the so-called "social media" or digital "social network" platforms, heralding the rise of a new Web that is sometimes called the "social" Web.

However, the economic models of this so-called Web 2.0 are still in place today:

– An attention economy and information capitalism take hold in a sustainable way. The resources that attract attention are co-produced with Internet users, and their recommendation becomes commonplace because its automation is based on the reputation generated by the opinions of the public (ratings, comments, etc.).

– Data are seen as a "new black gold" from which it is absolutely necessary to extract value, whose importance no one really knows, but which requires new forms of legal regulations.

To summarize this period, for organizations, websites sought to centralize content, to grab ever more attention in competition with the digital "social media" platforms that were developing, or even to become platforms themselves in order to provide complementary services. Organizations expanded their digital territories by using content producers, such as bloggers, and by offering content creation features on their platform sites. The various mechanisms offered to users of these sites to evaluate, comment and produce content were also part of a logic of valorizing the beneficial work done, providing a remuneration based on reputation and visibility: the more we produce contents for the site, the more votes and comments the productions receive, and the more visibility they achieve, thus encouraging them to produce more contents on large extent (and all of which, of course, is provided for free; see Figure 1.6).

These sites, whose data capture and processing are at the center of activities, as well as the production of content by users, require the deployment of increasingly massive storage infrastructures. These developments contribute to the development of a platformizing Web in which the public must stay on websites, and where they are put to work in order to produce content as well. The reputation and performance of the site are evaluated based on various interactions (ratings, comments, clicks, eye tracking, etc.) and the mobilization of users/producers. During this period, the samples, discussions and the sharing of opinions between Internet users, who have now become producers of knowledge and data, come to the fore. Organizations that develop their own discussion spaces recruit community managers to regulate the expressions and interactions of their users.

Figure 1.6. *Excerpt from the page "AlloCiné blogs" from the site www.allocine.fr, August 1, 2009[7]. For a color version of this figure, see www.iste.co.uk/massou/analyzing.zip*

1.6. The social Web (from 2010 to 2015)

As the dominant platforms (GAFAM and others) became omnipresent, particularly digital social networks, the website became an element of a social Web where the links of sociability between profiles of Internet users would structure the circulation and the visibility of content. It made it possible to centralize the profiles of organizations on other platforms, or conversely, to be transformed into a "showcase": a bit of content and a few services are produced and hosted elsewhere, and interactions with audiences are decentralized, to be transferred to the place where they make their thoughts known. Navigation came to be thought of as occurring between the different profiles or accounts of the organization that form its digital presence. The profession of community manager, which appeared in the

7 Available at: www.web.archive.org.

previous period, and was often associated with the activity of webmaster, would gain momentum: it no longer consisted of merely managing the content of the website and generating conversations, but in tying together all the profiles of the organization and developing specific content on those profiles. This position plays the role of mediator, facilitating the circulation within the digital territory of the organization:

> [Community management is] then defined as the set of policies and techniques intended to promote the emergence, development, and valorization of communicational activity produced by all interactions between member-users of an online community. Organizations that define and apply a policy of *community management* do so in order to manage as effectively as possible their image, the relationship with their users, their consumers, or their members, and to update their organizational culture or to find new ways of coordinating actions. (Galibert and Cordelier 2017)

The public is thus seen as a tool to propel the circulation of content between platforms, in the digital territory of the organization and within its own "communities". Bloggers on the so-called Web 2.0 are called "influencers": they are sought after to transform this circulation into propagation, to make available their attentional, reputational and emotional capital in order to ensure effective "virality" as well as to build affinity links between the organization and its audiences (Alloing 2016). But unlike the volunteer bloggers from the previous period, they are becoming more professionalized and gradually begin to ask for substantial payments.

The measurement of the performance of websites is fully integrated with that of the organization's digital territory, which itself depends on digital social media platforms: engagement on Facebook, impressions on Twitter, etc. (Alloing and Pierre 2019). Many software, applications and services were developed with this in mind, in order to associate the previous measures of the performance of websites with those of the platforms. The conventions are established by the dominant platforms on the Web. These will guide the development of websites, as well as their use in communications strategies. In this sense, like Facebook, AlloCiné chooses the term "friend" to designate the other members of its platform (Figure 1.7).

Here too, these developments reflect the changing digital economy. It is an economy that is reputational: the goal is no longer just to capture people's attention by creating visibility, but to direct it to the website, or to the rest of the organization's digital territory, to promote the circulation of useful opinions, information and recommendations. The (e-)reputation of organizations is central to this, because it has become an ordinary mechanism for selecting and consuming information because of the appropriation of the evaluation features of the previous period (Alloing 2016). It requires organizations to increase, evaluate and manage the visibility of their digital territories, the opinions that circulate and become attached to them, the influence of the content they produce on their audience's behavior and the affinity they develop with audiences through the conversational strategies of community managers or the use of "influencers". However, since the advent of the so-called Web 2.0, this ever-increasing collection of data on website users collected in order to try to "see everything" so as to better quantify communications actions and influence the behavior and opinions of the public, brings organizations into a kind of surveillance capitalism that:

> Begins when we claim the human experience as a free raw material intended to be translated into behavioral data. This raw material is seized and considered as a legitimate good that can be made profitable and sold at will, and from which we can derive all of its benefits. (Zuboof and Chalier 2019)

Partagez votre passion

Que ce soit via des articles sur votre blog AlloCiné ou via des contributions sur le site : faites partager vos connaissances à vos amis AlloCiné.
Profitez à fond d'AlloCiné pour faire vos commentaires :
Devenez fan de films, séries ou stars dans votre bibliothèque et retrouvez toutes les dernières news dans Mon AlloCiné !

Figure 1.7. *Extract from the "Allocated Service" page of the website www.allocine.fr, January 9, 2011[8]. "Share your passion whether via articles on your blog or via contributions on the site: share your knowledge with your AlloCiné friends. Take full advantage of AlloCiné to make your comments: become a fan of films, series or stars in your library and find all the latest news in My AlloCiné!". For a color version of this figure, see www.iste.co.uk/massou/analyzing.zip*

8 Available at: www.web.archive.org.

On the AlloCiné website like many others, this search for more qualified data promised by the so-called "social media" platforms is identified by the possibility of connecting to the site using Facebook or Google accounts. It also involves making mobile applications available which are designed to facilitate the collection of various data (geolocation, etc.). Essentially, it is not necessary to come to the AlloCiné website. Rather, it is the site that goes to the users, no matter where they are located (Figure 1.8).

Figure 1.8. *Excerpt from the home page of the website www.allocine.fr, October 17, 2014[9]. "AlloCiné everywhere! By email, on your mobile, on social networks, in podcast, via our RSS feeds". For a color version of this figure, see www.iste.co.uk/ massou/analyzing.zip*

To summarize this period, for organizations, the management of their websites sought to promote the circulation of the content they produced or had produced, to ensure an "informational anchor" or a showcase of their digital presence, as well as to diversify or develop ways of getting in touch and in conversation with "communities". The site is entirely an attribute of the digital territory of organizations. It participates in the reputational calculations necessary for the evaluation of the performance of digital communication, and in the deployment of automated algorithmic recommendations. The site becomes what users share, what they discuss, particularly where they go for specific actions (playing, discussing, sharing, being informed). It is no longer an obligatory visiting site for the organization's presence, but a resource for this presence. In the case of the AlloCiné website, which remains a portal and not a showcase site, many features developed in the previous period remained in place, while at the same time we see the appearance of links and connections to digital social network platforms.

---

9 Available at: www.web.archive.org.

1.7. An affective and artificial Web (2015 to the present)

The development of features that allow users to show our emotions (likes, hearts, etc.), to affect others who might feel affinity, to associate our conversations with emotional markers (emojis, emoticons), all coupled with techniques for analyzing our feelings and emotions, places websites in what can be referred to as an "affective Web" (Alloing and Pierre 2017). The website becomes an experiential space that reconfigures itself according to the emotions expressed or identified by the public: facial recognition of emotions, virtual and augmented reality, voice commands, chatbots, etc. The mix of interfaces created following to the precepts of "emotional design" (Norman 2005; Pierre and Alloing 2019), and automations based on machine learning (in other words, "artificial intelligence"), causes websites to base themselves on perpetual "A/B testing": with each new interaction with a user, the site is able to offer different, customized information or forms of browsing.

The conventions and utopias of this affective digital landscape have become more stabilized but were first brought to light in the mid-1990s (Picard 1999). They are based on a conception of audiences as irrational beings, dominated by their emotions, constantly seeking out sensations and new experiences to escape from their boredom. This new form of website development gives them the potential to participate in a digital emotional economy, where emotions are considered as a universal means of attracting attention and a relevant driver of segmentation. It is an economy that itself participates in "an affective capitalism":

> We use the notion of affective capitalism to describe a particular mode of capture where the resonances between bodies – both human and non-human – enter into systems of value and value production. Affective capitalism appeals to our desires. It requires social relations; it organizes and establishes them. Our abilities to affect and be affected are transformed into financial assets, property, services, and management strategies. (Karppi et al. 2016)

It is effectively a Web where the websites stimulate our emotions and evaluate what affects us. It is no longer solely or exclusively social relationships and data that count and are counted to direct attention or recommend content, it is the affections that this same content produces that direct their circulation. When we use Instagram, Facebook or Twitter, the platform selects for us what we should see, with the belief that what it shows us will please us, move us, annoy us, or in any case, will make us react. It is this automated selection, which goes much further than reputation or affinity calculations, which now dominates the circulation of information in the digital territories of organizations, and causes technical architectures to evolve (to promote machine learning, add elements of biometric recognition, etc.). Along these lines, since 2020, the AlloCiné website has been offering a "new index based on your tastes [which] is now displayed on movies and series"[10]. Though not revolutionary, this system built around the evaluations made by users of the site fits into both the conventions established by a platform like Netflix, but also into those specific to the affective Web through the use of experiential terms. And in the same vein, AlloCiné offers a *chatbot* on the Facebook Messenger app, with many emojis, providing various different types of information (Figure 1.9).

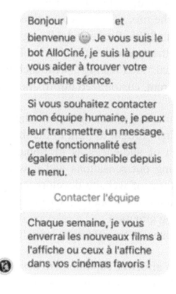

Figure 1.9. *Image of the Allociné chatbot. "Hello and welcome. I am the AlloCiné bot, and I'm here to help you find your next session. If you want to contact my human team, I can send them a message. This option is also available from the menu – Contact the team. Every week, I will send you the new movies showing or those showing in your favorite cinemas!". For a color version of this figure, see www.iste.co.uk/massou/analyzing.zip*

1.8. Conclusion

In conclusion, over time, the websites of organizations are a reflection of what digital technology is doing to communication. It is a strategic element, mainly because it can be adapted to public uses and to technical and economic

10 "How to find the movie or series that's the best fit for you: discover AlloCiné's affinity score", see: www.allocine.fr/article/fichearticle_gen_carticle=18688588.html.

developments. Organizations thus have access to a medium that can adapt to the latest trends of the moment, while constantly updating the ways they enter into relationships with audiences. Its evolution, as presented in this chapter, also shows that digital environments evolve by constantly reconfiguring themselves, more frequently than undergoing radical disruptions. The various "revolutions" advocated by the sellers of "digital" solutions, from 2.0 to artificial intelligence, generally serve to mask business models built on the exploitation of users' creative and communicational work, their privacy and their opinions. As an attribute of the digital territory of organizations, the website is a means of limiting the forms of dependencies generated by the centralization of data by the dominant digital players. The website thus acts like a ship in the middle of an ocean of information, where the waves caused by the anti-cyclones of GAFAM are not like tsunamis, but require constant change so as not to sink to the bottom of the 10th page of search results.

For researchers, the website is a way to follow societal and communication trends, to carry out an archeology of its evolutions to better understand those of the Internet in general. But this is not without many methodological challenges (Brügger 2012). One difficulty that seems to arise systematically during the study of websites, apart from any historiographical approaches, is the consideration of a "trans-contextual syndrome" (Pierre 2013): the website offers us a global vision of a set of localized uses. The interpretation that can be made of these uses (commenting, sharing, reading, etc.) is thus complex, depending on the contexts in which they were produced. For example, how can we understand the choice to use an advertising banner without at the same time analyzing the overall functioning of the regulations, the uses of the site and the objectives of the organization that owns this site? Even more so when sites become attributes that are transposed and reconfigured as they circulate from platform to platform, from device to device (phones, tablets, etc.). Thus, the choice was made in this chapter to approach these difficulties with a functionalist and pragmatic approach: what are websites for (for organizations, audiences, on the Web), and what does observing their uses in different contexts teach us about them? The primary objective is not to increase a performativity that is already at work: creating a category for the "website" whose attributes we would simply look for, at the risk of seeing websites everywhere, or not seeing any anywhere. In short, the analysis of websites is relevant, because it allows us to analyze plural models that are constantly evolving... especially if we use them as a lens and not simply an object.

1.9. References

Alloing, C. (2016). *La E-réputation. Médiation, calcul, émotion.* CNRS Éditions, Paris.

Alloing, C. (2020). Construire les publics numériques par leurs mesures. In *Les technologies et le gouvernement des marchés. Des algorithmes aux biotechnologies*, Kessous, E., Nau, J.-P. (eds). L'Hamattan, Paris.

Alloing, C. and Pierre, J. (2017). *Le web affectif : une économie numérique des émotions.* INA éditions, Paris.

Alloing, C. and Pierre, J. (2019). Une approche praxéologique des métriques numériques : mesurer le community management pour quoi faire ? *Revue Communication & professionnalisation*, 9, 85–108.

Austin, J.L. (1975). *How to Do Things with Words.* Oxford University Press, Oxford.

Boutet, C.V. and Amor, S.B. (2010). Vers l'active SEO 2.0. *Les Cahiers du numérique*, 6(1), 179–198.

Brügger, N. (2012). L'historiographie de sites web : quelques enjeux fondamentaux. *Le Temps des médias*, 1, 159–169.

Bullich, V. and Lafon, B. (2019). Dailymotion : le devenir média d'une plateforme. Analyse d'une trajectoire sémio-économique (2005-2018). *tic&société*, 13(1–2), 355–391.

Callon, M. and Law, J. (2005). On qualculation, agency, and otherness. *Environment and Planning D : Society And Space*, 23(5), 717–733.

Denis, J. (2006). Préface : Les nouveaux visages de la performativité. *Études de communication. Langages, information, médiations*, 29, 8–24.

Domenget, J.C. and Michel, J.L. (2014). Le métier de référenceur est-il pérenne et légitime en communication ? *Revue Communication & professionnalisation*, 2, 161–179.

Espeland, W.N. and Stevens, M.L. (1998). Commensuration as a social process. *Annual Review of Sociology*, 24(1), 313–343.

Galibert, O. and Cordelier, B. (2017). Animation et gestion des communautés en ligne : quelles rationalisations du social ? Une introduction. *Communiquer. Revue de communication sociale et publique*, 19, 1–8.

Jouet, J. (2004). Les dispositifs de construction de l'internaute par les mesures d'audience. *Le Temps des médias*, 2, 160–174.

Kaplan, F. (2014). Linguistic capitalism and algorithmic mediation. *Representations*, 127(1), 57–63.

Karppi, T., Kähkönen, L., Mannevuo, M., Pajala, M., Sihvonen, T. (2016). Affective capitalism. *Ephemera: Theory and Politics in Organization*, 16(4), 1–13.

Le Deuff, O. (2007). Le succès du web 2.0 : histoire, techniques et controverse [Online]. Available at: http://hal.archives-ouvertes.fr/docs/00/13/35/71/PDF/web2.0.pdf [Accessed 7 September 2022].

Muniesa, F. and Callon, M. (2008). La performativité des sciences économiques. *CSI WorKing Papers Series*, Centre de sociologie de l'innovation, Paris.

Muniesa, F. and Callon, M. (2009). La performativité des sciences économiques. *Traité de sociologie économique*, 289–324.

Nantel, J. and Berrada, A.M. (2004). L'efficacité et la navigabilité d'un site web : rien ne sert de courir, il faut aller dans la bonne direction. *Gestion*, 29(4), 9–14.

Norman, D.A. (2005). Emotional design: People and things. *Jdn.org* [Online]. Available at: https://www.academia.edu/download/30792320/M4_Emotional_Design.pdf. [Accessed 7 September 2022].

Paloque-Bergès, C. (2015). L'imaginaire du "grand public" au tournant du Web (1993–1997). *Revue française des sciences de l'information et de la communication* [Online]. Available at: http://journals.openedition.org/rfsic/1478 [Accessed 7 September 2022].

Peraya, D. (2008). Un regard critique sur les concepts de médiatisation et médiation : nouvelles pratiques, nouvelle modélisation. *Les enjeux de l'information et de la communication* [Online]. Available at: https://lesenjeux.univ-grenoble-alpes.fr/2008/supplement-a/12-un-regard-critique-sur-les-concepts-de-mediatisation-et-mediation-nouvelles-pratiques-nouvelle-modelisation/ [Accessed 7 September 2022].

Picard, R.W. (1999). Affective computing for HCI. *HCI*, 1, 829–833.

Pierre, J. (2013). Le cadre privatif : des données aux contextes : approche interdimensionnelle des enjeux de médiation de la vie privée. PhD Thesis, Université de Grenoble, Grenoble.

Pierre, J. and Alloing, C. (2018). Comment les émotions traversent le design ? Conception et usages d'une fonctionnalité du web affectif. *Revue des Interactions Humaines Médiatisées* [Online]. Available at: http://europia.org/RIHM/V19N2/2018-19(2)-1-Pierre.pdf [Accessed 7 September 2022].

Pinède, N. (2018). Du site web aux identités numériques organisationnelles : proposition d'un modèle d'analyse. *Questions de communication*, 34, 75–94.

Proulx, S. (2005). Penser les usages des TIC aujourd'hui : enjeux, modèles, tendances. In *Enjeux et usages des TIC : aspects sociaux et culturels*, Pinède N., Vieira, L. (eds). Presses universitaires de Bordeaux, Bordeaux.

Reynaud, J.D. and Richebé, N. (2007). Règles, conventions et valeurs. *Revue française de sociologie*, 48(1), 3–36.

Rifkin, J. (2001). *The Age of Access: The New Culture of Hypercapitalism*. Penguin, London.

Zuboff, S. and Chalier, J. (2019). Le capitalisme de la surveillance. *Esprit*, 5, 63–77.

2

Is the Web a Semiodiscursive Object?

Christine BARATS[1] and Julia BONACCORSI[2]
[1] CERLIS, Université Paris Descartes, France
[2] ELICO, Université Lumière Lyon 2, France

2.1. Introduction

Data from the Web[1] are at the center of many research works in the humanities and social sciences (HSS), and in particular in communication studies. The many different perspectives and issues addressed attest to the diversity of different methods and approaches, as well as the types of data put to use. However, the "websites"[2] are at the core of many social practices, but they are not an object in themselves. Thus, in various ways, content from the Web appears to constitute a gateway into analyzing communication processes in most social fields, at the risk of erasing the media-related and mediatizing nature of the research data gathered. Precisely, the apparent simplicity of pre-existing "content" is opposed by a laborious

---

1 To begin, we will establish a minimal definition of the Web as a hypermedia and documentary system, allowing access to the resources of the network of the Internet, to later focus on the media dimension of the Web through the study of the information–communication materiality at work ("websites", "writing appearing on the screen", "traces set of use"). For this reason, we will give preference to the notion of a "device" above that of the Web or a "website", as we will develop below.

2 We use quotation marks to emphasize the complexity of the expression "website", and the need for work on the defining and objectification to build observables.

Analyzing Websites,
coordinated by Luc MASSOU, Patrick MPONDO-DICKA and Nathalie PINÈDE.
© ISTE Ltd 2023.

work of selection and characterization of what will constitute the "data" of the survey, in connection with the objectives of the research. This task, while bolstered by the many publications on the production of the body of materials used (in discourse analysis) and the collection of sources (e.g. in the field of analysis of press speeches), is beset by difficulties in the case of computerized media. This is one of the difficulties faced by the institutions tasked with indexing and preserving the Web[3], as well as the researchers in this field. Indeed, it must be noted that the amount of change undergone by the content studied and the types of authorities is quite remarkable, an editorial activity that is based on layers of writing that are hidden but not devoid of the challenges of power, a heterogeneous granularity of the levels of observation and documentary collection, etc. It can be added that the apparent accessibility of the data is inversely proportional to the difficulties of the inquiry to be performed and requires diverse and expert-level skills. In using the term inquiry, we emphasize that the semiodiscursive research falls within the human and social sciences, and as such raises questions of defining a terrain, then choosing empirical methods to observe and analyze social phenomena.

In this chapter, we will be taking a look at some of these areas of skills and expertise so as to bring to light their theoretical and analytical coherence, especially with regard to the notion of "data". Thus, we will have a biased point of view. Our bias is not intended to describe a method of analyzing content from the Web: on the contrary, it highlights the points which should be viewed attentively, and the difficulties that will have to be faced, regardless of the prowess of the technology used or the abundance of "data". Research on discursive, enunciative, documentary, editorial and visual media – in other words, the "products" of communication and their socio-political effects – has for a long time led to a discussion on the delimiting of units of meaning, such as text, words and speech, in how they relate to the material nature of the media, as well as the different instances of it (the publisher, the author, the media organization). This discussion has been going on in a digital context for the past 20 years and has helped expand the methodological attention and reservations necessary for the interpretation of the statements made on the Web. This is the reflection that we will develop here.

Thus, the centrality of Web content invites us to pay attention to the way content is produced, where it is produced and how it is decentralized, dispersed and circulated. Analyzing Web content sheds light on many research questions, provided that we locate the data that are collected, question the methods and conditions of the

---

3 In the context of legal deposits in France, the Bibliothèque Nationale de France (French National Library, or BNF) and the Institut National de l'Audiovisuel (National Audiovisual Institute, INA) collect and archive numerous websites (Schafer 2018).

collection and do not underestimate the importance of the device within which they are produced. The heterogeneous nature of online content (texts, images, sounds, link hypertext, emoticons, architexts[4], the numbers of "friends", followers, retweets, etc.), their composited and sometimes ephemeral aspects present researchers with many difficulties and limitations that underscore the methodological and epistemological issues in constructing them as relevant data sets, as observables. As with any empirical approach, it involves a reflection on the place of technical mediation, and in particular on the criteria and conditions for collecting and analyzing data from the Web. We use the term "data" to include alphanumeric, visual and sound data, as well as data pertaining to interfaces and algorithms that are specific to Web devices. It is indeed a question of taking into account the specificities and peculiarities of the production of Web content. We propose highlighting the contribution of semiological and discursive approaches, as mobilized in communication studies, to apprehend online productions and grasp this complexity: the notion of socio-technical devices facilitates the construction of content from the Web as an object of research.

Far from proposing a way of doing things or a *vade-mecum* of good practices, we would like to point out the contributions of semiodiscursive approaches to the analysis of Web content. Indeed, the analysis of digital content, both that displayed on-screen (Souchier 1996) and found in techno-languages (Paveau 2017), cannot be envisaged without examining their conditions of production, spread and circulation, in other words, what devices do to data. In addition, the complexity of the contents, their heterogeneous nature and their composite aspect require us to go back and forth between the theory and the data. The accessibility of these data, as well as their material or scriptural dimension, are not a given but instead a construct in connection with a research question. There are also questions of scale and contextualization in the collection and interpretation of data, which requires a reflexive posture to choose relevant methods and tools related to a semiodiscursive research question.

2.2. How to do relevant data sets with Web data? The making of a complex object of research

2.2.1. *Sociotechnical devices and the construction of the object*

When our interest is political communication, the forms of expression online, or the circulation of forms such as Facebook's "like" feature, the data taken from

---

4 In other words, all the "computer objects that are in a position to govern the writing, to provide it with its formats and its resources" (Tardy and Jeanneret 2007, p. 24; Goyet 2017).

websites can be considered as observables, provided that we understand the website as a complex and composite device within which different types of data can be collected. This can suppose a true centrality of the website, thought of as a device socio-technical. By calling the device "socio-technical", the goal is to provide a reminder of the interdependence between the technical and social dimensions, emphasizing the complex ecology that contributes to the production of Web content. This notion borrows from the philosophy of Michel Foucault, who defined the concept of device ("*dispositif*" in French), as "a resolutely heterogeneous set comprising discourses, institutions, architectural arrangements, regulatory decisions, laws, administrative measures, scientific statements, and philosophical, moral, and philanthropic proposals; in short: from what is spoken as well as from what is unspoken, these are the elements of the device". "The device itself is the network that can be established between these elements" (1977, p. 62). The notion of a device has been used quite often and has sparked discussions in communication studies, which have given rise to several publications (Jacquinot-Delaunay and Monnoyer 1999; Call et al. 2010; Bonaccorsi and Julliard 2010; Gavillet 2010; Monnoyer-Smith 2016). As Violaine Appel, Hélène Boulanger and Luc Massou recalled in 2010, "in information and communication sciences, the device is a key notion that is closely linked to the analysis of mediation processes, an analysis that, among other things, allows us to associate the study of media and technological media with that of the challenges and players in particular social situations" (Appel et al. 2010, p. 9). This notion draws our attention to the composite dimension of the device and emphasizes the interconnection between discourses and practices, without underestimating the strategic dimension that any device can cover. Today, we can note that the central issue for the actors of the media and communication industries is the interface which makes it possible to organize the access to a diverse array of forms and content, speakers and industries. This has been shown by Vincent Bullich and Thomas Guignard in their article on connected TV platforms and the challenge of valorization for the players involved in the production process (Bullich and Guignard 2014). In this way, numerous studies have stressed the importance of taking into account the ecology of devices and their interfaces in order to contextualize the content and understand their production conditions.

For Laurence Monnoyer-Smith, observing and analyzing Web devices "represents a desire to see a technically complex and socially constructed reality, [...] it is necessary to properly ascertain the complex mediation relationships that contribute to shaping the Web to the extent they are constrained by it and to deduce the consequences, both theoretically and methodologically" (Monnoyer-Smith 2016, p. 13). The analysis of Web content therefore prompts researchers to reinforce a more reflexive posture, to take into account different discourses, technological imaginaries, interface design, software programs and databases, that is to say, the complexity of the device and the forms of mediation.

There are two pitfalls to be avoided: the reification of Web devices, as well as the naturalization of such devices.

Refusing to reify socio-technical Web devices eliminates the temptation to pretend that the Web can be considered a monolithic reality, which is essential from a methodological point of view, and in particular while interpreting the data. For example, if we take the case of online participation devices, Clément Mabi's work has shown a variety of uses for them, as well as the contrasting dimension of the interface and the importance of the context: depending on the issue discussed, the device and its design do not promote dialogue (Mabi 2016, p. 33). In the case of online petitioning, although the sites have common characteristics, there are many differences that depend on the device studied, such as the presence or absence of tips for filing a petition, the number and title of the headings proposed to classify petitions (presence or absence of a "health" category, for example), which affects the act of petitioning and the production of content, in this case the texts filed as well as their comments (Huré 2017; Barats et al. 2019). The notion of a socio-technical device would also allow us pay attention to whether or not the device is stable over time, and to the architexts, that is to say, to the "computer objects that are in a position to govern the writing, to provide it with its formats and its resources" (Tardy and Jeanneret 2007, p. 24; Goyet 2017). These architexts, to use the example of online petitioning, encourage or incite the act of petitioning through the highlighting on the home page of a selection of petitions, the ones that have the most signatures, the most recently, etc. (Barats et al. 2019).

The de-naturalizing of these devices helps to avoid a meaning of "the Web" that does not take into account the complexity of the mediation relationships from which it comes, in this case without taking into account the heterogeneous and evolving array of the components that make it up. From a methodological point of view, Web devices involve the processing of signs and symbolism, as well as technical and social elements. This involves deconstructing all that has been "wrapped up in the Web and that remains invisible on the surface in what is displayed on the screen", and thus linked to a socio-technical construct to be made intelligible. It is necessary to "deconstruct the evidence of these traces in order to highlight the fabric of the mediations which, like the tip of an iceberg, produces a trace which is given to the researcher to see. Going beyond and deeper within the Web is essential to understanding it" (Monnoyer-Smith 2016, p. 15). What can be seen at a time t is the result of a set of mediations that must be brought to light by paying attention to the conditions and context of production of the content and data from Web devices in order to guarantee the analysis of any interpretative bias, particularly in the case of semiodiscursive approaches that give a central role to the conditions of production.

2.2.2. *From the research question to the data sets: knowledge and documentation of the device*

As soon as the research question is posed, the socio-technical device that is the Web implies a back-and-forth between the research question and the criteria of the selection of data, that is to say, the things the researcher will observe, collect and analyze, without underestimating the limits and blind spots inherent in any empirical approach. In other words, it requires taking into account the porosity of the devices, their dynamic and sometimes ephemeral aspects, which can make collecting certain data difficult.

This requires the researcher to have good knowledge of the device, a form of inventiveness also to collect initial data and verify their relevance, and thus test the selection criteria in order to build observables related to the chosen problem.

The complexity of these socio-technical devices requires us to resituate their contents within a logical flow where measurements and algorithms play a central role. To illustrate this, we will examine a study conducted on online petitioning[5], which showed that the visibility on the home page of the site of the most recent or most signed petitions had an impact on the petitioning dynamics, which confirms the significance of the interface (Barats et al. 2019).

The documentation of the data collection conditions and the specific attributes of the device is thus central to situating the results and interpreting them. This involves the monitoring of the interface and its design (screenshots) in order to contextualize the data, to distinguish the data entered by Internet users and those generated by the device, and if necessary, to note the changes in the interface. What may be referred to as the stability of the device should be questioned.

Figures 2.1 and 2.2 illustrate the changes over time of the homepage of an online petitioning site, highlighting the importance of screenshots in examining the transformations of the device being studied.

---

5 Contrat ANR-14-CE29-0010, projet APPEL (Analyse pluridisciplinaire du pétitionnement en ligne – *Pluridisciplinary Analysis of On Line Petitioning*), Jean-Gabriel Contamin (CERAPS/ Lille 2, scientific coordinator). Available at: www.anr-appel.eu.

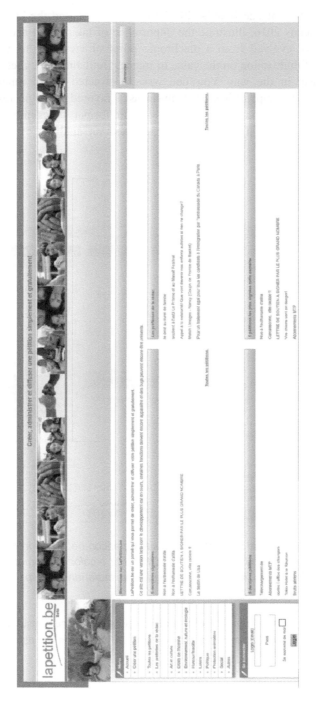

Figure 2.1. *Homepage of the website lapetition.be, retrieved from the Internet Archive archives, on 3 July 2007 (source: www.web.archive.org/web/20070703021331). For a color version of this figure, see www.iste.co.uk/massou/analyzing.zip*

The introduction of Facebook's "like" button in 2010, and the later addition of five new emoticons 2016, illustrate the importance of taking into account the way the devices have evolved from a diachronic point of view. In his thesis on the consequences of digitization on the value of music, Guillaume Heuguet analyzes the impact of music in the way YouTube was constructed as an innovation, and questions how the company has used music as a favored strategic resource. The semiological study of technical, media and aesthetic formats takes into consideration the successive transformations of interfaces based on analysis of Web archives (Heuguet 2018).

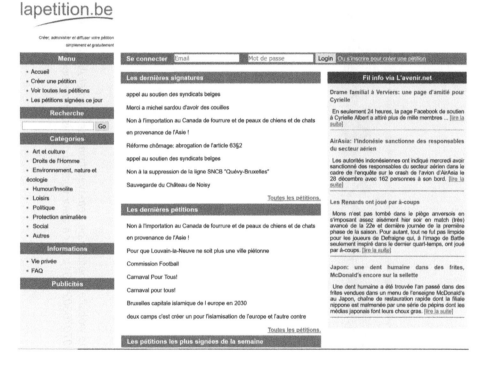

Figure 2.2. *Home page of the website lapetition.be, taken from the Internet Archive, January 7, 2015[6]. For a color version of this figure, see www.iste.co.uk/massou/analyzing.zip*

Depending on what is being researched, the question of the consultation terminal can also attract attention, as material support has an impact on the data, the analyzed

_____

6 Available at: www.web.archive.org/web/20150107075940.

contents and the communicational pretension (PC versus tablet versus smartphone, or conversely, a trans-media process). The notion of a device confirms its relevance since it contributes to greater attention paid to the ecology of the Web, which includes the visibility of certain content compared to others. Also, the anticipation of reception practices, as illustrated today by the nearly systematic subtitling of videos circulating on social networks such as Facebook, letting them be viewed without sound and confirming the importance of considering alphanumeric texts, including for videos. In a way, the devices format the statements of the Web and are formatted by the practices of consultation of digital content. In addition, the analysis of data and Web content cannot ignore the different forms of use, and the role of recommendation algorithms that provide content suggestions according to users' practices and make it difficult to build an "above ground" corpus, that is to say, without taking into account user profiles and algorithmic logic in making certain content visible.

To summarize the necessary consideration and knowledge of devices for analyzing Web content from a semiodiscursive perspective, the cited works focus our attention on:

– the tensions between the necessary stability and reproducibility of research versus the instability of the devices;

– the short time span of the rapid progression of websites and digital data versus the long timespan needed for research, hence the importance of the documentation of the research protocol for the interpretation of the results;

– the choices and trade-offs necessary to carry out the investigation: delimiting its "terrain", defining criteria for the data collection, and retaining different types of data, depending on the object of study and the assumptions used (screenshots, corpus of data, interviews with the designers of the device or documentation of the latter, etc.). We will discuss these precautions in detail in the second part.

Therefore, the device is far from being a concrete object that, to a certain extent, would perhaps be duplicated from a website, and is instead an effective conceptual tool for constructing the object of the research. The socio-technical device thus falls within a first instance of delimitation of the research field and the relevant observables. In this respect, this concept supports a social and material complexity that is quite crucial for integrating temporal dimensions into the defining of the problem, such as by taking into account the evolution of the interface of a social network and its diachrony, but also its spatial and situational dimensions so as to finely grasp the relationships between online statements and offline interactions, or for example, different media and display and dissemination sites in urban public space (Bonaccorsi 2020).

2.2.3. *Notional tools for semiodiscursive approaches*

Thus, the delimitation of research materials, as we have seen previously, is both a deconstruction and a reconstruction that the concept of the device allows us to carry out because it supports the problematization and makes it explicit. The research objectives of the studies we have mentioned are certainly heterogeneous, but they are located between two poles specific to communication approaches: understanding social phenomena and characterizing their mediatization. If the issues are divided between other poles according to the research, a structuring axis is the difference with the digital sciences, in particular through the development of notional tools that, in turn, shift the relationship to concrete objects.

In this sense, we can cite the foundational work of Yves Jeanneret: *"Y a-t-il (vraiment) des technologies de l'information et de la communication?" ("Do information and communication technologies (truly) exist?")* (Jeanneret 2011). Explaining the distinction between two irreconcilable values of information, the social value and the mathematical value, Yves Jeanneret highlights the challenge of conducting research on the breadth of social and cultural mediations at work, and on the way in which ICTs[7] imply interpretation, in the same way as a communication medium. This perspective, which is supported by established knowledge on media devices, is part of the tradition of text theory, and works on reading and writing, as well as publishing. Thus, attention is paid to the relationships between the technical and semiotic properties of digital writings and appropriation practices as they become standardized and modeled by Web devices, for example. The communities of researchers reveal distinct dimensions of the materiality of digital writings and their social operativeness: textuality, interpretation, editorial device and documentary strata. These notions make it possible to deconstruct such terms as interface, platform, application, or even site, by implementing qualitative approaches focused on limited and location-specific research materials. The methods developed seek to identify and qualify verbal and visual signs and their meaningful organization in the context of the screen. This qualification thus allows us to

---

7 Information and Communication Technologies, according to the syntax in use in France in the 1990s.

distinguish signs that have an editing and writing function, such as the hypertext link (renamed as a "signe-passeur"[8]), to identify processes of standardization of writing by templates and forms of *Content Management System* (renamed in architexts) which provide material for databases and editorialize content. The "digital" realm is thus characterized by its semiotic continuity, where contexts of spaces, objects and various signs are present where people act. Since the notion of the "écrit d'écran"[9], the analytical framework has been developing to take into account computerized media that addresses multiple granularities of Web services: from the Facebook like button analyzed as a circulating sign (Candel and Gomez-Meija 2017) to the editorial role of APIs (*Application Programming Interfaces*) described by Samuel Goyet as "tools that propagate a certain conception of the text and which are located in a contemporary economy where the text is processed to circulate, be taken up, and transformed" (Goyet 2017).

These works propose many empirical and concrete research avenues based on surveys situated so as to critically approach that which produces "content" and unity of meaning, and to think about the points of connection between the technical and symbolic domains. In fact, the layers of writing (computer processing by calculating the coded representation, and the formatting on the screen) and their social values have been studied since the 1990s as the modalities of construction, access and representation of texts and documents that constitute the digital realm.

It is worth focusing on the consideration given to the breadth of the documentary materials to qualify the new forms of writing, inscription, authority and memory, as well as their social life. Indeed, the use of the notion of the "document" is not anecdotal, and is supported by the knowledge developed in the information–documentation field of the communication studies (Cotte 2004). A "document" can essentially be envisaged by the recognition, in a social project, of an indexed and detachable unit of meaning. Thus, it, which constitutes "data" or "traces", depends on this recognition (or these different degrees of recognition), by researchers, the publisher of the site or by its reader (Jeanneret 2020).

Approaching the Web through documentary economies thus requires two behaviors: on the one hand, recognizing the materiality of "sharing", the "circulation" of "content" and on the other hand, understanding and interpreting the information structures and documentary organizations of Web devices as social constructs. In a collective study that we are conducting on the ordinary media

---

8 In English, a "sign for passing or acting" (Davallon and Jeanneret 2004, p. 53).
9 Literally, "écrit d'écran" refers to the text written by and for the screen as a display surface.

displays in the urban space that our analysis focuses on how unprofessional photographic statements on the Web "become archives", and their potential transformation into documentary traces of the territory. This investigation allows us to understand the different editorial and material operations of the documentary enhancement of photographic representations of urban space shared on digital social networks (DSNs)[10]: operations industrialized by the architects of digital media in the form of DSNs and documentation operations tinkered with by the authors of the images; valorization operations by institutions for the preservation of heritage wishing to make these semi-private documents as commons (Navarro and Bonaccorsi 2018).

Beyond giving a state of the art and an inventory of the digital tools, at the end of this first part, we will essentially note some of the major avenues opened up by these cumulative studies on the transformations of written culture and the media, in a broad sense. Firstly, the recognition of the editorial dimension of Web devices which directs the questioning toward instances, authorities and enunciators in a very judicious way, also making it possible to think about contemporary mutations of authorship[11]. Secondly, the voluntary notional shift with categories that conceal semiotic operativeness, such as "hypertext link", "interactivity", or even "content"; third, the emphasis on the foundations of Web devices insofar as they already contain writings: databases and their documentary breadth (which also give rise to a kind of arms race between possible algorithms to produce calculated statements or links); fourth, the predominant issue of circulation as a model (of writing and dissemination): of media variation, and that which is "shareable".

However, the presentation of a semiology of Web devices broken down in this way fails in part to be structured as a methodological protocol, in particular for the formulation or elaboration of a corpus in phase with a field, a space of practices, or an investigation leading to multiple adjustments and iterations. In our second part, the collection and constitution of observations in corpora and research materials, as well as the knowledge issues that are identified, will now be questioned, from a critical perspective specific to semiodiscursive approaches.

---

10 Projet IDENUM – Identités numériques urbaines. LabEx Intelligence des mondes urbains, Université de Lyon (2016–2020). Unités de recherche impliquées : ELICO EA 4147, ERIC EA 3083, EVS UMR 5600, LIRIS UMR 5205.

11 The amateur contribution, instances without institutions, such as automatic or semi-automatic writing algorithms called "bots", are analyzed in particular by Marie-Noëlle Doutreix (2019).

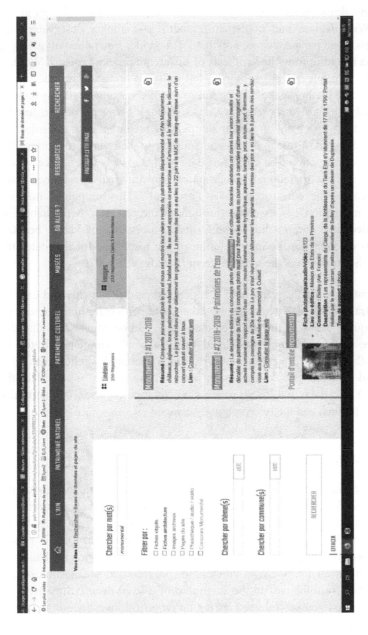

Figure 2.3. *Integration of photographs from the #Monumental competition into the heritage databases of the Ain Departmental Council, 2019 (source: www.patrimcines.ain.fr/archive/resultats/globale/n:559?RECH_libre=bassin&RECH_typedoc%5B0%5D= Objet&RECH_typedoc%5B1%5D=Architecture&RECH_typedoc%5B2%5D=concoursphoto&type=globale). For a color version of this figure, see www.iste.co.uk/massou/analyzing.zip*

2.3. Standing the test of time: surveys and methods

This section deals with the main methodological issues involved in understanding Web devices and constructing them as complex observables, as relevant data sets. Our perspective is not that of a guide, but rather of giving a critical panorama resulting from the synthesis of different research projects. We thus seek not principally to put forward solutions, but rather to bring to light the salient points that have come to oppose the conception of the Web as a pre-existing thing, a gateway to social worlds. On the contrary, it is through being put to the test by conditions in the field, space and time that sharpen the methods, from the selection decisions and the fixation of research data and sources, to their very production. We will approach the construction of a corpus of data as this always takes place within an investigation, subject to rational, geographical, institutional constraints: each investigation involves the construction of a "protocol". The scrupulous notation of this (its "documentation") is essential throughout the research: beforehand and during the collection, during the storage and processing of data, because documentation is essential for the interpretation of the results, and it facilitates the intelligibility of the approach in the medium term (Schafer et al. 2020).

This documentation and the reflexivity it engages then make visible and explicit the sets of constraints in which decisions are taken, and participate in the selection, production and qualification of the research data. It should be emphasized that this conception of research operations articulated in a "survey" has demonstrated its effectiveness in the context of certain multidisciplinary research studies, making it possible to avoid an overly marked division between the players involved in the collection of "Web" data and their processing (computer sciences, and also conservation institutions) and the interpretative sciences.

2.3.1. *Tangled temporalities*

In the HSS, defining the problem of the social requires thinking about the relationship to time following at least two forms of logics: first, the temporality of the research conducted, and second, the temporality of the data. For this reason, the terrain outside the Web is captured in an artifactual way. It is also for this reason that data are collected and qualified, which is to say interpreted (such as data from the people present in an interview as enunciation in recorded oral testimony are contrasted with data from the past in the statement of a lived event). Similarly, the value of a documentary source collected during an empirical investigation is related to its symbolic value in the present, for the social actors who have preserved it, or by contrast, who have forgotten it. In other words, the quest, just like research on written corpora, requires thinking about the articulation between the moment of data collection (a duration, a predefined sequence) and the temporalities of the social phenomena to which they refer. Surveys conducted based on or using Web devices are obviously infused by this reflexivity over time, but in a more ambiguous way, particularly due to the updating and evolution of certain Web devices, the never-ending metamorphosis of some observables, and the disappearance of others.

Firstly, the instability of the observables highlighted in the first section induces an iterative and pluri-semiotic practice of fixing and collecting research materials to consolidate their temporal relevance. It must be said that the conditions are rarely ideal, and even before a decision is made on a reasoned and pragmatic protocol, various operations are carried out for exploratory purposes but can also continue: screenshots, collection by hand, the formation of a corpus, the selection of extracts, automatic collection and making recourse to existing collections (the National Library of France [BNF], the National Audiovisual Institute [INA]). The attaching of data may depend on various operations that then involve different types of analysis and processing: for example, the screenshot may differ from a "hand-picked" collection of textual statements, or from the automated collection of data and metadata.

Secondly, this tension between the temporality of research and the temporality of Web services is particularly exacerbated by the very conditions of research practice, both from the point of view of social demand and also the need for "emergency excavations". These are the work of researchers proposing to examine data almost in real time, such as example in the case of the attacks in France in January and November 2015, or in 2020 during the time of the Covid-19 pandemic[12]. However, this research implies that the importance of the Web's document architectures and their instability over time must not be underestimated, especially the long times for indexing and processing these data.

Similarly, the values aggregated by notation and evaluation practices do not constitute a data item without a fine-level understanding of the time span of the assigned notations. In other words, just as the analysis of media content requires a rigorous understanding of the temporal modalities of publication and the relationship to the event they define, research on materials from Web publications requires the same rigor, in addition to being alert to any possible changes to the sites. However,

---

12 For example, see the challenges faced by the "emergency collections" conducted by the BNF: www.asap.hypotheses.org/168. See also the historiographical issues surrounding the collection conducted by Frédéric Clavert involving Covid-19: www.c2dh.uni.lu/thinkering/traces-et-memoires-en-devenir-dune-pandemie.

despite all efforts, accurately dating the statements studied is not always possible, which requires the additional use of other sources and the producing of hypotheses[13].

The issue of temporalities is thus at the very heart of the definition of the protocol (what, when), of the production of data (what is fixed, archived to be processed) but also of their indexing (what temporal relationship they have to the "reference reality"), and requires diversifying empirical inputs and scales, that is to say, to approach data sets and observables with a flexible and iterative granularity. Semiodiscursive approaches, whether based on quantitative or qualitative empirical approaches, share situated objects of knowledge that involve addressing entangled temporalities.

2.3.2. Defining the right way to select and collect data sets

As we mentioned in previous sections, the variety of status types of the potentially collected or collectable data is infinite, and it would be very difficult to seek to determine the various associated tricks that could be played beforehand. What seems particularly salient to us is not so much the homogeneity of the types of materials entered into the survey, but rather the stability of the theoretical postulates that give rise to the definition of proper data: we consider it to be "proper" in the sense that it is valid, from the point of view of the survey conducted and the objectives of knowledge.

In the same way that the study on how the culture of amateur gardening is spread can give rise to the notation of the types of tools used, to the study of layouts of gardens or speeches on the soil and its quality, or even the numerical comparison of the diversity of vegetables planted according to the gardener's experience, the semiodiscursive approaches of Web devices are not predisposed to a single type of data; these can arise from a very qualitative and situational approach, or from an extraction of quantified values. However, it is essential to insist that researchers always keep an eye on the concrete object (the website, tweet, Facebook wall, etc.) in its social coherence, as a publication, or on the very contexts of production and reception (interviews, observations, etc.).

We will point out two sets of difficulties related to the collection of research materials since they never quite correspond to the famous "Web content" whose socio-political and symbolic operativity we wish to understand.

---

13. The problem of the temporal aspects of data was the subject of a seminar since 2019 led by Agnieszka Smolczewska Tona, "The thousand-count Data" (Enssib, ELICO).

The first set concerns the selection and attention to the margins, to the alternating cases ("crumbs") which, according to the surveys, can turn out to be useful and significant. In other words, the points of view that we defend do not predetermine types of data that are "valid" for some issues more so than for others. For example, the question of the algorithmic manufacturing of cultural prescription by online recommendation sites can give rise to the collection of very varied types of data, from the textual statements of published opinions, the collection of ratings and genres of evaluated content, the metadata associated with cultural objects, the algorithm's software, screenshots, etc. The semiodiscursive perspective, regardless of the nature of these data, leads us to question the way in which, in the very practice of collecting and preparing corpora, certain entries will be selected that necessarily involve choices and thus contain blind spots: data entered by Internet users, those related to the device (architexts) and those generated by the device (algorithms, measurements, automatic writing by bots). This will require the questioning of the conditions in which texts, sounds, still or animated images, etc. are produced, and taking into account their enunciative plurality (device, advertising advertisers, Internet users with or without anonymity and pseudonym, etc.).

There is nothing new in this comment on the relationship between data and the limits of knowledge horizons, but a reflection on what is excluded from the analysis is all the more necessary with regard to the Web, which is prone to many pitfalls: the survivability of certain particularly high-profile phenomena, the editorial and semiotic complexity of web pages, gaps in archives leading to a bias toward the present, the power of the promises of digital companies, etc. The effects of taking a closer look at the formats, statements or processes, or the invisibilization of others, presuppose the taking of scrupulous precautions in the identification, selection and prioritization, implying a slow-down of pace in the investigation, which is a welcome change.

The second set highlights the necessary qualification of the collected data on the basis of knowledge of the production contexts of these data, the instances that predispose them to collection, which in the investigation is a use of data, as well as the manufacture of these data. On the one hand, the intent to form a base of knowledge from these mass-scale data generation sources, such as the social networks Twitter, Instagram and Facebook, constitutes to a certain extent a turning point in HSS research, "directed from now on by the existence of data, and not by its prior point of view on the object it is questioning, if only from its investigative device" (Bonaccorsi and Tardy 2019). For example, Marta Severo and Timothée Giraud have shown the risks and perils of social science research in the angelic recovery of data from the social digital network, to analyze them as traces of the social (Severo and Giraud 2019). The transfer of data sets from one social context (that of platforms and their own objectives) to another (that of scientific research and the objectives of the survey) is particularly sensitive and absolutely a major issue. This qualification of the relationship of data to a "reference reality" (Olivier de Sardan 1996) has been the subject of publications that have highlighted the ambiguity of the value of the "trace of the social" (Jeanneret 2020). On the other hand, the qualification of the collection of data is also affected by the issue of archives and conservation: other entities, those in the public service sector such as the BNF or the INA, are thus intermediaries in the collection and selection of data that participate in their mode of existence, and prefigure the types of research or objects for collection a priori, even if this reflection on Web archiving is carried out in close collaboration with researchers (Schafer 2018). The source then takes on relative and consistent values, underlining the extent to which the investigation on/by the Web is part of the continuity of the difficulties and pitfalls of semiodiscursive analysis (Lécossais and Quemener 2018; Anquetil et al. 2019).

The two sets of difficulties that we have noted here directly highlight some of the ideas received on the Web, envisaged as a repository of data (which would be used), direct and easily accessible (available), especially by the apprentice researchers who are students. There are many blind spots here, which lead us to reaffirm, among other things: the data are always produced by the survey conducted.

2.3.3. *From the notion of corpus to the notion of digital corpus*

The notion of the corpus, central to linguistics and language sciences, is also essential for other disciplines in the HSS, and in particular in communication studies. In language sciences, the use of a corpus is mandatory operation and attests to the diverse nature of the criteria selection: by speakers, themes or pivotal words, moments of speech (Moirand 2007), etc. There is also a review devoted to this notion: the *Corpus* review[14]. Very often, one or more exploratory corpus is necessary in order to verify the validity and relevance of the collection criteria and avoid biases. In the case of a digital corpus, the exploratory corpus makes it possible to refine the collection criteria and is part of an iterative approach, which can result in lengthy periods being devoted to this stage (combining criteria, excluding them, evaluating blind spots in the search, etc.).

The notion of the corpus helps to shed light on the methodological issues for the construction of digital corpora, given the heterogeneity of the data. It implies an objectification of the criteria for the constitution of the corpus, whether one single corpus or multiple ones. When we are looking at a semiotic form and its circulation,

---

14 Available at: www.journals.openedition.org/corpus.

such as the Facebook like button, it is thus possible to constitute a corpus of screenshots according to criteria which include the date, enunciators, types of devices, etc., "to understand the symbolic powers attributed to the like as a written and therefore social object: as an object of computer practices for Internet users, this clickable button can alternately arouse admiration, empathy, infatuation, curiosity, fear, distrust, or astonishment" (Candel and Gomez-Mejia 2017).

Alphanumeric and semiotic data can also be collected in a corpus in the case of an analysis of the semiodiscursive exchanges present in a discussion thread or in the case of reactions to a hashtag, for example, and this presupposes a good knowledge of the device. The criteria for selecting the data can be linked to an enunciator and/or a form and/or a period, and can be based on principles of representativeness, traditionally implemented in the HSS. The criteria vary according to the objectives of the research and can be combined in order to narrow down the content that is collected and guarantee the coherence and relevance of the corpus (one or multiple). It is important to remember that the corpus is constructed, that is to say, it is constituted in accordance with specific criteria, defined according to the problem set out by the researcher. There is no such thing as a "turnkey" corpus or a "corpus reservoir", and any corpus requires a clear definition of the collection criteria. The availability of massive amounts of digital data does not imply the pre-existence of a corpus that is "naturally" ready for analysis (Barats et al. 2016) because all collections assume an objectivized set of criteria. If the hypermnesia of the Web, in part related to the policies of systematic archiving, makes it accessible to many corpora, it renews the reflections on the terms of the definition of criteria for the collection of a corpus compiled from data that is both heterogeneous (alphanumeric data, sound, visual, time stamped, etc.) and ephemeral – including a short duration – and constraints for the design of delivery devices (sites, social-digital networks, etc.), as well as for their reception (computers, tablets, smartphones). This requires making a choice depending on the objectives of the research and excluding certain data in order to guarantee the coherence of the corpus and of the data collected.

The digital corpora are usually part of a logical flow that should not be underestimated. The use of data collection tools makes it necessary not to blindly delegate to the software because any collection program is based on choices and assumptions that must be made known. It must be added that the time taken for the research does not coincide with that of the devices, which are often unstable and short-lived, and it involves anticipating these difficulties so as not to artificially freeze a dynamic temporality. The researchers may need to obtain new skills.

In the case of using the archives, the knowledge of the conditions for the establishment of the database is necessary. Virginie Julliard and Thomas Bottini, who have used the archives of the INA to examine the dimension of semiotics of the controversy on Twitter around gender studies, emphasize that we must "take into account the logical archiving of these databases which are not always explicit, as well as the changes in architecture and editorial policies" (Bottini and Julliard 2017, p. 47). The reliability of the analysis depends on the intelligibility of the conditions of collection and the limitations inherent in any collection. The choice of the data and their readability in the medium term therefore involve a detailed documentation of the archiving logic to document the corpus. However, a knowledge of the methods of collecting and archiving can be complex in the case of digital materials.

Traditionally, different criteria are used for the constitution of the corpus:

– keywords or critical words for a so-called thematic corpus;

– an enunciator or a discussion thread;

– dates or periods for synchronic versus diachronic corpus;

– so-called open corpus (without closure) versus so-called closed corpus that make it necessary to resort to computer tools for automatic processing;

– so-called representative versus exhaustive corpus;

– transversal (different arenas) versus longitudinal corpus, etc.

It can be useful to combine criteria. However, it is necessary to ensure the consistency of the corpus, especially in the case of automatic processing, and compare what is comparable.

In the case of digital data, the criteria can be linked to a semantic form or a hashtag to better observe its circulation. Maxime Cervulle and Fred Pailler (2014) have shown that certain hashtags have a high conversational efficiency and are characterized by peaks in their frequency of use. Looking at public media spaces, and in particular digital ones, they analyzed the use of the hashtags #mariagepourtous ("marriage for all") and #manifpourtous ("demonstrations for all") on Twitter in the context of the debates in France in 2013 around the reform to open marriage to same-sex couples. These hashtags show schisms: the analysis of the corpus has revealed enunciative and argumentative positions that shed light on the semiodiscursive characteristics of the arenas studied and the role of hashtags. The use of corpus and the consideration of morpho-syntactic characteristics confirm their heuristic dimension, and attest to the importance of situating and contextualizing the data in order to interpret the results.

2.4. Violence against data: issues of interpretation

To borrow again from the anthropologist Jean-Pierre Olivier de Sardan in his analysis of the "violence against data", we return in this third part to the interpretative operations that base the very practice of SHS research: "Interpretative processes, as omnipresent as they are, recognize empirical constraints and give themselves procedures of (relative) methodological vigilance (and not only logical vigilance) that try to preserve a certain level of adequacy between empirical referents and interpretative assertions" (Olivier de Sardan 1996).

This attention to interpretative processes has been mentioned previously about the "collection" of data, and we have clearly specified how problematic their treatment of the "traces" of the social has been. We thus see that the question of interpretation cannot be relegated to a final sequence (which would be in a linear perspective: "I have my data, I process them, then I finally analyze them by interpreting them"), but concerns the approach as a whole, from the definition of the object of research to the selection of observables and materials, their qualification in data and corpus, to categorization and analysis. This point to look out for is fundamental in that it imposes a constant denaturalization of data as a means of understanding social phenomena.

2.4.1. Formatting of issues by research instrumentation

The virtuosity and innovation in the development of computerized tools for analysis on/by the Web is now quite remarkable (a participant in the digital methods), supported by an institutional dynamic of development of the digital humanities (in France, in the Research institution, etc.) and by the growing injunction to constitute radically multidisciplinary project consortia: because the materials are digital, this would therefore also require computer tools. Conversely, some disciplinary fields such as discourse analysis have been working with computerized tools for a long time and remind us of the importance of returning to the text and context for the interpretation of results, in other words, combining the quantitative approach with a fine qualitative and situational analysis (Born et al. 2017). As such, we consider that a certain critical maturity of the HSS communities regarding these dynamics is observable today and that it can be quite effective, scientific and fertile, in areas such as the exploratory part of the investigation, or even for the analysis as a whole, to work with the following tools: screenshots, notes, hand-indexing of small corpora and reading or viewing the analyzed statements in their entirety.

However, the Web device has been seized on in particular as a socio-technical observable since the 1990s by the joint exploration of its socio-semiotic properties and the tools for observing them; for example, the trend toward Web mapping depends both on a conceptual predefinition of the Web as a territory and on computerized instrumentation in terms of data collection and visualization of spatialized data. We may note that the methodological monitoring evoked by Olivier de Sardan is particularly difficult to carry out in this context, even though this method (Web mapping) stands out as being a "tool" for objectification, compared to "hand-crafted" methods. The study of the relationships between online publications (between websites) is central, but the qualification of a "map" and "territory" is a metaphor that, even before the data visualization, introduces a first theoretical interpretation of the social value of the relationships between the data produced, what Jeanneret refers to as "chimeras" (2020).

Likewise, the analysis of controversies currently constitutes another example of this pre-interpretation of phenomena through a theoretical model, encapsulated by the collection and processing software used for this analysis. Thus, controversies are less of an outcome (which would eventually lead us to consider that the issue was not in fact a controversy but something else instead, or to refine what defines a controversy), and more of a prerequisite – in other words, a ready-made thought pattern within a machine designed to represent and visualize controversies. Obviously, this caricature is quite simplistic, but it makes it possible to emphasize (though admittedly, along very general lines) the fragility of the readings of the social world a priori, which are embedded within the tool. Our experience in the collective task of carrying out the survey and producing a digital instrument to do so goes in this direction, an experience that we have been able to have in various contexts of research. For example, the monitoring then focuses on the increasingly frequent use (and production) of automatic processing tools – as in the case of automation tools for *opinion mining* or sentiment analysis (Boullier and Lohard 2012) – which sometimes reduce the textual data (partially erasing their diversity and heterogeneity) and standardize the potential results.

This gives rise to two important points in the monitoring of the formatting of the issues by the software tools to keep in mind: the first concerns the pre-existing notions which can be grouped under an initial conceptual interpretation of "the Web", definitively prefiguring the analytical and theoretical framework (a public space, a territory, the contributing factors, etc.); the second concerns the reflexive analysis of the operations and representations produced as a crutch in their interpretation (Compagno 2017). Our second point will thus focus on the way in which semiodiscursive approaches, through their expertise which also bears on the processes of meaning, take into account what makes the collected materials meaningful and significant (Compagno and Treleani 2019) to respond to issues in the HSS.

2.4.2. *Limits and challenges of interpretation: taking the illusion of immediacy and standardization of meaning into account*

Works in the field of discourse analysis and in semiology have long focused on social frameworks and issues of meaning from a perspective that seriously considers languages as a social practice (Burger 2018).

We will note three interpretative operations so as to highlight their limits and issues, by linking them to distinct but correlated horizons of knowledge such as social facts, categorization and computerized media. Society, concepts (opinion, identity, etc.) and media (writing, editorialization, etc.) are three means for carrying out the interpretation and specifying of the types of knowledge that can be produced and the purposes of knowledge. The importance given to the conditions for gathering and collecting data is at the core of semiodiscursive approaches. The question at hand is that of situating data and examining their condition of production and diffusion in order not to consider data as a reflection of opinions and not to grasp the Web as a mirror of what is seen as a digital public sphere, one that is homogeneous and immediately readable, obliterating the issues related to meaning, the opacity of data and their meaning.

First, digital data require taking into account the context, insofar as the meaning is neither transparent nor unambiguous and is part of the social relations, the power issues that depend on the context, both production and reception. As we have pointed out, returning to the text and the socio-political context is essential. Romain Badouard has focused on the hashtags #jesuischarlie and #jenesuispas-charlie ("I am Charlie" and "I am not Charlie") and their roles in the dynamics and structuring of the online public debate after the January 2015 attacks on the editorial office of *Charlie Hebdo*. He recalls that the creation of the hashtag #jesuiskouachi ("I am Kouachi", the name of one of the terrorists) is linked to being used by the extreme right in order to denounce and stigmatize immigrant populations. He also draws attention to the limits of a strictly quantitative approach that would infer the movements of opinions: "On Twitter, the number of uses and the virality of a hashtag in a conversation are not sufficiently reliable data to be considered as indicators of changes in opinion" (Badouard 2016).

Romain Badouard's comments lead us to our second interpretative operation, which involves the categorization, and more broadly, the use of concepts to designate (and therefore qualify) the phenomena observed: the notion of opinion, as we have shown in this chapter, constitutes a very significant example of this reference to data which are then "considered as indicators". We must not give in to the temptation to make misleading reflections that would disregard the conditions and means employed in speech (Raynauld et al. 2020), and update the critical questions in HSS and communication studies on the effects of categorization: overinterpretation or anachronisms, the importing of terms (the "participative", the "community", the "virtual"), borrowings from common places. The critical deconstruction of these preconceptions requires great care within a context where the predefinition of communication processes by digital promoters is often naturalized. This deconstruction itself represents a possible site for new knowledge and new problems.

The third interpretative operation on which we would like to focus responds to the aim of knowledge concerning the media and media-related areas of the Web as a socio-technical device. We have developed this horizon of fundamental knowledge in semiodiscursive approaches at greater length in our first part. A fine-grained and measured elaboration of the corpora of data will contribute to this knowledge of symbolic materiality and the making of meaning in computerized media, based on epistemological and empirical frameworks that place Web devices as part of a long history of written culture and languages, information and public space. It is constructed within a vast space, one that is constantly being reconfigured by the rapid transformation of industries, technologies and formats, which means that what is written over long time periods and within cultures is rendered invisible, while also creating an illusion of novelty. The desire to know of the Web as a medium would be like going from bad to worse, that much is clear. Conversely, a fine level of understanding of the processes of mediatization (e.g. that of "sharing") is an essential knowledge project, carried out on the basis of precise empirical studies describing the documentary and enunciative mediations involved, taking note of the layers of writing and the power of their effects.

2.5. Conclusion

Tasked with the elusive challenge of capturing "traces of the social" from analyses of Web devices, we wish to revisit the contributions of semiodiscursive approaches in order to contextualize the data, situate these data and prioritize an iterative approach allowing us to test the choices that are made and stabilize a research protocol that is, above all, an investigation.

In advance of the research done, we have highlighted that, from an epistemological point of view, it is necessary to take into account the constraints imposed by technical mediation, without underestimating the effects of social practices on technology, thus avoiding the pitfalls of a technocentric, logocentric or sociocentric vision. This is the contribution made by the notion of a socio-technical device, which emphasizes the interdependence between the technical and social dimensions. The text, visual, graphic and alphanumeric elements, etc., are thus the product of a complex connection between the technical and the social domains, between technical prescriptions and constraints and social practices, but also between online and offline practices.

This perspective, from a methodological point of view, leads us to question the notion of "data" and the observable, as well as the "mechanisms of practice" for collecting and analyzing Web content. Moreover, within a context of so-called big data, the questions inherent in the choice of observables related to a problem, whether or not they occur prior to a research project, remain during the construction of the object and the problems, or during the collection and analysis of data. For example, if some tools claim to "make the data speak" almost automatically, they must be questioned and examined. In this way, many researchers have recalled the illusion of a digital hermeneutics (Boullier and Lohard 2012; Born et al. 2017) based on an automatic and software-assisted processing that would ignore technical mediation and the conditions for selecting and collecting data, and in particular the areas of in-person interaction, as in the case of the media or digital arenas related to the "yellow vest" protest movement[15] (Souillard et al. 2020). From this point of view, we think it is essential to highlight the contributions of the semiodiscursive approaches developed in the communication studies, since they pay attention to the conditions of production and distribution of data in analyzing the contents of Web devices. They also show the value of being interested in the hapax and rare forms, and not focusing solely on salient or dominant features. Finally, they show the relevance of combining quantitative and qualitative methods in a flexible way.

Thus, the complexity of Web devices as observables is always stimulating, both from an epistemological and methodological point of view. It requires situating the data in a way that takes into account the specificities of the devices and their instability, as well as their temporality, thus inviting us to reinforce the reflexive posture inherent in the survey. If the data from the Web imply rethinking the categories of analysis and taking into account the weight of instrumentation, they open up new perspectives for observing and analyzing social phenomena as a space for publication and mediatization.

2.6. References

Anquetil, S., Duteil-Mougel, C., Lloveria, V. (2019). *Le sens des données. Le statut du corpus et herméneutique à l'aune des humanités numériques*. L'Harmattan, Paris.

---

15 Protest movement that began in October 2018 in France after the announcement of the fuel price increase and spread via social networks.

Appel, V., Boulanger, H., Massou, L. (2010). *Les dispositifs d'information et de communication. Concepts, usages et objets.* De Boeck, Brussels.

Badouard, R. (2016). "Je ne suis pas Charlie". Pluralité des prises de parole sur le web et les réseaux sociaux. Le Défi Charlie. Les médias à l'épreuve des attentats [Online]. Available at: https://hal.archives-ouvertes.fr/hal-01251253/document [Accessed 29 September 2022].

Barats, C. (2014). Le Web : outils de communication, objet de connaissance. In *Sciences de l'information et de la communication*, Olivesi, S. (ed). Presses Universitaires de Grenoble, Grenoble.

Barats, C. (ed.) (2017). *Manuel d'analyse du web.* Armand Colin, Paris.

Barats, C., Dister, A., Gambette, P., Leblanc, J-M., Peres-Leblanc, M. (eds) (2019). Ce que les données textuelles disent du pétitionnement en ligne : entre contraintes et appropriations du dispositif. *Questions de communication*, 36(2), 123–146.

Bonaccorsi, J. (2020). *Fantasmagories de l'écran. Nouvelles scènes de lecture, 1980-2012.* Presses Universitaires du Septentrion, Villeneuve d'Ascq.

Bonaccorsi, J. and Julliard, V. (2010). Dispositifs de communication numériques et nouvelles formes de médiation du politique, le cas du site web d'Ideal-EU. In *Usages et enjeux des dispositifs de médiation*, Aghababaie, M., Bonjour, A., Clerc, A., Rauscher, G. (eds). Presses Universitaires de Nancy, Nancy.

Bonaccorsi, J. and Tardy, C. (2019). Analyser les données urbaines comme de nouvelles cultures de savoirs. *Questions de communication*, 36, 7–23.

Bonnafous, S. and Krieg-Planque, A. (2014). L'analyse de discours. In *Sciences de l'information et de la communication*, Olivesi, S. (ed.). PUG, Grenoble.

Bottini, T. and Julliard, V. (2017). Entre informatique et sémiotique. Les conditions techno-méthodologiques d'une analyse de controverse sur Twitter. *Réseaux*, 204, 35–69.

Boullier, D. and Lohard, A. (2012). *Opinion Mining et Sentiment Analysis.* OpenEdition Press, Paris [Online]. Available at: https://doi.org/10.4000/books.oep.198 [Accessed 29 September 2022].

Bullich, V. and Guignard, T. (2014). Les dispositifs de "TV connectée". *Les Enjeux de l'Information et de la Communication*, 15/2, 5–19.

Burger, M., Thornborrow, J., Fitzgerald, R. (2018). *Discours des réseaux sociaux : enjeux publics, politiques et médiatiques.* De Boeck, Brussels.

Candel, E. and Gomez-Mejia, G. (2017). Le bouton like : poétique du clic, vertige des discours. *SEMEN*, 42, 71–92.

Cervulle, M. and Pailler, F. (2014). #mariagepourtous : Twitter et la politique affective des hashtags. *Revue française des sciences de l'information et de la communication*, 4 [Online]. Available at: http://journals.openedition.org/rfsic/717 [Accessed 29 September 2022].

Compagno, D. (2017). Signifiant et significatif. Réflexions épistémologiques sur la sémiotique et l'analyse des données. *Questions de communication*, 31, 49–70.

Compagno, D. and Treleani, M. (2019). Special Section: Meaningful data/Données signifiantes. *Semiotica*, 230, 1–17

Cotte, D. (2004). Le concept de "document numérique". *Communication et langages*, 140, 31–41.

Croissant, V. (ed.) (2019). *L'avis des autres. Prescription et recommandation culturelles à l'ère numérique*. Éditions des archives contemporaines, Paris.

Davallon J. and Jeanneret Y. (2004). La fausse évidence du lien hypertexte. *Communication et langages*, 140, 43–54.

Doutreix, M.-N. (2019). Les bots wikipédiens peuvent-ils aider à penser l'automatisation dans le journalisme ? In *Journée d'étude – Les pratiques journalistiques face aux algorithmes et à l'automatisation*. Université de Lorraine, Metz [Online]. Available at: https://www.youtube.com/watch?v=AssAVRb9ET8 [Accessed 29 September 2022].

Foucault, M. (1977). Le jeu de Michel Foucault (entretien avec Colas, D., Grosrichard, A., Le Gaufey, G., Livi, J., Miller, G., Miller, J., Miller, J.-A., Millot, C., Wajeman, G.). *Ornicar ?, Bulletin Périodique du champ freudien*, 10, 62–93.

Gavillet, I. (2010). Michel Foucault et le dispositif : questions sur l'usage galvaudé d'un concept. In *Les dispositifs d'information et de communication. Concepts, usages et objets*, Appel, V., Boulanger, H., Massou, L. (eds). De Boeck, Brussels.

Goyet, S. (2017). Outils d'écriture du web et industrie du texte : du code informatique comme pratique lettrée. *Réseaux*, 206, 61–94.

Heuguet, G. (2018). Métamorphoses de la musique et capitalisme médiatique. Au prisme de YouTube (2005-2018). PhD Thesis, Celsa Université Paris Sorbonne, Paris.

Huré, I. (2017). Change.org, autorités et processus d'autorisation. *Communication & Langages*, 192, 83–102.

Jacquinot-Delaunay, G. and Monnoyer, L. (1999). Le dispositif. Entre usage et concept, *Hermès*, 25, 9–14.

Jeanneret, Y. (2011). *Y-a-t-il (vraiment) des technologies de l'information ?* Nouvelle édition revue et corrigée. Presses universitaires du Septentrion, Villeneuve d'Ascq.

Jeanneret, Y. (2020). *The Trace Factory*. ISTE Ltd, London, and John Wiley & Sons, New York.

Moirand, S. (2007). *Le discours de la presse quotidienne. Observer, analyser, comprendre*. PUF, Paris.

Monnoyer-Smith, L. (2016). Le web comme dispositif : comment appréhender le com-plexe. In *Manuel d'analyse du web*, Barats, C. (ed.). Armand Colin, Paris.

Navarro, N. and Bonaccorsi, J. (2018). Documenter le renouvellement urbain : le devenir-archive des énonciations ordinaires de la ville. In *Colloque international franco-brésilien – Médiations des savoirs : la mémoire dans la construction documentaire*. Lille.

Née, E., Barats, C., Fleury, S., Leblanc, J.-M., Sitri, F., Veniard, M. (2017). *Méthodes et outils informatiques pour l'analyse des discours*. Presses universitaires de Rennes, Rennes.

Olivier de Sardan, J.-P. (1996). La violence faite aux données. De quelques figures de la surinterprétation en anthropologie. *Enquête*, 3.

Paveau, M.-A. (2017). *L'Analyse du discours numérique*. Hermann, Paris.

Raynauld, V., Richez, E., Wojcik, S. (2020). Les groupes minoritaires et/ou marginalisés à l'ère numérique. Introduction. *Terminal*, 127 [Online]. Available at: http://journals.openedition.org/terminal/5656.

Schafer, V. (ed.) (2018a). *Temps et temporalités du Web*. Presses universitaires de Paris Nanterre, Nanterre.

Schafer, V. (2018b). Les archives du web entre science et artisanat. In *En quête d'archives. Bricolages méthodologiques en terrains médiatiques*, Lécossais, S., Quéméner, N. (eds). INA Éditions, Bry-sur-Marne.

Schafer, V., Barats, C., Fickers, A. (2020). Fading away... The challenge of sustainability in digital studies. *Digital Humanities Quarterly*, 14(3) [Online]. Available at: http://www.digitalhumanities.org/dhq/vol/14/3/000484/000484.html [Accessed 29 September 2022].

Severo, M. and Giraud, T. (2019). La fabrique de la donnée géolocalisée. Une analyse socio-technique de Twitter pour les études urbaines. *Questions de communication*, 36, 43–61.

Souchier, E. (1996). L'écrit d'écran, pratiques d'écriture & informatique. *Communication & langages*, 107, 105–119.

Souillard, N., Sebbah, B., Loubère, L., Thiong-Kay, L., Smyrnaios, N. (2020). Les Gilets jaunes, étude d'un mouvement social au prisme de ses arènes médiatiques. *Terminal*, 127.

Tardy, C. and Jeanneret, Y. (eds) (2007). *L'Écriture des médias informatisés. Espaces de pratiques.* Hermès-Lavoisier, Paris.

3

Expertise from Websites: Pedagogical Perspectives in Information and Communication

Luc MASSOU

CREM, Université de Lorraine, Metz, France

3.1. Introduction

We begin this chapter with a two-fold observation: despite the placement and growing influence of digital social networks and mobile applications in the Web-based communications of organizations (companies, communities, media, associations, etc.), it must be understood that the desktop versions (to be used on computers) of their websites still remain in place. In most cases, they still remain an anchor point for their digital communication strategy, to which their social networks and mobile versions are anchored. And this has remained the case as responsive Web design (adaptation of a website in three main formats: for computer, tablet and smartphone) has become widespread, and a shift to mobile first design, to use an expression increasingly popular among Web design professionals (Drouillat 2016; Nogier and Leclerc 2016), has become the norm over several years. Indeed, recent audience figures or surveys on digital uses attest to this trend: according to the Alliance for press and Media Figures (APCM 2020), the mobile Web traffic for the top 10 media sites in France most often (in nine cases out of 10) exceeds that of their fixed websites, whose figures are also increasingly closer to those of their mobile and tablet applications. And according to the annual survey on the spread of information and communication technologies within society according to the French Electronic communications and Postal Regulatory Authority (ARCEP) in 2019, the devices most frequently used by the French to connect to the Internet are mobile devices (51%, +9 points compared to 2017), followed by computers (31%, –7 points compared to 2017) and tablets (6%, –1 point compared to 2017).

In this chapter, we would like to put forward a perspective of educational experiences on several supervised works at the levels of bachelor 2 (L2), bachelor 3 (L3) and master 1 (M1) degrees in information and communication, the training received by future Web communication managers or digital project managers, and focusing on the analysis of websites (in institutional, media, or commercial communication) and online socio-digital networks (social media, community sites). For this qualitative analysis work, our approach is based in particular on the work of Pignier and Drouillat (2004), on the socio-technical analysis grid devised by Josiane Jouët and Coralie Le Caroff published in the co-authored book *Manuel d'analyse du web* edited by Barats (2013), but also on Web analysis grids from research teams in ergonomics and communication (Millerand and Martial 2001) or professional publications in Web project management (Bordage 2003). Our goal will be to formulate a reflective and critical assessment on both the contributions and limitations of this type of external expertise of websites in terms of the choice of criteria and angles of analysis, methodological constraints, but also on the skill sets intended for future digital communication professionals enrolled in training in the information and communication sciences (ICS). Finally, with these issues, we will also draw parallels with our experience from analyzing websites in several research works on different corpora (Massou 2007, 2009, 2016, 2017; Massou and Morelli 2009; Massou et al. 2011). This chapter is therefore written from both a disciplinary (ICS) and personal perspective, due to our participation in specialized courses on the expertise of multimedia products from the time of their emergence in the early 1990s (CD-ROMS, then websites) to today, and our scientific work on the subject.

3.2. What is the role of website expertise in information and communication?

First, it is important to clarify here that our purpose is not to generalize about the place occupied by website analysis on all information and communication education programs in French universities. We will rely on our feedback from our experience in Bachelor's and Master's level information–communication courses at the University of Lorraine (Metz site), in courses or specialty programs specializing in the creation of digital projects that have been open since the 1990s, that is, since the emergence of consumer multimedia technologies. In their current versions

(2018–2022), the lessons oriented toward this topic start from L2 and go up to M1. They represent specific skills, listed in the sheets of the national directory of professional certification (RNCP) of these degrees:

– Bachelor's degree: "To be familiar with the different categories of socio-technical systems available on the Internet and their audiences" and "To implement theoretical and conceptual tools for the analysis of communication practices".

– Master's degree: "To understand the professional, economic and marketing issues of communication on digital media" and "Advanced knowledge of theoretical tools for the analysis of technological innovations and the evolution of their uses".

These expert skills fulfill the needs of several digital professions targeted by this education: webmaster, designer/director/content manager of websites or Web communities and multimedia/digital content or projects, digital communication manager/advisor, Web/digital project manager.

3.2.1. *Example of a 3-year educational program*

The introductory and advanced courses in website analysis are currently based on three years of study: L2, L3 and M1. Table 3.1 gives a summary and global overview.

	Semester	Approach	Field
L2 (lecture/tutorial group, initiation)	2	Analysis of socio-technical systems	Community site (social media, sharing, training, entertainment, publishing, or online services)
L3 (tutorial group, initiation)	1	Editorial, graphic, and ergonomic analysis	Institutional communication website (public or private sector)
L2 (lecture/tutorial group, refinements)	1	Editorial expertise	Media sites (television, press, radio)
M1 (lecture/tutorial group, refinements)	1	Competitive analysis, communication and semiotics expertise	Institutional communication (public or private sector) and commercial (brand) websites

Table 3.1. *Educational program for lessons on website analysis*

The pedagogical progression is considered at several levels:

– A diverse array of approaches and analysis criteria (from scientific and/or professional sources: see below), in order to cover the primary design and strategy choices in Web communication.

– A diverse array of analyzed fields (community, institutional, media or commercial sites), in order to address several areas of activity present on the Web.

– Single site analysis in L2 and L3, then comparative analysis in M1 (on two or three sites of the same category), in order to gradually lead to a competitive, benchmarking-type approach.

– Criteria grids provided and sometimes designed by the instructor (L2, L3, M1), then co-designed with the students (M1) in order to place them in a more active position.

In the second semester of L2, the analysis of socio-technical devices (which are constituted by all websites) is based on the grid proposed by Jouët and Caroff (2013, p. 150) for social networks such as Facebook. It is divided into two columns for each set of criteria: the technical dimension (that of the systems) and the social dimension (that of its uses). On this basis, the grid is then divided into three main sections:

– site architecture and operation: editorial policy (site morphology and attention capture), site management (moderation and "netiquette", audience and visibility tactics);

– participation: contributions (participation tools and forms of contribution), personalization (personalization tools and display methods);

– social connections: discussion (discussion tools and forms of exchange), sharing (sharing tools and circulation methods).

The main interest of this approach is its continuous connecting of technical criteria (tools and functionalities included in the Web system) and uses among Internet users, in each section of the grid. This analysis is coupled with another lesson introducing the concept of the *dispositif* (Appel et al. 2010) and the socio-technical approach (Akrich 2006).

In the first semester of L3, we then offer all students (in all courses combined: "journalism", "communication of organizations" and "digital creation") an introduction to website analysis based on two main sources, the first professional, the second scientific: the editorial and graphic analysis grids by Bordage (2003), and the text *Guide pratique de conception et d'évaluation ergonomique de sites Web*

("A practical guide to ergonomic website design and evaluation") from the Montreal Computer Research Center (Millerand and Martial 2001). The grids proposed by the Web project consultant Stéphane Bordage are presented in the form of Excel files listing several dozen analysis questions, by sections and subsections, inviting students to evaluate them down individually, in order to automatically calculate a general average (out of 10) for their three main sections. For example, the editorial analysis grid is broken down as follows:

– general organization: first impression (four questions), topic names (two questions), information structure (five questions);

– valorization of content: updating (six questions), access to information (three questions), added value (five questions);

– quality of editorial content: who (three questions), what (seven questions), when/where (two questions), graphic content (four questions).

The approach is therefore both entertaining and precise, provided that the students then argue their answers, and illustrate them with carefully chosen screenshots. The second grid, based on a state-of-the-art scientific research in Web ergonomics, proposes a so-called heuristic evaluation of websites, that is to say, revealing whether or not they take into consideration the primary rules of Web usability. These rules are first explained in the guide (Millerand and Martial 2001, pp. 16–53), then presented in the form of a checklist that is immediately operational (Millerand and Martial 2001, pp. 54–73). For this second introductory exercise, we have selected the following four main criteria (out of the eight available in the guide):

– information architecture: the choice of an appropriate architecture, levels of depth, organization and prioritization of information, categorization of information;

– home page: home page functions, home page content, home page style, home page length;

– presentation of pages: presentation in accordance with a graphical charter, presentation in accordance with the layout rules on the Web, presentation in accordance with the user perspective;

– navigation: principles of site navigation, principles of page navigation, principles of link design, search function, site map, site index.

This analysis is both specialized in its ergonomic approach while also remaining accessible to non-specialists as is the case here (because ergonomics initially depends on the fields related to psychology). It is also complementary to other approaches more specific to CIS, such as editorial, graphic or communication analysis, and approaches the scientific work on hypermedia writing that we will discuss hereafter.

In the second semester of L3, we offer students enrolled in the "Digital Creation" course an advanced module based on an editorial analysis grid of media websites (for a detailed presentation of this grid, see Massou (2017)). This was designed based on various scientific works on the models of information publication on the Web (Altman 2000; Gaudreault and Marion 2000; Ringoot 2002; Utard 2002; Chartron and Rebillard 2004) and online press organization (Attias 2007), from which we extracted the following five main criteria of analysis:

– Publication models: classic editorial model (upstream regulation), authoritative publication (self-publication), distributed publication (decentralization of the circulation of content), meta-editorial level (aggregation of content from different sources).

– Web organization models: own or subcontracted Web content production capabilities, editorial and commercial partnerships, distribution on own site and/or on third-party sites, advertising financing, visibility strategies, brand assets (notoriety).

– Intermediality and integrative birth: continuity and/or editorial ruptures between the traditional media and the website, complementarity of digital media and versions, added value of the website.

– Enunciative unity: enunciative coherence of the screen pages, risks of editorial overload and loss of unity.

– Temporality: periodicity (pace of content updates) and historicity (archives, stock logic) of the website.

This grid is the first to have been constituted ad hoc by us, on the basis of criteria considered relevant to qualify the editorial choices of media websites, which are among the most visited sites on the Web for information or entertainment. It prepares L3 students for an approach that we will offer them at the beginning of M1, in connection with their first methodological lessons on the preparation of their research thesis: creating their own analysis tools, based on scientific literature.

3.2.2. From analysis to website expertise

The first semester of the specialty "Creation of digital projects" of the M1 thus marks a double turning point: co-designing a grid of expertise of websites with students, and entering into a comparative benchmark-type approach. For co-designing a grid, we propose three keywords to them that are representative of multimedia and interactive writing, which they each must use to suggest precise analysis criteria: multimodality, hypertextuality and interactivity. After a period of reflection, based on a collaborative framework shared by all students (of the Etherpad type), a grid is thus stabilized and exploited by the entire promotion (see the example below), to carry out a comparative expertise of three "competing" institutional communication sites (positioned in the same field of activity). The goal here is to avoid the juxtaposition of three parallel analyses of websites, and to promote the identification of common points and differences in digital communication strategies.

	Criteria for expertise
Multimodality	– Presence of multimedia content (videos, sounds, etc.)? – Typology of the multimedia content present: what form? What type? – Media quality (image, sound, animation, video): technique, content, originality – Consistency of the media with the content: relevance, adequacy, redundancy, complementarity – Identification of sources/authors – Positioning of multimedia content in the site tree: which sections?
Hypertextuality	– Typology of hypertext links: internal (to other pages of the same site), external (to other sites), incoming (which direct to the site: backlinks) – Functions of links: (content) repositories, navigational, application – Quality of links: relevance, coherence, meaning, structuring/organization, effectiveness (impact on navigation) – Clarity of links: explicit, identifiable, in excess – SEO: optimization, choice of URL
Interactivity	– Contact tools: contact form, email, online help (chat), subscriptions (newsletter, RSS feeds, push tools), FAQ – Exchange/participation tools: forums, games, contests, surveys, comments, sending multimedia content, use indicators (number of subscribers, comments posted, etc.) – Personalization tools: navigation preferences or interface, interests – Community tools: social networks, online community – Tracking tools: internal search engine, site map or index – Mobile versions (smartphones, tablets): features? differences, similarities with the Web version?

Table 3.2. *Example of a grid co-designed by M1 students*

Finally, the M1s carry out a second comparative expertise of websites from two competing commercial brands (regardless of the field: agribusiness, sports, luxury, industry, etc.), based on criteria extracted from the book by Pignier and Drouillat (2004) on Web design.

The goal here is to familiarize them with a semiotic approach, coupled with the study of the communicational context specific to the two selected sites, which is necessary to contextualize their expert point of view.

The choice to compare two commercial brand sites is justified by the care generally taken in their graphic identity on the Web, and their creativity in terms of Web design. Here are the primary criteria of this final grid:

– Communication context and objectives of the site: identity of the advertiser, sector of competition, targets, previous axes of communication strategy, placement of the site within the global communications system.

– Promises of the interface and enunciation: typology of the site (persuasive, incentive, informative, fulfilling), dominant enunciation strategy (mimetic or demonstrative representation, figurative or pictorial presentation, mythical or symbolic evocation, exotic or exploratory implication).

– Information architecture: tree structure, zoning, mode of spatial structuring of the page (unity, totality, plurality), mode of qualitative structuring of the page (exclusive or partitive zones).

– Staging of information: scriptwriting, actors and roles assigned to Internet users, degree of interactivity.

– Visual and graphic continuity: aesthetic choices, sensitive and graphic identity, instances of reception by the Internet users (foveal, parafoveal, or peripheral vision).

Among the points shared between the different approaches proposed in L3 and M1, we emphasize the importance of avoiding any approach overly focused on current trends that sees all technical objects as a revolution, as suggested by Gueguen (2014). As an introduction to their analysis and expertise of websites, they are then asked to search for older versions of the sites, available in particular on the largest open archive on the Web: the Internet Archive Wayback Machine[1] (archiving 771 billion web pages worldwide, from 1996 to 2022). Their task will be to identify historical evolutions in the editorial and graphic choices of these sites, in order to identify the most significant changes.

---

1. Available at: www.archive.org/web.

3.3. What are the benefits of semio-rhetorical, critical and socio-technical approaches for the learner?

From an educational standpoint, we see training in website expertise as an interesting option in several ways. First of all, it requires students to deconstruct Web design choices that have been made upstream (by the creators and sponsors of the sites) from the downstream point of view, thus explaining and interpreting editorial, graphic and ergonomic choices related to a Web communication strategy. In this way, it promotes the learning of digital literacy as an ability to implement digital writing to achieve communication objectives (Crozat et al. 2011), through specific elements of metascriptural knowledge. Thus, it fully forms part of a semio-rhetorical approach to "understand the new writing modalities inherent in the digital medium, in order to analyze, teach and anticipate the related practices and systems", "intention to communicate a meaning" which is made concrete by the website, as "support for the manifestation of content in a perceptible semiotic form and through the interaction it allows" (Crozat et al. 2011, p. 2). According to Jacques Fontanille, in his preface to the book *Penser le webdesign. Modèles sémiotiques pour les projets multimédias* (Pignier and Drouillat 2004, pp. 10–12), the semiotic approach considers design as a "reception-oriented design process". It then proposes a "science of the possible" (or "knowledge of the possible": know-how and the ability to create) to lead to choice, decision, "the will to do". According to Jacques Fontanille, the semiotic approach is not only descriptive and explanatory, it also contains a dimension of critical or evaluative intervention, with recommendations and suggestions, which is precisely at stake in the assessment of website analyses carried out by our learners.

Indeed, analyzing a website is also part of a critical perspective, a process of emancipation that requires hindsight in order not to be trapped by the ideological discourses conveyed by the Web and its systems, which we know are abundant. According to Giroux et al. (2011), this critical thinking of the Web is an evaluative practice, based on criteria (as proposed by the analysis grids cited above):

> Based on a reflexive, self-critical, and self-correcting approach implying the use of different resources [...] in order to determine the beliefs which can be reasonably held [...] or to do so [...], carefully considering the criteria of choice and the contextual diversities.

As concerns our students, this is a matter of "going beyond one's personal impression by relying on decisive reasons, or to put it another way, on criteria", without applying them blindly, becoming aware of their "relative importance according to the contexts and aims pursued" (Giroux et al. 2011). This is why self-correction and self-criticism are important for Giroux et al. (2011), as this applies to the ability of learners to return to their own ways of seeing things, on the one hand, and to reflect on the processes of elaborating information and its value, on the other hand. This is all the more necessary since the Internet constantly raises the question of its novelty compared to other communication media. As Rebillard (2007) explains, it is a "total", universal and convergent communication system, including different registers and communication mechanisms (mass diffusion, interpersonal exchanges, etc.) in all socioeconomic and cultural sectors. In his view, this evolutionary, cumulative and plural process requires historicizing mutations, and clarifying the uncertainties of self-publication (how much freedom? For which audiences?) and the role of the reader-author on the Web (what commitments?), among others.

Finally, website analysis is fully part of a socio-technical approach for digital devices. It requires the students to ask themselves the question of the prescriptions that form part of the technical object (Akrich 2006): what are the design choices? What are the rules and conditions for navigation and interactivity? What is the framework of the action? What degree of activity is possible for the user? We can therefore consider the website as a socio-technical system, articulating preprogrammed and/or co-constructed functionalities with users, such as "negotiable objects" (Massou 2010). The objective of website expertise is therefore also to identify this relatively important delegation between technical objects and users' abilities, which is illustrated in particular by the level of interactivity offered to Internet users.

3.3.1. *An "external" expertise to put results into perspective*

Despite the many contributions cited above, and the proposed pedagogical progression from L2 to M1, our approach to website expertise includes several limitations that the teacher must take into account in order to put the results obtained by his learners into perspective. First of all, for purely pragmatic reasons (duration of teaching time, available student work time), the choice of the sites to be analyzed should favor medium-sized sites, neither too poor nor too complex (in terms of the number of sections, content, and web pages), so that it is possible to analyze them within a limited period of one semester of study. The fields observed also fall into categories that are among the most representative of Web communication in organizations (community, institutional, media, or commercial sites), but they exclude other categories that are sometimes very creative (from a semio-rhetorical point of view) such as digital art sites.

Then, the analysis is primarily carried out "on screen", taking into account the observable elements of the digital device and how they are used by Internet users (e.g. published content, comments submitted, personal pages). Despite some attempts, and in some cases for understandable competitive reasons, making contact with the site design teams is usually not very beneficial, which forces students to deduce the production context on the basis of the clues visible on the screen. They must then make prudent interpretations, in order to avoid any risk of the naturalization of uses and design choices made simply through their digital imprints.

Finally, in our view, the main difficulty for our students lies in their position of being caught between two extremes: they must both try to evaluate the website from the point of view of their audiences, who in most cases are not digital experts, and also to do it as students who are being educated on Web communication strategies. The relevance of their expertise will therefore rest, among other things, on their ability to extract themselves from this position of future specialist, in order to succeed in evaluating Web design choices according to an "imagined audience" that is as faithful as possible to the "real audience" of the site (Assogba et al. 2016). On this point, we believe that misinterpretation is one of the potential risks of this "external" analysis.

3.3.2. *Several points in common with our scientific analyses*

These different findings are similar to those of the methodological approaches that we have been able to experiment within the context of scientific analyses of websites on various fields: media sites and institutional or commercial communication sites. In fact, even if most of these only confirm the contributions made by external experts, on the basis of an ad hoc criteria grid (Massou 2007, 2009; Massou and Morelli 2009; Massou et al. 2011), others have also demonstrated the interest of a cross-comparison of the analysis data with interviews of designers or decision-makers to find out the context of production and design of the websites being studied, or with research resulting from surveys and professional data on the subject. As part of the project entitled "Sterility and the use of AMP in the context of globalization (Pretoria, Ouagadougou, Paris)" done in the ANR Les Suds II program (2010–2013), we conducted an analysis of the digital communication strategies of health professionals (Massou 2016), based on the study of a corpus of websites comprising six French-speaking African clinics (in Togo, Mali, Burkina Faso, Ivory Coast and Cameroon) and 27 clinics and health centers for English-speaking donors (in South Africa), involved in the management of medical procreation assistance (MPA). To accomplish this, we have combined a criterion-based analysis (see grid 1 in section 3.5) of the corpus concerning the communications choices (hypertext links, management of interactivity with Internet users, interface of the pages on-screen) and the editorial choices (nature and format of published content, sources of the content) selected by health institutions, with seven interviews with managers and doctors from four clinics in the French-speaking corpus, to ask them about their choices in terms of Web design and communication. In bringing together two methods of data collection, one "external" on the pages of the websites, and the other on the discourse of the socio-professional actors involved, we were able to both verify the relevance of our analyses of the screen pages, and to identify (or confirm) the underlying socio-professional and media issues. Indeed, in the case of these clinics operating in a very sensitive (or even taboo) field – medically assisted reproduction – the communication issues concerned both the medical domain (a very low success rate, patient follow-up, the quality of care), the societal domain (financial cost of care, cultural acceptance of the approach) and also the professional domain (communications to peers, the fight against misinformation).

In another study conducted on editorial strategies of media websites (television channels, print media, radio; Massou 2017), we have also coupled a proposal for a criteria grid (see grid 2 in section 3.5) structured into five main criteria (Web organization models, publication models, intermediality, enunciative unity, temporality), with a documentary research on emerging trends in the context in which these websites have been operating since the 2010s: multi-screen consumption, mobile uses and interaction with social networks. This documentation, based on both statistical data from organizations such as Médiamérie, the Alliance for Press and Media Figures (ACPM), the Interactive Advertising Bureau (IAB) or the Pew Research Center, and scientific data on the evolution of digital uses, allowed us to better contextualize our web page analyses by situating them in a rapidly changing socioeconomic environment. The editorial choices of media websites could thus be explained by their inclusion in trans/cross-media, community and/or participatory strategies, creating a new way of being "together alone" (Mc Gill et al. 2015). Indeed, according to some authors (Van Cauweberge et al. 2014), the goal would be to offer additional online content, as well as tools for sharing or interacting with the content broadcast, and to diversify activities on each digital medium used (PC, mobile, tablet) as a second (or third) screen. For others (Cailler and Masoni Lacroix 2014), this is a question of saturating the relationship with audiences with digital technology (to retain them, and to maximize audiences) but also to renew creation (e.g. with transmedia storytelling, Web documentaries, viral content, etc.).

The other main point in common with our scientific analyses is the need to develop criteria grids specifically built according to the chosen field, based on the scientific literature of the field and sometimes on more professional data (surveys, reports). For example, the analysis of online press sites involves editorial analysis criteria specific to journalistic practices (such as the prioritization of news, or the choice of editorial angle, for example), while that of health institution websites must take into account particular ethical issues (such as the confidentiality of medical data, the prohibition of commercial practices, or the quality of published information). In section 3.5, we provide four examples of grids that we have developed for different fields of study: grid 1 for health institution websites, grid 2 for media websites (TV or radio channels, print media), grid 3 for TV channel websites and grid 4 for institutional websites, press sites and information blogs. Each time, the choice of criteria is based on an aggregation of sub-criteria selected during our state of the art, whether scientific or sometimes from professional sources (specialized press, statistical studies), and which we have cross-analyzed with our own criteria. For example, Grid 2 (Massou and Morelli 2009) was intended to study the production and dissemination of online information on a corpus of African websites of different types (institutional sites, press sites, blogs), to assess whether the editorial forms chosen were specific to French-speaking African countries or identical to those generally observed in France. The grid was thus formulated around the six functions of the communication model of Jakobson (1963), to which we added several criteria and sub-criteria from website analysis grids published by Western authors (Tixier 1996; Bennett et al. 1997; Pignier and Drouillat 2004; Hardy 2005). Without going into the details of the sub-criteria, here are the six main criteria chosen: expressive function (identity and quality of the issuer, characteristics of the site, objectives targeted by the issuer), referential function (built context, typology and quality of content), poetic function (format of content and interface), meta-linguistic function (code used, help), phatic function (access modes, interactivity) and conative function (questioning of the receiver, mode of involvement of the receiver). By adapting each criteria grid to the objectives of the research, and drawing inspiration from work already existing in the scientific and also professional fields, our approach allows us to propose different grids adjusted according to the fields studied, in order to take into account the specificity of the communicational and also social context in which they are part.

Among the limitations in these different approaches we can identify, whether applied in pedagogy or in research, is the absence of quantitative approaches in the analysis (e.g. metric analysis of link networks, proportions and quantity of different content published on the screen, typology of uses among Internet users, etc.) or taking into account more "macro" analysis factors (socio-political or socio-historical, for example). Indeed, the latter pose the central question of the "relative autonomy" available to the user and the designer "in relation to the technical-economic system" (Georges 2014) in which they exist. We asked this question explicitly during our study conducted on the corpus of French-speaking African news sites cited above (Massou and Morelli 2009), where our posture remained Western, and was not based on a specific research related to the local context of realization and publication of the eight sites and 12 blogs selected, unlike that which was conducted on the establishments practicing MPA (Massou 2016), where we interviewed the designers and managers of the sites selected for the analysis. In the first case, our neutrality was thus completely relative, not formed a priori but using analytical tools used in the West, which was also pointed out to us by our African colleagues at the international symposium "Culture, communication and globalization" in Brazzaville in 2007, where we presented the results of this study.

For another communication study (Massou et al. 2011), this time conducted on nine sites of Tunisian companies exporting to France to analyze how the construction of meaning takes place in their websites with an international focus, we were able to observe the importance of more "macro" factors, such as the intercultural element, in the choices made by the designers of the sites. Several sites of industrial companies have highlighted their technical capabilities in this way (European-made machinery, well-trained personnel, high production capacity, etc.), bringing to mind the conception that Europe is associated with a mastery of technologies and modernity (with European machines considered to be the archetype of reliability). In order to win over Internet users, they appear to have internalized these representations and translated them into expectations, by creating an image in line with European technical requirements and quality standards, or by referring to their foreign partners (and their brands), in order to strengthen their own credibility. Thus, the removal of or the discretion in displaying the cultural elements specific to Tunisia in these websites owes more to the impressions that advertisers have of their target audience, even if our analysis, which remained "external", could not confirm it through additional survey data (such as through interviews with their designers).

3.4. Conclusion

The goal of this chapter has been to use feedback from teaching experiences explained in detail as the basis for identifying several pedagogical contributions for students in information and communication: skills in digital semio-rhetorical analyses, socio-technical analyses of Web devices, critical thinking and competitive intelligence capacity. Several of these are also relevant in training courses that are not only registered in information and communication. Indeed, the teaching of the analysis of websites can also be useful in training courses related to the use and/or design of online digital resources: in human–computer interaction (HCI), Web ergonomics, education, computer science or management. For example, we have experimented with these for several years in a professional degree in Information systems and software (ISS), which trains e-commerce site developers, and in a digital option for a Master's degree in teaching, education and training professions (TETP) for primary and secondary school teachers in continuing education. In each case, we have adapted the proposed grids of analysis criteria to the specificities of the field and the targeted professions, as well as the field chosen for them to be carried out. In this chapter, we have also highlighted a potential connection between training and research by using grids created in an educational framework, perhaps established on the basis of scientific work (as in the case of grid 2 cited in the section 3.5, for example). We think it will be important to expand on these connections in the future by continuing this transfer, or even by considering connections in the other direction as well: the educational uses in the training of future experts in digital communication could allow us to modify, improve or adapt grids initially designed in relation to scientific issues and fields. This transposition of a tool of scientific analysis into didactic applications also raises the question of the propagation of grids potentially available for such use. We have provided four such grids in the annex that have originated from our own work, but the list could be expanded to broaden the current state of the art. Will we need to arrive at a grid that is more "generic", at least in its common base, and then made available in alternatives (or options) according to the type of sites and web of communicative contexts for which they would be used? Though the task may be complex, for the reasons that we have mentioned above (the need to adapt to the specific concerns of the field in question), it deserves to be established and expanded upon. This would allow for the potential transferability to different fields of study (scientific and/or pedagogical) of a "universal" but flexible grid to be facilitated.

However, one question remains: how much longer will we be able to apply such approaches? While they have shown and continue to show their relevance since the emergence of consumer multimedia in the early 1990s, and in the rapid transition between off-line media (on CD-ROMs) and on-line media (on the Web), the coming years are likely to see this situation gradually change. Indeed, it will be necessary to keep an eye on the future impacts of several recent trends mentioned in the introduction to this chapter, and which have been gaining in popularity since 2015: the dominance of mobile access among Internet users (known as "mobile users"), the exchanges and dissemination of Web content through digital social networks, the simultaneous consumption on several screens (television, computers, tablets and mobile devices) and the Internet of things (which no longer require a computer or a mobile device to act as an intermediary to connect). Depending on their future changes, it will most certainly be necessary to orient the Web expertise criteria more toward the increasing interconnection and interlocking of digital media (computers, tablets, mobile applications, connected objects), and toward digital communications strategies that are either crossmedia (transmitted using several media types) or transmedia (bringing together several different media) by also adding surveys or observations of uses among the target audiences of these websites, even if this approach requires more time to be carried out.

3.5. Appendices

	Criteria
Website	– Identities and contact information of the issuer and the host
	– Primary and secondary targets
	– Frequency of data refreshes
Types of information provided	– Editorial policy: writing style, means of processing information (scientific, popularization, testimonials, opinions, etc.)
	– Publication model: classic (regulated) or Web-specific (self-publishing)
	– Authors and sources of information: data collection from the Web, writing by the sponsors
Analysis of information regarding the targeted audience	– Presence or absence of specific cultural and social references: community of origin, diaspora, local content, etc.
	– Image of the health facility provided
	– Patient/medical staff relationship: autonomy/dependence of the patient
	– Representations of the couple and gender relations
	– Representations of sterility, AMP, adoption
Level of interactivity	– Forums: dynamics of discussion threads, references cited
	– Moderation methods for comments submitted
	– Degree of involvement by Internet users: visible traces, registration methods, self-presentation, etc.
Hypertext network	– Link typology: internal links, outgoing links, incoming links (*backlinks*)
	– History of presence on the Web: possible connections or partnerships with other sites (medical institutions, associations, etc.)

Table 3.3. *Grid 1 (Massou 2016)*

	Criteria
Overview of the site	– Media history – History of Web versions
Web organization models	Organizational model: – Vertical integration – Partial integration – Dual distribution – Total outsourcing Typology of site: – Large specialist – Quality general service provider – Aggregator – Niche publisher
Publication models	– Authoritative publication – Distributed publication – Editorial model – Meta-editorial level
Intermediality	– Continuity – Complementarity
Enunciative unity	– Dilution – Fragmentation
Temporality	– Periodicity – Historicity – Temporal hybridization

Table 3.4. *Grid 2 (Massou 2017)*

What content?
– Local?
– "Niche"?
– Variety of sources?
– Amateurs? Professionals?
– Modified? Commented? Enriched?
– Experienced? Tested?
– What metadata?
– Individual or collective authorship?
What publication and communication practices?
– Which audiences? Strong or weak audience?
– What exchanges between Internet users?
– What visibility?
– What editorial choices?
– What kind of intermediation through the sites?
– What control of the content? How much freedom do Internet users have?
– What is the connection with TV programs?
What media communication strategies?
– Several public spaces? Publicization of private practices?
– The Internet as a universal communication medium?
– Multidimensionality of information and culture?
– Complementarity with existing audiovisual systems?
– System in transition?

Table 3.5. *Grid 3 (Massou 2009)*

	Sub-criteria	Questions
Expressive function	Identity of the issuer	– Individual or collective? – Group/institution/community it belongs to? – What status? – Contact information displayed?
	Capacity of the issuer	– Expertise in the subject addressed? – Authority/recognition? – Commitment on the topics covered? – Personalization/individualization of the subject?
	Characteristics of the site	– Personal or professional creation? – Identity of the host? Part of a portal? If so, what type of portal? – Does it use a standardized publication template?

	Sub-criteria	Questions
Expressive function	Objectives of the issuer	– Communication objectives (to inform, entertain, bear witness, denounce, explain, etc.)? Are they clearly stated? – Target audience (profile)?
Referential function	Built context	– The blogger's own situation – Topics/themes addressed – References invoked (cultural, political, etc.)? – Choice of proposed links (internal and external)? Semantic network constructed in this way? – Angles chosen (editorial choices)?
	Typology of content	– Content categories (informative, fun, documentary, etc.) – Multimedia content? – Ranking/organization of content?
	Quality of content	– Interest/added value of the published content (use value)? – Quality level (completeness, accuracy, etc.) – Update frequency?
Poetic function	Format of content	– Language/directory of language – Writing style/tone – Formats adapted to an online publication (conciseness, contextualization, deepening, quantity, etc.)? – Multimedia writing (articulation, etc.)?
	Format of the interface	– Visual quality (aesthetic choices)? – Consistency (stability of the interface)? – Clarity/readability (ergonomics of the interface)? – Originality/creativity?
Metalinguistic function	Code used	– Specific codes used (symbols, etc.) – Allusions/level of connivance (jargon, etc.)
Phatic function	Assistance	– Tools for helping to use blogs/websites (guides, FAQs, plans, demos, etc.) – Support messages for a user (form and content of help messages)

	Sub-criteria	Questions
Phatic function (cont'd)	Access types	– Access types (paid/free, with/without registration/identification, total/partial/temporary, etc.)
		– Personalization tools (display options, preferences, browsing history, etc.)
	Interactivity	– Transparency of exchanges and contents?
		– Exchanges between Internet users (form and content)?
		– Communication tools (forums, posting messages/comments, forms, etc.)
		– Tools for maintaining contact (newsletters, emails, exchange of banners/links, polls/surveys, downloads, threads RSS, etc.)
Conative function	Interpellation of receiver	– Means for directly addressing the Internet user (signals, messages, announcements, etc.)?
		– Methods for generating interest in the site (updates, management of forums, creation of events, etc.)
		– Tools for interacting with the content (configuration, control, manipulation, etc.)
	Form of involvement of the receiver	– Use of communication tools (when? How? To say what?)
		– Degree of involvement (low, medium, high)?
		– Signs of involvement (yes/no, what types)?

Table 3.6. *Grid 4 (Massou and Morelli 2009)*

3.6. References

Akrich, M. (2006). La description des objets techniques. In *Sociologie de la traduction. Textes fondateurs*, Akrich, M., Callon, M., Latour, B. (eds). Presses de l'École des Mines, Paris.

Alliance pour les chiffres de la presse et des médias (2020). Classement unifié des sites grand public [Online]. Available at: https://www.acpm.fr/Les-chiffres/Frequentation-internet/Sites-Grand-Public/Classement-unifie [Accessed 27 June 2020].

Altman, R. (2000). Technologie et textualité de l'intermédialité. *Sociétés & Représentations*, 9, 11–20.

Appel, V., Boulanger, H., Massou, L. (2010). *Les dispositifs d'information et de communication. Concept, usages et objets*. De Boeck, Brussels.

Autorité de Régulation des Communications Electroniques et des Postes (2019). Baromètre du numérique 2019 [Online]. Available at: https://www.arcep.fr/uploads/tx_gspublication/rapport-barometre-num-2019.pdf [Accessed 10 May 2019].

Assogba, H., Coutant, A., Domenget, J.-C., Latzko-Toth, G. (2015). Les publics imaginés et réels des professionnels d'internet. *Communication*, 33(2) [Online]. Available at: https://communication.revues.org/5704 [Accessed 15 June 2020].

Attias, D. (2007). L'impact d'Internet sur l'économie de la presse : quel chemin vers la profitabilité ? PhD Thesis, Université Paris-X Nanterre, Paris.

Bennett, L.T., Oliver, K.M., Wilkinson, G.L. (1997). Evaluation criteria and indicators of quality for Internet resources. *Educational Technology Archive*, 37(3), 52–59.

Bordage, S. (2003). *Conduite de projets web*. Eyrolles, Paris.

Cailler, B. and Masoni Lacroix, C. (2014). Industries narratives et publics de télévision : le défi de la logique transmédia. *Télévision*, 1(5), 27–45.

Chartron, G. and Rebillard, F. (2004). Modèles de publication sur le web. Rapport final AS 103/RTP 33 – Documents et contenus : création, indexation, navigation, CNRS, Paris.

Crozat, S., Bachimont, B., Cailleau, I., Bouchardon, S., Gaillard, L. (2011). Éléments pour une théorie opérationnelle de l'écriture numérique. *Document numérique*, 14(3), 9–33.

Drouillat, B. (2016). *Le design interactif. Du web design aux objets connectés*. Dunod, Malakoff.

Fontanille, J. (2004). Préface. In *Penser le webdesign. Modèles sémiotiques pour les projets multimédia*, Pignier, N., Drouillat, B. (eds). L'Harmattan, Paris.

Gaudreault, A. and Marion, P. (2000). Un média naît toujours deux fois. *Sociétés & Représentations*, 9, 34–35.

George, É. (2014). Quelles perspectives critiques pour aborder les TIC ? *TIC&société*, 8(1–2) [Online]. Available at: http://ticetsociete.revues.org/1365 [Accessed 27 June 2020].

Giroux, P., Gagnon, M., Cornut, J., Lessard, S. (2011). L'exercice de la pensée critique. Réseau d'information pour la réussite éducative [Online]. Available at: http://rire.ctreq.qc.ca/lexercice-de-la-pensee-critique/ [Accessed 05 January 2020].

Guegen, H. (2014). La critique et le possible. Le rôle de la catégorie de possible dans la critique des TNIC. In *Critique, sciences sociales & communication*, George, É., Granjon, F. (eds). Éditions Mare & Martin, Paris.

Hardy, J.-M. (2005). Grille de contrôle de la qualité des contenus en ligne. *Yellow Dolphins* [Online]. Available at: https://yellowdolphins.com/publications/articles/grille-de-controle-de-la-qualite-de-contenu/ [Accessed 15 March 2021].

Jakobson, R. (1963). *Essais de linguistique générale*. Éditions de Minuit, Paris.

Jouët, J. and Le Caroff, C. (2013). L'observation ethnographique en ligne. In *Manuel d'analyse du web*, Barats, C. (ed.). Armand Colin, Paris.

Massou, L. (2007). Stratégies éditoriales des sites web des chaînes de télévision française. Le cas de TF1 et France 2. In *Enjeux et usages des Technologies de l'Information et de la Communication. Médias et diffusion de l'information : vers une société ouverte*, Meimaris M., Gouscos, D. (eds). Gutenberg, Athens.

Massou, L. (2009). Web 2.0 et stratégies éditoriales des sites web de TF1 et France 2. In *International Conference. New Media & Information: Convergences & Divergences*. Athens.

Massou, L. (2010). Dispositif et enseignement à distance. In *Les dispositifs d'information et de communication. Concept, usages et objets*, Appel, V., Boulanger, H., Massou, L. (eds). De Boeck, Brussels.

Massou, L. (2016). Construction d'un discours médiatisé et d'un public sur l'AMP. Le cas des sites web de cliniques et centres de dons africains. In *Procréations médicales et mondialisation. Expériences africaines*, Bonnet, D., Duschesne, V. (eds). L'Harmattan, Paris.

Massou, L. (2017). Stratégies éditoriales numériques et sites web de médias. In *Site internet : audit et stratégie*, Rouquette, S. (ed.). De Boeck, Brussels.

Massou, L. and Morelli, P. (2009). Sites web et blogs africains : modèles de publication en ligne. In *Communication et dynamiques de globalisation culturelle*, Kiyindou, A., Ekambo, J.-C., Miyouna, L.-R. (eds). L'Harmattan, Paris.

Massou, L., Morelli, P., Simonnot, B., Zamit, F. (2011). Analyse communicationnelle de sites d'entreprises tunisiennes. Stratégies et confiance en contexte interculturel. In *Hypermédias et pratiques numériques. H2PTM'11*, Saleh, I., Massou, L., Leleu-Merviel, S., Jeanneret, Y., Bouhai, N., Morelli, P. (eds). Hermès-Lavoisier, Paris.

McGill, M., Williamson, J., Brewster, S.A. (2015). A review of collocated multi-user TV. Examining the changing role of the TV in the multi-viewer, multi-screen home. *Personal and Ubiquitous Computing*, 19(5–6), 743–759.

Millerand, F. and Martial, O. (2001). *Guide pratique d'évaluation d'un site Web*. Centre de Recherche Informatique de Montréal, Montreal.

Nogier, J.-F. and Leclerc, J. (2016). *UX Design & ergonomie des interfaces*. Dunod, Malakoff.

Pignier, N. and Drouillat, B. (2004). *Penser le webdesign. Modèles sémiotiques pour les projets multimédia*. L'Harmattan, Paris.

Rebillard, F. (2007). *Le web 2.0 en perspective. Une analyse socio-économique de l'internet*. L'Harmattan, Paris.

Ringoot, R. (2002). Périodicité et historicité de l'info en ligne. *Médiamorphoses*, 4, 69–75.

Tixier, M. (1998). Les entreprises sur l'Internet : rêve et réalité. *Communication et Langages*, 116, 58–76.

Utard, J.-M. (2002). Du portail au site. Le repli énonciatif de la presse en ligne. *Médiamorphoses*, 4, 83–88.

Van Cauweberge, A., Schaap, G., Van Roy, R. (2014). TV no longer commands our full attention: Effects of second-screen viewing and task relevance on cognitive load and learning from news. *Computers in Human Behavior*, 38, 100–109.

PART 2

The Website as a Semiodiscursive Device

4

Semiotics of Digital Design: From Ethos to Ethics

Nicole PIGNIER

EHIC, Université de Limoges, France

4.1. Introduction

The 21st century began with the emergence of webdesign[1], the field of design that at the time was dedicated to the creation of Web interfaces offering new information and communication experiences. At the very beginning of the 2000s, every organization – institutions, companies, and associations – was eager to create its own website, using the skills of Web designers to create it. The outpouring of creativity was in full swing: designers explored all the possibilities of Web interface design and "content" design. This desire to interact with multimodal information, combining enunciative forms such as images, sounds, linguistic texts, and movement within the "screen page", was symbolized by the success of the Macromedia Flash software which, over the period of a decade starting in 1996, made it possible to design animations and bring together artistic creation and

---

1 The definition of the term "webdesign" as used in French is significantly different from the English definition of "Web design" written either as two separate words or as a single word and referring to the semantic languages used for the technical development of interfaces and content such as XHTML, HTML, object-oriented languages such as Javascript or CSS (Cascading Style Sheets), which are sheets that determine the appearance of HTML and XML documents. Today, in French, the term "webdesign" refers to both creative and technical skills, information architecture, user experience and accessibility to different audiences and through different terminals.

Analyzing Websites,
coordinated by Luc MASSOU, Patrick MPONDO-DICKA and Nathalie PINÈDE.
© ISTE Ltd 2023.

communicational originality. In Web agencies, a considerable amount of time was spent on creative research and development. While this period also suffered from unreliable digital security and laborious updates requiring manual changes to the code, it was marked by curiosity, the opening of possibilities, and the creative impulse both artistic and artisanal, to produce something "handmade".

With this in mind, our goal is to question the "meaning-making" of webdesign: to what extent and in what ways do these new types of enunciations make it possible to create a link between an instance of enunciation (such as a brand) and an instance of co-enunciation,[2] the users? Beyond the quality of the information that is enunciated, which elements are taken into account in the process of perception and interpretation of websites? Is it possible to orchestrate the native multimodality of digital technologies, or is it an evolutionary legacy? Does the use of "page-screen" metaphors at home, in a book or on a theater stage by brand websites contribute to how the co-enunciators create meaning? How?

Over the course of multiple events and meetings, we have established a semiotics of webdesign, one that is not an applied semiotics that would have consisted in "tacking" Greimas's methodologies onto corpora of websites, but a semiotics that is open to what it has learned from the creation methods of the time.

In these meetings, we recall that held with Benoît Drouillat in 2003, at the time the artistic director of a large Parisian Web agency; he worked for L'Oréal, *Le Monde*, etc. Étienne Mineur, the director of Incandescence, a Parisian creative agency, was in charge of creating a website for the Japanese stylist Issey Miyake[3]. Each year, he created a multimodal experience specific to the new collections. Benoît Platre, director of the Web agency Ici la lune[4], worked on the creation and development of the website for chocolate maker Patrick Roger where he was able to provide a fresh look[5], and also did work on Web communications for champagne

---

2 In the language sciences, enunciation is what makes speech perceptible; an utterance, whether gestural, linguistic, auditory or visual. This is its manifestation. This includes its form, materiality, circulation in social life or mediation. Co-enunciation refers to the dynamics or tensions that emerge during exchanges between enunciators. The enunciator is the one who enunciates; the co-enunciator is the one who perceives an utterance as it manifests itself. Echoing the words of the linguist Dominique Maingueneau in his paraphrasing of Culioli, we can say that the user is a co-enunciator and not a simple receiver: "That is why, following the linguist Culioli here, we can no longer speak of a 'recipient' but of a co-enunciator. Used in the plural and without hyphens, co-enunciators will design the [different] partners of the speech" (Maingueneau 1998, p. 40).

3 Available at: www.my-os.net/isseymiyake/archives/spring_summer_2007/index_women.html.

4 Available at: www.icilalune.com/fr/experiences/clients.

5 Available at: www.experience.patrickroger.com/fr/chocolat/jardin.

houses. His work has given special attention to the sound design elements, and to accomplish this, he has cooperated with sound engineer Charles Vannier. With a talent for both programming and design, his group sought to create Web interfaces that transport the enunciative instance into the universe of values. Another notable figure in this area is Ariel Malka, an Israeli developer, whose work involved experimental research linking art, writing and coding[6]. All of these professionals have questioned the true meaning of their creations and put them to the test through public scrutiny, particularly during the WIF (World International Festival), an annual event launched in Limoges, in Limousin, by the Regional Development Agency in 2004.

With Benoît Drouillat, a contributor to the WIF, participant in its organization and an intermittent collaborator in analyzing the meaning of websites, we have established a methodology for the semiotic analysis of multimodality as well as the interface design of websites. What do these methodologies consist of? Are they still relevant? This contribution will focus on these issues first. Second, we will then identify the limits of such an approach considering the evolution of the Web and digital information or communication devices. Third, we will question the enunciative and ethical interrelations from which digital design is formed. In conclusion, we will consider the terms to be used in asking the question of how to "make meaning" in digital design.

4.2. Semiotics of webdesign: from 2004 to 2021

In *Penser le webdesign. Modèles sémiotiques pour les projets multimédia* (Pignier and Drouillat 2004), we questioned the forms of multimodal writing used in stating the "content" of the sites. How does each mode of orchestration of kinetic, visual, auditory and linguistic modalities give rise to the perception of objects enunciated in a specific form, and in what way? And is this still the case in 2021? Have they evolved, and if so, in what way?

4.2.1. A realistic or hyper-realistic form of multimodal writing

When we zoom in on a satellite photo or on a picture of shoe to observe its texture, or a rendering to see its colors, when we listen to the sound of a car engine or when we use virtual reality to see what a piece of furniture or another would look like in our kitchen or living room, and when a video of protesters or simple passers-by posted online is reviewed by police officers, realistic multimodal writing

---

6 Available at: www.chronotext.org/TextTree/v1.htm.

gives a presentational or demonstrative function to the picture. Like a transparent window on the real world, the picture and visual enunciative form plays a predominant role here, with the other mechanisms acting to complement it. For instance, the sounds of horns honking, engines or the cries and from a conflict serve as a "realistic" reinforcement of the image, with linguistic texts acting as a referential function (i.e. dates, place names, prices, technical and practical characteristics). Movements, interacting with the gestures of the user, allow for the observation of the object.

This form of multimodal orchestration is based on an aesthesia, or sensibility, of existing in the world (Pignier 2017, p. 169) which is intended to be objective; an enunciation is not presented as a discourse on reality, but as a reality itself placed before the eyes of the perceiving subject to facilitate identification and categorization.

This multimodal form of writing tends to evolve toward a realistic utterance that is intended to be omniscient: there is no detail that has not been included in such a virtual tour and even recreated in three dimensions, there is no place on the planet that appears not to be covered by Google Maps[7]. During this Covid-19 era, the service allows the user to display a "trace" on the satellite photo of a given city to determine the number of infections. This produces an effect of omniscience, giving rise to a perception that feels augmented in comparison with what we would have physically without digital tools by looking at an object or walking down a street, which comes to construct a kind of hyperreality. This sensation relates to our control over objects: zooming in, zooming out, changing the view angle, the perceiving subject is invited to utilize the haptic ability of the view, in the sense that Gilles Deleuze[8] uses this qualifier to describe any pictorial configuration that "allows the eye to proceed as touch", through a "frontal and close-up view" (Deleuze 2002 [1981], p. 115).

But unlike Egyptian paintings or the work of Francis Bacon that Deleuze studied, the haptic sense that we find in virtual tours of museums as offered by Google's Arts

---

7 Available at: www.google.fr/maps/@45.95956,0.9665754,13z. The "Covid-19" service is presented on www.support.google.com/maps/answer/9795160?hl=fr as follows: "Information about the Covid-19 pandemic on Google Maps. If your region is affected by the Covid-19 pandemic, Google Maps allows you to obtain relevant information about the places involved. Suggestion: In some regions, additional information about Covid-19 may be available. If you select the alert on the Google Maps home screen, relevant links related to the area currently displayed on the map can be found".

8 According to Deleuze, the "haptic adjective" ("*adjectif haptique*") is a French translation of the term haptisch, coined by the Austrian art historian Aloïs Riegl at the beginning of the 20th century, taken from the Greek term haptein, meaning "to touch".

and Culture site[9], in places such as Google Maps Street View[10], maps such as Google Maps, or even car configurers such as that offered by the brand Jaguar[11], are all part of a multimodal writing that is intended to be hyperrealistic. The high-resolution shots, the editing techniques and the interior design all call upon the haptic sense by setting the image in motion between circular, vertical and horizontal contraction/dilation and distancing/concentration. With their hands "at the controls", the users control its animation, setting reality into motion as if it were following their own fingers and eyes, etc. However, all these photos, montages, and selections all represent choices, transformations and statements about reality, as do the Covid-19 data shown on Google Maps. Given the number of people who are tested, the reliability of the tests, the time when they take place and the means by which the data are stated and communicated, the figures displayed are not the number of actual contaminations at the time the user clicks on a place.

Of course, realistic and even hyperrealistic writing is not what is real, it is only an elaborate fabricated effect, but one that creates an illusion. It calls on the user to share an ethos, that is to say, an imaginary, sensitive and moral representation in the sense of mores, life in society, values and domination (Pignier 2008, pp. 50–55). It tends to reinforce the feeling of the Cartesian subject who stands in front of objects in order to submit them to his/her thought, by his/her thought. The notion of "I think therefore I am", in the hyperrealistic multimodal mechanism of orchestration becomes "I click therefore I am".

4.2.2. A mythical or symbolic multimodal writing

Nominal expressions written in a fine and elegant typography, a smooth dissolve between poetic landscapes of Aubrac with a slow rhythmic pacing alternating between close-ups and panoramic views, the site of the chef restaurateur Michel Bras[12] enunciates a cosmo-poetic ethos anchored in a mythically portrayed Aubrac. This form of writing places the auditory, visual, kinetic and linguistic modalities in harmony. The power of images is not intended to be preponderant here compared to other modes. On the contrary, visual expression works together in its composition with text, sound and movement to symbolize, that is to say, represent that which is absent; a cultural universe, an artistic sensibility, etc. Each modality composes

---

9 Available at: www.artsandculture.google.com.

10 Available at: www.google.com/maps/d/u/0/viewer?ie=UTF8&hl=fr&msa=0&ll=46.3469280000 00005%2C3.7792970000000103&spn=13.316091%2C38.496094&z=5&mid=1YvFTZQ9zC-9-c7UeVo3b1AuoVM4.

11 Available at: www.jaguar.fr/jaguar-range/xe/index.html.

12 Available at: www.bras.fr/fr/le-suquet.

together with the others, echoing, not to show or demonstrate an object of reality, but to suggest the perceptual world in which it is located. Far from an enunciation that is intended to be omniscient, here we find a suggestive form of writing that leaves an interplay, an empty space between the visible and invisible, between presence and absence, placing the real in a relationship that is both concrete and symbolic between people and places.

This type of multimodal writing structures the enunciation of the Rainforestfoods brand, which manufactures and markets food products from the Amazon rainforest. On its website[13], it invites the co-enunciator to share a dream-like perception of the Amazon. The alternation between close and panoramic shots of the forest suggests an original world that connects us to the Earth. As the user moves using the arrows on the keyboard, the plant life appears to be enveloped in the mist rising from the bends in the river up to the sky. The mist, obscuring what would be a clearer shot, instead allows for a dream-like view: an imagination of that which is absent or far away, which then brings us to the forest with its cacao trees, berries and birds. The text displayed in bold at the center of the screen, stated in the form of precepts, does more to suggest a mythical world than it does to give characteristics of the products sold: "Nature does nothing uselessly", "Nature sustains those who sustain her".

Each scene invites viewers to discover one of the brand's products connected to the mythical world of the Amazon through a parallax effect, that is to say, an optical effect that stems from the displacement of the observer. The superposition of the flat planes creates a depth effect inviting the co-enunciator to project himself into the *mythos*, the myth designating a narrative that sets the stage with creatures symbolizing forces of nature. Rainforestfoods thus presents itself as the brand that connects humans to the mythical Amazon, rejuvenating bodies and souls by tapping into the original cradle of the Earth. From the stereotypes of the intense, passionate culture of Italy that are associated with Nespresso coffees[14], to the woman portrayed as the object of desire on perfume websites, to a more original mythical writing, this mode of multi-modal orchestration calls for reflection. It plays on allusive enunciation rather than illusory enunciation.

4.2.3. *A readable and redundant multimodal writing*

The third mode of multimodal orchestration consists of unifying the linguistic text and the image, what David Gullentops refers to as the "readable" (Gullentops 2001). Words and numbers, while keeping their linguistic nature, become visual

---

13 Available at: www.rainforestfoods.com/experience/#!/slide-intro.
14 Available at: www.nespresso.com/fr/fr/experience-cafe-original.

figures so significant due to either their plastic expression (highlighted by typography, their cover) or by their figurative expression (highlighted as an object of the world). This mode of orchestration, occurring frequently in the graphic design of off-Web logos, also occurs on the Web. We can find examples of this in the many "doodles" published by Google: the verb *to doodle* referring to the search engine's logo being redrawn on the occasion of the birthday of an artist, such as the Turkish sculptor Ilahn Koman[15], or an event, such as Mexico's Independence Day celebrations[16]. In the case of the former, the letters forming the word "Google" remain legible, but they also each take the form of a sculpture. In the latter, the word "Google" remains just as legible, but the letters are transformed into festive figures, garlands and trumpets, in the colors of the flag of Mexico.

This orchestration mechanism can also be found in data visualization. In this way, the *Datageule* video series, a production by Premières lignes Télé in partnership with France TV, gives a presentation in each of its online episodes of a topic representing an important societal challenge. The goal is to present them in a playful style to make them easier to understand[17]. To do this, each sentence is spoken orally through a voice over, which is both:

– displayed on the screen;

– illustrated with simple and entertaining in solid-color vector images;

– accompanied by sounds that punctuate the displaying of key words and figures that can be seen as well as to read, creating a "shock" effect.

The *Datageule* video "Industrial agriculture: producing to death"[18] explains in this way the absurdity of the global industrial agricultural system, where the more it produces, the more counterproductive it is, making farmers disappear, decreasing their income, increasing their debt and polluting the environment. On the screen, the dates and comparative key figures between 1940 and 2014 show that at the beginning of this period, 1 calorie of energy made it possible to produce 2.3 calories of food, while in 2014, to produce 2.3 calories of food, it was necessary to consume 7 calories of fossil energy. These figures, made to stand out on the screen by their

15 Available at: www.google.com/doodles/ilhan-komans-98th-birthday.

16 Available at: www.google.com/logos/doodles/2019/mexico-independence-day-2019-598619565 2739072-law.gif.

17 The presentation of this program can be seen on the website www.france.tv/slash/datagueule/: "Every day we are bombarded by thousands of molecules of information. These facts, names and figures all pile up and collide, yet they never come together to create anything. So for once, rather than remaining passive in the face of this onslaught, let us play with it."

18 Available at: https://www.youtube.com/watch?v=_7z4.

size and their color, are accompanied by drawings of fuel cans that stack up to power the global system. Conversely, the number of food baskets decreases. This chiasm effect between the two dates is connected to a redundant enunciation in which each modality draws from the other, re-enunciates it, synthesizes it and then highlights it in a playful, simplified narrative. The data are read aloud so that they are unambiguous, unquestionable and made known advance: industrial agriculture is increasingly counterproductive. Through their multimodal redundance, the choices of enunciations short-circuit the interpretative path of the co-enunciators, placing a clear interpretation before their eyes, hitting their senses with a blow of what appears as "common sense".

This mode of writing does not pretend to be a transparent window on reality. On the contrary, it is firm in its game of enunciation, but at the same time that it simplifies and gamifies the intake of information, it also interprets it (Pignier 2020a).

4.2.4. *A reality-removing and subversive multimodal writing*

We are visiting the mini-site[19] for *Le Dernier Gaulois*, the animated film by Samuel Tilman, released in 2015. Apator, a wealthy aristocrat and a Gallic leader, is exhausted after Alesia has been under siege for 40 days. His armies are preparing to charge against the Roman legions that have surrounded them. Apator recalls his journey. The mini-site created for the website of France TV is structured into six sequences that "immerse" the co-enunciators in the memory of this narrator-character. By browsing the site with the keyboard, users can perceive the memories of people, places and scenes from Apator's point of view, which are formed and deformed by continuous variations. This allows the visual image to become substance and matter, taking shape in the character's memory through anamorphosis, that is to say, by re-ascending time and metamorphosis. The enunciation subverts the form conducive to the categorization in the opaque and intimate rhythm of memory. A surreal writing, added to by a deep voice seeming to arise from the depths of the ages, along with the gestural interactions; at the keyboard, the users immerse themselves in a visual abyss. Reality is undone by this game of syncretic, multimodal language, a kind of language-matter.

The reality-erasing form of writing founds, to a lesser extent, the experimental site of Google Lines Chrome Experiments[20]. On a black background, the following text appears: "Start with a line, let the planet complete the picture". Users are invited

---

19 Available at: www.lederniergaulois.nouvelles-ecritures.francetv.fr.
20 Available at: www.lines.chromeexperiments.com.

to draw lines, curves and informal shapes without knowing where these will take them. Using the shapes that are sketched, satellite photos from Google Maps then appear representing geographical locations, from which some of the curves are analogous to the ones made by the user. The linguistic text that appears at the bottom left of the screen gives the name of the place. These cosmo-poetic games of chance give shape to algorithmic abstraction, phenomenologically and by metamorphosis.

The reality-deconstructing multimodal mode of orchestration is anchored in the subversion of surrealist poetry, the objective of which is to revive the world, to bring out a new world. In the case of Google, would subversive writing not be an invitation to believe in the demiurgic capabilities of the digital technologies it offers? This would then offer us a subversive use of surrealist poetry, loaded with a counter-power. In other words, it would amount to recovering a resistant form of writing by a brand that symbolizes the limitless power of digital technologies.

4.2.5. The semiotic functions of Web interfaces

The keyboard navigation through a rectangular grid, offering a perceptual continuity of the Amazon on Rainforestfoods, a roll over coupled with animated statements on a modular grid made up of boxes with graphics suggesting poetry as used by Aubrac with Michel Bras, a sequential grid structured into six episodes to be navigated through by keyboard on the website for Le Dernier Gaulois: these examples question the phenomenological relationships between multimodal writing modes and the semiotic functions of Web interfaces. In *Le webdesign, sociale expérience des interfaces web* (Pignier 2008), we specified how these examples, far from being reduced to the function of a frame simply displaying "content", play the following roles:

– Figurative material support or interface metaphor. The most common metaphor is the "screen page", but this can be a terrestrial or interstellar landscape as proposed by a Swiss website for the exploration of songs from the 1950s[21]. On the website for *Le Dernier Gaulois*, the metaphor of the interface is an intimate world, that of memory. These figurative material displays, which can be navigated ergonomically, make anthropological sense to the extent they anchor digital statements in a physical world.

– Formal supports or modes of organizing content within the space of the screen. Grids or other structured forms allow information to be re-stated in the perception space.

---

21 Available at: www.50-jahre-hitparade.ch.

– Ergodic support or work path. The neologism "ergodic", coined by Aarseth (1997), derives from the Greek *ergon* (work) and *hodos* (path). An ergodic support refers to the modes of gestural interaction required to browse the digital spaces, with the functionalities made possible with these spaces.

In our 2008 book, we explained the origin of the semiotic concept of support, highlighting different modes of figurative, formal or ergodic material supports. In 2012, we developed the semiotic scope of the types of gestural inter-action at work in many hardware and software digital devices (Pignier 2012). We considered that the design of Web interfaces or mobile applications brings together design, graphic forms, functionalities, sketches of interactional modes, etc., with a desired goal (the objective of the site or application, the platform). Related to multimodal writing mode(s), it enunciates an ethos in a more or less voluntary way; the world of cosmo-poetic authenticity of Aubrac for Michel Bras, osmosis of the Amazon for Rainforestfoods, the creative media for France TV with the mini-site *Le Dernier Gaulois*, etc.

Interface design and multimodal writing are an essentially specific experience of information input and communication. Thus, each more or less stereotyped or singular case comes to form perceptual styles (Pignier 2014, pp. 53–61); as a co-enunciator, the user is invited to assume the role of explorer on the Google Culture and Arts website, of contemplator on Michel Bras's website, to identify with the character/narrator on *Le Dernier Gaulois*, to be immersed in the Amazon rainforest on Rainforestfoods.

The few examples analyzed in the first section show that while digital technologies are constantly evolving, paradoxically, the ways of phenomenologically "meaning-making" are not being created at the same rate. In fact, the exact opposite trend is most prevalent with Content Management Systems intended to automate content editing, and more broadly with the industrialization of the Web, which nonetheless invites us to redefine webdesign within digital design, to expand our semiotic approach to design.

4.3. Beyond its ethos, the ethical aim of digital design

We have briefly defined design as the association of a drawing, sketch, outline, storyboard, plan, etc., used to create a design and a desired practical outcome (the goal or objective of the design). But both drawing and practical design are based on an ethical purpose; a conception of better living and individual and collective well-being animating the creation of a platform, an object, a software, etc. (Pignier 2017, pp. 12–13).

4.3.1. *Divergences between ethos and ethics*

The website Chromelinesexperiments, connected to Google Maps, offers a surreal, subversive entry on Google Maps, a hyperrealistic site configuring a perceptual experience that is intended to be omniscient, showing the entire planet at the click of a button. These two websites state the ethical goal of Google: the belief that digital technologies, capable of digitizing the real as well as our own imaginations, are the path to progress, well-being, better living. Therefore, we find no gap here between the ethos stated in the design of the sites and the ethical aim of digital solutionism according to the expression of Evgeny Morozov[22] (Morozov 2014), sometimes resulting in horrific actions by companies[23]. But in the case of Rainforestfoods, the ethos of living in osmosis with the Amazon rainforest, is perhaps out of step with the ethical goal; in 1994, in a personal communication, the director of the London-based brand wrote about violations of the territories and indigenous populations of the Amazon: "A company that owns a trademark has the right either to disregard violations or to register the names of users when it believes that this will advance the cause of ethical marketing"[24].

Is the Rainforestfoods brand so concerned about the Amazon rainforest that it states this through its ethos? An ethos is the enunciative staging of a universe of values, of an imaginary. The ethical goal is the belief that drives the brand, the institution, as a participant in society. The foundational ethical aim of the design of a site, a platform, an application or any object cannot be understood in isolation from the interactions of the actors involved in digital design.

---

22 The expression above criticizes the logic of digital technical progress consisting of seeking a technological solution to each problem that technology has generated. In this way, the more automated our gestures are, the more we accelerate our rhythms of life, and the more we come to rely on automation to free up time.

23 In 2019, under pressure from its employees, Google had to abandon a project to design an artificial intelligence mechanism intended to identify "subjects in video rushes captured by military drones in the field". To do this, the company hired "little hands" to retrieve data, allowing "Google's AI to better detect human targets, while the workers in question obviously had no idea what type of project they were working on as employees" (www.lesnumeriques. com/vie-du-net/google-a-fait-travailler-petites-mains-sur-project-maven-n83675.html).

24 Cited by Posey and Dutfield (1997). The global intellectual property market. Rights of traditional and indigenous communities (www.idrc.ca/sites/default/files/openebooks/823-6/index.html).

4.3.2. *Websites in a tense relationship with other players in digital design*

As a consequence of what has been seen above, the analysis of websites cannot be understood without questioning the use of Content Management Systems such as Wordpress for content editing, as well as the creation of websites from pre-designed templates. These tend to focus on interface design. We are seeing the proliferation of elements such as modular grids, for example, for any type of site, application or platform. For sites for shoe brands or publishers on Instagram or Facebook, the modular grid, structuring the space of the page-screen into boxes and modules, a hierarchical grid, or any other formal support can be the subject of special graphic attention, as we have seen for Michel Bras' site. Conversely, these types of formal supports can be implemented without any graphic work, impoverishing the enunciative ethos. This applies to the hierarchical grid of the newspaper *Le Monde* whose website trivializes its ethos to the extreme, with no distinction between it and a free-distribution newspaper covering superficial topics, like the publication *20 minutes*[25].

By mobilizing things such as the organization – brand, association, institution, etc. – at the origin of a website, its ethical goal is brought into dialogue with that of free software, whether this is intentional or not. The defenders of "free" software envisage a better form of indivisible and collective living based on the sharing of computer knowledge, on the collaborative writing of code, and the co-creation of software. Here, we also see an attitude of do-it-yourself with others that prevails. We are then at the opposite end of the spectrum from the unintelligibility of the codes and algorithmic logic of the GAFAM. But the ethical aim of free software does not guarantee that users will contribute to the development of the software; to save time and money, many are content to put the proposed models into practice, working unwittingly toward a creative impoverishment and a loss of the enunciative meaning of design.

Beyond the software used, the analysis of websites requires taking into account other actors such as search engines, whose SEO strategies all content publishers must be familiar with if they want to see their sites appear prominently in specific keyword searches. The ethics of Google, based on the automation of SEO processes according to the popularity of keywords, comes to configure formatted modes of utterance. The online press is thus incentivized to formulate its information in a syntax that can easily be picked up by Google's Web crawlers. Moreover, it must take into account topical thematic orientations for the search engine, those prevalent in the "auto-complete" function, which by facilitating searches, has a tendency to

25 Available at: www.lemonde.fr et www.20minutes.fr.

guide the linguistic intentions of users. Unwittingly, organizations find themselves in tension with Google's ethical goal, one involving technological solutionism but also linguistic capitalism, as Kaplan (2014, pp. 143–156) explains. It is therefore not only a question of capturing the attention of users through the design of public spaces, but also of orienting their intention, formatting their thinking.

With the multiplicity of participants influencing the design and modes of enunciation, the semiotic analysis of websites cannot produce meaning in isolation in an immanent way. We therefore propose questioning the interplay and tensions between the enunciative ethos, the ethical goals at work in the design of a platform, a site or an application. In their global communications, an organization, brand, institution or association is most of the time forced to format its enunciations as required by Google, but also according to the popular social networks, Facebook, Instagram, Twitter, TikTok, etc. However, the grids of these platforms in modules or windowing configure perceptual experiences that are not only reminiscent of the attention capitalism described, among others by Gomez-Mejia (2014, pp. 77–94) or Saemmer (2020, pp. 9–23), but also of the linguistic capitalism that Frédéric Kaplan questions.

4.4. Interrogating the semiotic interrelations between the strata of digital design

How can an organization whose ethical goal is not that of corporate capitalism build its digital communication differently? Our understanding of digital design is based on a non-deterministic thesis. This thesis holds that a platform, an RSN that makes up such an attentional regime, such a communication experience, does not mechanically close the user's initiative. We have found that the way of in which usage is made, or is not, raises the question of meaning, of the ethical goal. The enunciation instance can thwart or counter-represent the formatting, which leads us to talk about usage design. We have also highlighted (Pignier 2020b, pp. 163–174) the enunciative strata that are interrelated in digital design, by questioning their function of prefiguration, configuration and figuration.

4.4.1. *The notions of prefiguration, configuration and figuration*

These three notions are used by Jean-Jacques Boutaud, who himself reframed the concept of figuration devised by Goffman (1974) to designate the moments during which meaning is made in the practices of gathering around a table and eating meals. According to Goffman, figuration or *face work* refers to the way in which a person proceeds in order not to lose face during a conversation. Thus, face work means to "fend off 'incidents', that is to say events whose symbolic implications are indeed a danger to one's image", for respecting the ego of the people conversing. The figuration is thus based on the modality of know-how. In order to save face for themselves and the others present, a person draws on a "figurative repertoire" which includes avoidance, assurance and repair (Goffman 1974, pp. 15–16). The goal is to put on a good face; it raises the question of the meaning of the relationship. While unique to "each person, each group, each society", Goffman's "figurative repertoire" refers to a "structured, unique, coherent set of possible practices, as if one's face, by its very nature, could only be saved in a certain number of ways, and that each social group had to make its choice in a unique matrix" (Goffman 1974, p. 16).

Within the framework of eating and table manners, Jean-Jacques Boutaud adapts the concept of figuration to designate the way in which diners "perform, that is to say achieve, authentic and appropriate relationships to animate the relationships around the table [...]" (Boutaud 2004, p. 14). By doing this, the structuralist understanding of figuration is erased so as to favor the development of a relationship of the process rather than the system. Figuration is thus understood as a notion designating the "process of formation, figuration of relations, beyond the given form or pre-constructed by the device" (Boutaud 2004, p. 15). For the guests, it is an issue of bringing the exchange to life, reactivating it phenomenologically. Figuration thus becomes the third moment of meaning-making, the way to take oneself "in the game of interaction, reinforced or confirmed in 1,000 ways with respect to others" (Boutaud 2005, p. 18).

From stereotype to creative singularity, the moment of figuration carries out what the time of sitting at the table and serving the food configures – the second moment of meaning-making – makes possible and selects, within global, general and virtual food interactions, because they are latent in a social background. These latter elements, which constitute a structural framework, allow us to imagine different possibilities. The framework, understood as dynamic forms, is structural but not structuralist here. In Jean-Jacques Boutaud's work, it is not understood as a functioning system but as a dynamic, evolving, virtualizing ensemble within which the entries onto the scene may possibly take place. These are "the restaurant", the "official setting"; the meal "with family", "with friends", etc. (Boutaud 2005, p. 17). The frame forms the first moment, the one where the stage entrances are prefigured (the second moment) which configure the performances of the participants without determining them. These participants, in turn, appear at the table or at the meal time in ways that range from conformity to inventiveness (the third moment). Erving Goffman's concept of figuration becomes a notion broken into three stages: prefiguration, configuration and figuration. This is no longer a question of merely exploring the abilities to "save face", to survive on the social scene, but of exploring the process that leads everyone to live and flourish concretely, symbolically, socially, on the occasion of "eating". For our part, we utilize the notions of prefiguration, configuration and figuration to question the strata of digital design as a process.

4.4.2. Semiotic interrelationships between the strata

We have also specified how digital design consists of continuous and reversible interrelations between three strata:

– the stratum of the founding sciences of digital technology that laid the groundwork for informational and communicational transformations;

– the stratum of designs of digital hardware and software objects used to configure information and communication experiences;

– the stratum of designs of uses or non-uses representing/counter-representing information and communication experiments (Pignier 2020b, pp. 166–173).

Stratum No.	Denomination of the proper enunciation at every stratum of the design	Function of the stratum in the information-text communication experience	Aesthesia at play
1	Enunciation at play in the design of digital technologies	Moment of prefiguration	Technesthesia
2	Enunciation at play in the design of hardware–software objects and devices	Moment of configuration	Esthesia related to the design of hardware-software objects
3	Enunciation at play in the uses of technologies and hardware, software supports	Moment of performance/counter-performance of the practices of the texts as configured by the previous strata	Aesthetics linked to the gesture of use to the design of use

Table 4.1. The different strata of meaning of usage technologies

The ever-evolving specificities of digital technologies: coding, tracing, counting and cross-linking are the foundation of the structural mechanics from which digital hardware or software objects can be designed. This stratum states a technesthesia (Couchot 1998, p. 8) or sensibility belonging to an objectifying ontology, that of digital computing. It is not a system or a repertoire where we draw to design digital objects, but a kind of moving totality, a dynamism, a field of enunciative forces arising from the interrelationship between mathematics, cybernetics, biology, telecommunications, economics, information and communication sciences and electronics. A tensed structure is made up of forces and enunciative forms in tension, the first stratum prefigures possibilities as virtual dynamics, virtualities or forces in a basic state, and not as a structuralist system. The other strata in return cause it to evolve, such as the stratum of the design of uses. As an example of this, if the uses of connected objects, computers and mobile phones had not been adopted on a mass scale, telecom companies would not have invested in the search for new generations of networks such as 5G. Similarly, the stratum of the designs of hardware and software objects, while it configures uses, is itself affected by the stratum of the design of use or non-use (stratum 3). For example, the limited adoption levels of robots for home use outside of Asia, or the lack of enthusiasm for self-driving cars Lesniak (2020) have given rise to designs of automated household objects or spaces whose automation is phenomenologically discreet, not apparent. This lets users have the feeling of continuing to do things with their own hands, to enjoy the pleasure of driving or traveling.

In short, these strata constitute enunciative structures that manifest and deploy forces in tension. They are interrelated from the point of view of modalization, ranging from virtualization (germinating, latent forces) to actual realization through potentialization, namely that which presents itself as giving shape to possible uses. But these moments are not linear; they are reversible. Thus, as the third stratum comes to realize, represent, counter-represent, through the design of use, the previous strata, in return, it brings out forces or virtual aspects that tend to cause evolutions in the design of objects as well as the sciences behind the technologies.

4.4.3. *Digital design: from ethos to ethics*

In addition to this, each stratum is a moment during which designs with practical and ethical aims are enunciated in contrary, contradictory and complementary tensions, but that gradually lead to dynamic "totalities-events" where dialectical polarities interact. These can be called "force fields", using Herman Parret's definition of structure (Parret 2018, pp. 54–55). As part of a publication on our shared existence together "in the digital age" (Pignier 2020d), we have put to the test the areas covered in the co-authored work *Manifeste convivialiste. Déclaration d'interdépendance*, published in 2013. The authors call for an ethic of conviviality, defined as effectively caring for others and for our environment. According to the authors, digital technologies form the condition *sine qua non* for the advent of convivial societies, from the moment when these technologies, including the Internet, become freely accessible and governed by the principle of neutrality. We conducted a qualitative study related to the peasant and agricultural uses of digital technologies. Here, we will partially summarize our analysis in order to compare the founding ethical aim of the design of two free agricultural software programs.

One, named Qrop, is dedicated to the planning of market gardening activities; the other, named Ekylibre, allows users to manage cultivation and livestock activities. The first was *designated* by L'Atelier paysan, a cooperative that designs and manufactures free agricultural tools, adapted to the practices of its members. These tools are cataloged and are distributed under a Creative commons license, free of any intellectual property rights. Training courses are organized within the territory of France based on the requests of farmers, to help them design and produce tailor-made tools. The other, Ekylibre, was designed by the company of the same name. This company is a member of the Agilibre association, which promotes the development of free software in the agricultural field.

At the level of ethos, both of these programs lay claim to the values of free access: sharing, access to knowledge and a "do it yourself" attitude. However, the ethical aims implemented by the designers in the specific areas of the first stratum diverge. One of the designers of the Qrop program specifies that the program was designed "to help, and not to dictate what we should do". He adds: "At the Peasant Workshop, we have developed a critique of technologies that can alienate us. We don't want to be dispossessed of our know-how[26]". Thus, Qrop does not use any automated tracing of peasant gestures, nor does it use the interconnection of digital objects, but it makes it possible to visualize graphically and on a year-by-year basis the spatiotemporal distribution of crops – lettuce, radishes, carrots, etc. – their rotations, and how they perform. This is done so as to take advantage of previous experiments and to predict the sufficient amount to be grown for each "series" of vegetables. This design allows for a rigorous work structure, and at the same time preserves the "homemade" gesture. Such a design is based on a critical ethical goal of tracing, counting and interweaving. The concrete, perceptual and creative link to the soil and plant life remains paramount.

Conversely, the Ekylibre software opts for remotely controlling activities. It allows for making "intervention declarations" on "products", a term that can be used interchangeably to refer to things such as a tractor that is refueled, wheat to be treated or an animal to be cared for.

---

26 For a video presentation of the Qrop software (www.latelierpaysan.org/QROP-Logiciel-de-planification-des-cultures-maraicheres).

With the help of an "appli-tracking" application used by the operator, the actions and gestures of this operator are filmed, and the application pre-interrogates the farmer to make responses easier. In addition, Ekylibre makes it possible to receive data from drones that photograph the land plots, taking measurements to delimit the quantity, timing and location of treatments and irrigations. These data are stored by the software and can be shared with other farms and sent to the machines, such as to a connected sprinkler, which in this case automates the irrigation. Such a design is based on an ethic of the automation of gestures and farmer enunciation through tracing, counting and cross-linking. The mechanical enunciation remotely controls the decision-making. In this way, the design sets the configuration for a phenomenological break with the soil, where living beings, seen from above, are reduced to data points. It is exactly such an ethical goal that is rejected by farmers who remain supporters of traditional agriculture. This is not out of technophobia, but rather out of an aspiration for a phenomenological, concrete and existential link to plant and animal life (Pignier 2020d, pp. 53–56).

The way in which users take hold of one digital object or another, or refuse to take hold of such objects, does not consist simply of putting on an attractive face, but states an aesthesia, a form of existing in the world, an ethical goal and not just an ethos. This could be seen in December 2018 when, during a congress on "smart agriculture" in Toulouse, peasants and other citizens burst onto the stage of a large amphitheater and interrupted a presentation being given by a representative of the American tractor manufacturer John Deere. They posted the slogans: "Peasants are animals, not robots"; "Collective farm lands, not selective robots"; "Disconnect them all". Then they read a text addressed to the various participants in the convention, explaining their refusal of an ethics of automation:

> We who have opposed the electronic killing of animals for years and are worried about the growing addiction of humans to screens, have come here to interrupt your (d)ebates with machines and loudly proclaim the outrage caused by your activity: for the culture of the soil, as for those of companies, you here, the engineers, startups, and other experts in development support – you are pests. What will be the result of your innovations (weed-picking robots, connected farms, or automated tractors)? In the immediate future, gains in power and precision for those who will use them. But the most massive and lasting result will be the even greater dependence of farmers on large industries. For several decades now, they have been dependent on an immense banking and industrial complex: Crédit Agricole, and the giants in the chemical, seed, and agribusiness sectors, etc. Those have the brilliant idea of acquiring/accepting your electronic toys for their

own exploitative ends will be given special benefits by the GAFAM (Google, Amazon, Facebook, Apple and Microsoft) and the many capitalist actors in their orbit. More than ever, they will have lost all control over everything on their farm; they will understand less and less how their tools work; they will be cut off from the sensitive and living reality of the fields, plants, and animals.[27]

Signed by its authors, "Some of the chimpanzees from the future Occitans", the above quote clearly claims a resistant ethos.

The staging is very present, carefully planned but also done to enhance an ethics based on a concrete and existential, phenomenological link to the earth, to others, to one's place, to living beings. An ethic that fully overlaps with that of the peasants that we have seen in the area of peasant seeding (Pignier 2020d).

4.5. Conclusion

Our approach to webdesign questions, on the one hand, the ways in which the different modalities are orchestrated. We have thus been able to clarify how each type of multimodal writing brings about meaning, by causing objects to be perceived in a specific way. Making meaning, or making a realistic or even hyperrealistic, mythical, subversive or reality-deconstructing, readable world, these modes of writing are not native to digital technologies, yet they nevertheless evolve with them, often in the direction of standardization where they are frozen into stereotypes. In this regard, our corpus mainly focuses on organizational sites, but the question of making meaning, creating a world according to multimodal orchestrations, remains relevant for social networks and platforms; it allows us to question the enunciative ethos at play in webdesign, the co-enunciative link between the DSN or the platform and users. This also makes it possible to understand what kind of ethos between users the webdesign configures. The extension of the analysis to the question of the semiotic functions of interfaces as supports makes it possible to understand not only the ethos at stake, for example, is that of sharing, communication openness, the pleasure of interacting with others on mainstream RSNs. It also makes it possible to question the way in which these media capture attention, intention and often, paradoxically, promote the withdrawal of communication on exchanges within oneself.

Our approach does not have the same goal as user experience (UX design). This design seeks to "meet the exact needs of a customer" by taking into account "all

---

27 Available at: www.terrestres.org/2019/01/16/disruption-dun-forum-de-robotique-toulousain.

aspects of the end user's interaction with a company, its services, its products" (Agence pour la promotion de la création industrielle et al. 2013, p. 58). UX design is based on a quality approach and a market logic, while our approach to webdesign questions the things left unconsidered that nonetheless work unnoticed in creating meaning out of digital utterances. That said, such apprehension cannot be enough on its own. The design of sites, platforms and applications constitutes an enunciative stratum in interrelation with the others. The first stratum states a technesthesia (Couchot 1998, p. 8) or sensibility belonging to an objectifying ontology, that of digital computing. It prefigures and makes possible the second stratum, that of the designs of hardware and software objects, the mediators of information and communication. These express a special relationship to digital aesthetics and cause the research to evolve. The second stratum consists of information and communication experiences that users make use of on the basis of whether and what they intend their use for. These express a special relationship to the previous strata. We envisage digital design as an interrelated enunciative dynamic between different strata that do not consist of chronologically ordered levels or deterministic causal relationships. They are semiotic, insofar as they form reversible moments of modalization. Indeed, each stratum expresses a certain perception of others and recurs, but it also generates the emergence of uses, technological evolutions and new objects in a non-deterministic and at least partially unpredictable way. These enunciative interactions between strata are added to the dialogism of ethical aims within each stratum.

This proposal not only has the will of a retrospective, but also intended to be prospective in view of the ethical questions posed by the evolutions of the three strata. The development of 5G by telecommunications companies and other sciences within the first stratum allows for the design of new digital software and hardware objects and materials (stratum 2) at the same time that these are the expressions of them, or that they echo aspirations on the part of potential users (strata 2 and 3). The debates that it provokes go beyond technical questions of power, speed and cost; they express high tensions between radically different, divergent ethical aims. Our semiotic approach to digital design places the analysis of websites within the grouping of "digital society" to better question its multiplicity, the issues of meaning and power that animate it. Even more broadly, on the basis of the statements at play in digital design, from the ethical aims in tension, we wish to break with the thesis of "the digital" as a medium, as a non-questionable entity that proceeds inexorably toward its destination with a procession of elements that go unnoticed.

We wish to point out the relative spaces of freedom of meaning and choice in the design of each stratum and within each stratum, including the choice, as an individual or collective enunciative instance, to make use, counter-use or not to use a given platform, a given RSN, facial recognition system, connected object, etc. The reluctance in France to use the first StopCovid application designed at the request of the government in spring 2020, the existential void that pervades in students forced to study in front of their screens, enunciates the fact that the "digital" is neither uniform, nor our only environment. As human beings living among the rest of the living beings on Earth, we need to reconnect with our environments in an eco-techno-symbolic relationship (Pignier 2020c). This means the anthropological need for a concrete, existential link to places, people, languages, arts, gestures, sciences and techniques. But what can a closed-off humanity give in an above-ground techno-symbolic environment, proclaimed as universal while it obeys the logic of tracing, counting and automation, that has the tendency to format our gestures, languages, lives and environment? Is it not possible for us to open up other digital possibilities? To acquire a methodology capable of questioning the semiotic, practical and ethical complexity of digital design means allowing for reflexive questioning in order to scientifically seek a new path.

4.6. References

Agence pour la promotion de la création industrielle, Designers interactifs, Mov'eo, Systematic (2013). *Le design des interfaces numériques en 170 mots-clés*. Dunod, Paris.

Boutaud, J.-J. (ed.) (2004). *L'imaginaire de la table. Convivialité, commensalité et commmunication*. L'Harmattan, Paris.

Boutaud, J.-J. (2005). *Le sens gourmand. De la commensalité-du goût-des aliments*. Éditions Pascal Rocher, Paris.

Couchot, E. (1998). *Des images, du temps et des machines dans les arts et la communication*. Éditions Jacqueline Chambon, Nîmes.

Deleuze, G. (2002). *Francis Bacon : la logique de la sensation*. Éditions de la Différence, Paris.

Goffman, E. (1974). *Les rites d'interaction*. Les éditions de Minuit, Paris.

Gomez-Mejia, G. (2014). De quoi le "nuage" est-il le nom ? *Communication et langages*, 4(182), 77–93

Gullentops, D. (2003). *Poétique du lisuel*. Éditions Paris Méditerranée, Paris.

Kaplan, F. (2014). La question de la langue à l'époque de Google. In *Digital studies : organologie des savoirs et technologies de la connaissance*, Stiegler, B. (ed.). FYP Éditions, Paris.

Latouche, S. et al. (2013). *Manifeste convivialiste. Déclaration d'interdépendance*. Le Bord de l'eau, Lormont.

Lesniak, I. (2020). Google Glass, drones, robots: The five failures of tech. *Les Échos*, October 21 [Online]. Available at: www.lesechos.fr/weekend/high-tech-auto/google-glass-drones-robots-les-5-echecs-de-la-tech-1257633. [Accessed 12 December 2022].

Morozov, E. (2014). *Pour tout résoudre, cliquez ici. L'aberration du solutionnisme technologique.* FYP Éditions, Paris.

Parret, H. (2018). *Structurer, Progrès sémiotique en épistémologie et en esthétique.* L'Harmattan, Paris.

Pignier, N. (2012). Le plaisir de l'interaction entre l'usager et les objets TIC numériques. In *De l'interactivité au(x) interaction(s) : Interfaces Numériques 1*, Mitropoulou, E., Pignier, N. (eds). Hermès-Lavoisier, Paris.

Pignier, N. (2014). Questionner le sens du lien entre supports numériques des textes, dispositifs d'information-communication et styles d'usage. In *Former ou formater, les enjeux de l'éducation aux médias*, Mitropoulou, E., Pignier, N. (eds). Éditions Solilang, Limoges.

Pignier, N. (2017). *Le design et le Vivant. Cultures, agricultures et milieux paysagers.* Connaissances et Savoirs, Paris.

Pignier, N. (2020a). L'éthique énonciative au cœur du design d'information et du data-journalisme. *Interfaces Numériques*, 9(3) [Online]. Available at: https://www.unilim.fr/interfaces-numeriques/4418 [Accessed 12 December 2022].

Pignier, N. (2020b). L'éducation critique aux médiations informationnelles et communicationnelles en milieu numérique. In *Éducation critique aux médias et à l'information en contexte numérique*, Saemmer, A. (ed.). Presses de l'ENSSIB, Lyon.

Pignier, N. (2020c). Le sens, le vivant ou ce qui nous relie à la Terre. In *Le design de "l'Intelligence artificielle" à l'épreuve du vivant*, Pignier, N., Marcela, L., Durán, L. (eds.). *Interfaces Numériques*, 9(1) [Online]. Available at: https://www.unilim.fr/interfaces-numeriques/4144.

Pignier, N. (2020d). Approche éco-sémiotique du convivialisme à "l'ère du numérique". In *Inter-connectés ? Numérisme et convivialisme*, Wallenhorst, N., Mellot, S., Theviot, A. (eds). Le Bord de l'eau, Lormont.

Pignier, N. and Drouillat, B. (2004). *Penser le webdesign. Modèles sémiotiques pour les projets multimédias.* L'Harmattan, Paris.

Pignier, N. and Drouillat, B. (2008). *Le webdesign, Sociale expérience des interfaces web.* Hermès-Lavoisier, Paris.

Saemmer, A. and Jehel, S. (eds) (2020). Introduction. In *Éducation critique aux médias et à l'information en contexte numérique*, Jehel, S., Saemmer, A. (eds). Presses de l'ENSSIB, Lyon.

5

Social Semiotic Approach of Press Websites: Genesis of a Method

Alexandra SAEMMER[1] and Nolwenn TRÉHONDART[2]

[1] *CEMTI, Université Paris 8 Vincennes-Saint-Denis, France*
[2] *CREM, Université de Lorraine, Metz, France*

5.1. Introduction

For several years (Saemmer 2017; Saemmer and Tréhondart 2020), we have been involved in the development of a social semiotic approach of cultural and media productions (press images, television series, press websites, etc.). Our framework is rooted in pragmatic semiotics, taking an analytical method that includes, on the one hand, the material characteristics of signs, and on the other hand, the central role of the subject who perceives and interprets these characteristics. It raises a certain number of methodological difficulties when taking into account the way in which the mediating role of the subject operates, which plays the role of an "instance of junction between sign and sign" (Fabbri 2008, p. 114) and raises a number of methodological difficulties. Some semiotics respond by assuming an immanentist based on the constraints related to the reception text, which the analyst has circumscribed. Other semiotics favor the juxtaposition of different points of view gathered on the field. But the expert's outlook is often a kind of overhead view, as it pretends to reveal the material characteristics of the object that are not spotted by average viewers. In both cases, the way in which points of view are constructed in a semiotic situation is not central to the analysis.

Analyzing Websites,
coordinated by Luc MASSOU, Patrick MPONDO-DICKA and Nathalie PINÈDE.
© ISTE Ltd 2023.

Without questioning the relevance of interpretative semiotics, which are the starting point of our approach, the social semiotics that we propose seeks to shift the focus of the interpretative result to the analysis of its construction process. The identification of units of meaning in a cultural production is no longer an end in itself, but instead serves as a springboard for a reflection on the way in which the interpretative filters that constitute all subjects operate in reaction to signs. These filters that orient the glance of any subject can include, on the one hand, cultural knowledge (such as intertextual references, reminders of current events, scientific knowledge) mobilized in a conscious way, and on the other hand, habits of thought (political and religious convictions, beliefs, values, ideologies, etc.) acting in a more implicit way in the semiosis. In this context, our definition of ideology is based on that of Louis Althusser, who defines it as the functional action of "perceived-accepted-suffered cultural objects" on humans (Althusser 1965, pp. 239–240).

We attempt to give a new centrality to the pragmatic principle that the materiality of a cultural production is inaccessible as it is, and that any access made to signs is mediated by the filters of the subjects' viewpoints, of which they have varying levels of awareness. The tools of interpretative semiotics can help the participants in our experiments to obtain a sharper view of the materiality of a cultural production, and in particular, to better understand the strategies and power issues that structure it. We also consider that, through a structured collective debate, forms of ideological introspection can be initiated that allow, at least in part, for subjects to recognize and become aware of the actions of their interpretative filters.

After several years of experimentation, we have come to the conclusion that the organization of interpretative debates can support the subject in this awareness. In order to be able to circumscribe the composition of the interpretative filters that mediate subjects' access to reality as accurately as possible, a comparison with other interpretative hypotheses supported by the members of a group, and especially a collective analysis of their rationales, proved to be a conclusive experience. Thus, from a methodological point of view, our approach is based on the commitment – by the individual participant, the researcher and the group – to engage in a reflexive investigation that gives a central role to convictions, beliefs and social affiliations in the way a cultural production is viewed, and makes it possible to account for habits of thought that are so internalized that a person's self-analysis alone is not enough to detect them.

In recent years, we have conducted experiments with this method on various fields and corpora: press photographs, trailers for TV series, press websites and social platforms. Based on the analysis of the website of the television channel BFM TV – a French media outlet that is both very popular and divisive – this chapter proposes to re-trace the genesis and evolution of the method from two experimental fields: one conducted in 2017, the other in 2020, with students from the professional Master's degree programs in digital communication and project management at the Paris 8 Vincennes-Saint-Denis university. We will show how our method, which was initially close to an interpretative semiotics centered on the identification and critical decoding of editorial units from a methodical exploration of interface design, has evolved gradually, seeking to answer the more complex question: "Why does an editorial unit mean something to a specific receiver?", or even more accurately, to lead the subject to question what is the ground of his or her interpretation process, and to try to verbalize it.

For students studying professions related to "digital communications", this viewpoint gymnastics, between ideological introspection and materiality of signs, appears essential to us: indeed, communicative uses tend to be naturalized by accompanying discourses, which, like "anticipatory narratives" of practices (Jeanneret 2014, p. 258), orient the ways of perceiving and interpreting websites and social platforms. The use of Web design vocabulary in conducting the analysis reinforces a globalized hegemony, which acts as a guarantee of sufficient and secure scientific knowledge among young communicators. However, for us, the point is not to use the analysis of the materiality of the signs alone, but to identify the ideological processes used in carrying out the interpretative act. This conviction was further reinforced when we were met the students' apparently unanimous rejection of the idea of working on the BFM TV website which they consider as semiotically "poor", and perceive in a negative manner. We felt it was all the more relevant to work with them on the ideological motivations explaining this rejection.

First, we will present the epistemological framework of our method. We will then break down and analyze the results of the two experiments in the field conducted in 2017 and 2020 to show how the evolution of the methodological framework has led to a shift. Initially focused on an interpretative semiotics promoting the identification of major editorial units and how they can be critically decoded, we chose to focus in 2020 on questioning the interpretative filters activated by the subject. It is this methodological evolution that we will qualify as a social semiotic approach.

5.2. Epistemological and methodological issues

5.2.1. *Genesis of a method*

One of the most important trends in semiotics in recent decades has undoubtedly been to focus primarily on social phenomena, as Lorusso (2019) explains. Many approaches in semiotics have indeed positioned themselves in the field of social practices, with frameworks in sociosemiotics (Landowski 1984; Hodge and Kress 1988) or more recently (Julliard 2013) in semio-pragmatics (Odin 2011). In line with the social turn of semiotics, our approach forms part of the legacy left by the works of Peirce (1978), who argues that our access to signs, even if it is pre-structured by their material configuration, is always carried out through the filter of knowledge and socially ingrained habits of thought (Peirce 1878) that guide the interpretive process.

In 2015, *La Rhétorique du texte numérique* formulated by Alexandra Saemmer worked on the basis of the theories of reception (Iser 1995) in order to show how hypertexts prefigure reading practices. The analysis starts from a semio-rhetorical approach of the specificities of the hypertext, contextualized by the circumscription of the horizons of expectations of readers tested during field surveys. While the attention paid to the reactions by empirical audiences was affirmed, the study's placing of the respondents in front of a hyperlink in a journalistic article led to the observation most notably of the discrepancy between their often restricted representations of the rhetoric of the digital text and the true diversity of figures that the expert analysis was able to reveal.

Following her doctoral work on the socio-semiotic analysis of a corpus of enhanced digital books, nourished by points of view from interviews with designers and publishers, Tréhondart (2016) questioned this separation of tasks between experts and professionals: the semiotician tends to retroactively superimpose his/her point of view in the results, without having previously discussed it with his/her interviewees.

These approaches, although bolstered by a pragmatic approach, ultimately fall within a semiotics of unveiling that we have sought to move beyond through the development of a new methodological framework based on co-interpretation workshops. During these debates, the analysts act not to impose their point of view, but instead to share questions with the participants as much as possible, or even to recognize that their own view can be modified by the perception of other people. Because of successive sessions, we attempt, through the comparison of views facing a cultural production, to make the filtering action of cultural knowledge and habits of thought more visible.

The purpose is not to guide the group in accessing an exhaustive interpretation of a text, a film or a digital production – which would imply the possibility of "unveiling" a pure semiotic object – but rather the more modest goal of showing that the perceptible reality (Berger and Luckmann 1997) of a cultural production is always socially constructed. Within our fields, we have found that this questioning has encouraged the participants to develop forms of reflexive thinking concerning not only the role of cultural knowledge in the interpretative process (such as familiarity with the main concepts of Web design), but also of more fundamental factors such as primary and secondary socialization processes, belonging to a social class, an ethno-racial or gender group or political and religious convictions.

5.2.2. Foundational concepts

How can we delimit the cultural knowledge and habits of thought that are implemented by the receiver when he develops interpretative hypotheses? We determined empirically that the concept of recognition grammar created by Verón (1995) was suited to our approach. Nevertheless, we gradually began to replace it with "interpretative filters", a concept that would seem more spontaneously understandable to the participants.

According to Eliseo Verón, all cultural production is innervated by communication issues, which govern the connections between signs in the form of a "production grammar": this refers to the set of discursive operations that constitute the rules for framing a discourse. For example, in the context of a museum, the production grammar results both from the project of cultural communication, the constraints of architectural space and the choices of the curators (Jacobi 2018). However, as Eliseo Verón explains, the access to the production grammar is conditioned by the social conditions of reception as well as by the perceptual and cognitive apparatus of the subjects, which structures what the author calls recognition grammars.

Recognition grammars make use of knowledge that is assured, instituted, recognized or legitimized within a given society: references drawn from books, films, paintings and photographs, in history, or in political news. But they are also made up of habits of thought stemming in part from the positions occupied by the subject in social structures and the systems of belonging and belief with which he more or less consciously identifies – a social class, a nation, a company, a family environment, a religion, a political party, etc.

Peirce (1878) defines habits of thought as an active rule within ourselves – an intelligent habit which we follow when the opportunity arises, and which has is clear and obvious. Comparisons have already been made with the concept of "*habitus*", as defined by Pierre Bourdieu. As Lorusso (2019) explains, Pierre Bourdieu's "habitus" are implicit patterns that function within the life of subjects as behavioral matrices, but also as socially established and accepted interpretative resources, forged by collective representations that are revived and reconfigured by encounters with signs. Habits of thought can resist spontaneous verbalization during a collective discussion: on the one hand, participants do not usually have the habit of arguing an interpretation based on their personal interpretative filters; on the other hand, their exhibition can be destabilizing.

However, in the field, we found that the term "grammar" used by Eliseo Verón tended to suggest the existence of a rigid framework in which the interpretative process takes place, and that the term "recognition" tended to reduce the interpretative process to that of perception. The concept of the interpretative filter appeared to us as both more suitable and more telling: it implies that the process of recognition and semiotization acts as a filter (and therefore a selection) when given the multiple material vibrations emitted by a cultural production; it refers also to the idea of a less rigid framework by suggesting that recognition is not always structured as a language with grammatical rules.

Interpretative filters are therefore defined as reading grids mobilized by the social subject in a situation of semiosis. Made up of conscious cultural knowledge and internalized habits of thought, they act in the perception, categorization and interpretation of the material vibrations that surround us. Some can be based on primary and secondary socialization processes and patterns of thought and action related to education, social origins, professional habits, psychological dispositions, personal and shared opinions, and convictions.

5.2.3. *Semiotic tools introduced in the field*

To prepare for the co-interpretation workshops, and to immediately break apart any hierarchies that may be found between interviewees and investigators related to a possible lack of training in methods, we utilize interpretative semiotics tools with the participants who are intended to sharpen their focus and to facilitate and clarify the verbalization of the perception of the material vibrations emitted by cultural productions. These tools structure the debate by providing a framework for reflection and a shared vocabulary; they also make it possible to present the methodological basis to the participants in which we situate these workshops, in order to establish bonds of trust based on the idea of sharing knowledge. We first ask them to note individually how they combine certain vibrations into meaningful units, and to propose an interpretation of their strategic configuration as considered by an instance of an enunciation. For example, we draw their attention to what can be meaningful in a website: the way in which the economy of digital text is anchored in practices of memory, historical forms (books, pages, etc.) which, while facilitating cultural appropriation, are also evolutionary; the way in which forms recurring within the designs structure perception by normalizing uses and processes of industrialization of the Web, this impression of repetition, being particularly related to the weightings used in "architexts" (Souchier et al. 2019).

Jeanneret and Souchier (1999) use the concept of architexte[1] to mean the forms, menus and other formatting options in digital editorial tools that prompt creators to enter texts, images or videos into predefined fields, and then automatically apply the desired formatting. This separation between the production of form and content in editorialization tools has given rise to new editorial units[2] on web pages which can, for example, host content updated in real time, such as a "front page" article that is refreshed several times per day, or a news feed.

Acting like an "editing table" (Gomez-Mejia 2016, p. 35), architext facilitates the production and editing of content – creators are no longer required to be adept at coding – but in this way imposes the views of the company that owns the software onto the final form of the content and its layout as displayed on the screen-page. Architext "provides representation devices that tie together multiple perspectives, all of which hold the power to give us a view of society" (Jeanneret 2014, p. 508).

The appearance of the content is formatted by the architexts. However, it is becoming increasingly common that the order of appearance in certain sections is calculated by algorithms, which take into account not only the chronology but also the "popularity" of certain topics. We use the term "computext"[3] (Saemmer 2020) to refer to this algorithmic structure that calculates the order in which the contents appear, according to a number of criteria and without the direct intervention of the creators. For instance, the appearance of *hit-lists*, the most read or clicked articles or videos, is based on an automatic quantification of readers' behaviors by the computer text.

Nevertheless, once the strategic issues of architexts and computexts were explained and discussed with the participants in our experiments, we found that there were nevertheless different interpretations of the editorial units, such as the news feed or the *hit-list*. While some participants recognize the hit-parades within

---

1 "We have given the name architexts (from the term *arch*, referring to origination and commands) to the tools that allow the existence of the written word on the screen and which, not satisfied with simply representing the structure of the text, control how it is executed and realized. In other words, the text is created from the architext that tags the writing" (Jeanneret and Souchier 1999, p. 103).

2 We define editorial units as the bricks used in constructing the design of websites and digital platforms.

3 Though we were already using the notion of "computext" during these experiments, it was only published for the first time in 2020.

the hit-list, others instead associate it with the idea of a democratic accounting of the tastes and preferences of the public. We arrived at the observation of these differences in 2017. In 2020, we investigated the reasons in more depth.

Beyond the concepts of an interpretative semiotics of display writing that allows us to better understand how a website is produced behind the scenes, before presenting a specific digital production, we discuss certain forms with the participants that we consider to have become recurrent in the design of websites (such as flows or *patchwork*) or that are becoming less common (such as a menu).

While the design of the website for BFM TV does not necessarily follow all these trends, the development and disappearance of these forms nonetheless tend to bring about new modes of understanding them by users, who are mostly accustomed to recognizing and identifying them.

For example, while the menu shows the principles of structuring the contents of a site, with its graphic forms that at times recall the contents of a book and the world of documentation and archiving, this is now beginning to disappear, with newer designs instead favoring a culture of flows and a post-hypertext design (Lloveria 2015), characterized by infinite scrolling and materialized in the form of chronological feeds of social networks. For its parts, the patchwork forms, another dominant editorial unit in contemporary Web design, refers to a mode of assembly composed of multimodal semiotic materials – short texts, still images and videos – and weaving a hierarchy between the materials by presenting the contents in frames of different sizes.

In 2017 as in 2020, for each form, we hypothesized about the reading practices that were modeled (early reading, scattered reading, etc.) and the communication and market strategies that they materialized. In 2020, with the goal of associating these significant elements with interpretative hypotheses, this step was used as the starting point for the approach, followed by returning to the analysis of the interpretative filters.

5.3. The first field: a critical decoding of interfaces

5.3.1. *Experimental protocol*

Our first experiment took place in the spring of 2017 and was carried out with 21 students enrolled in the first year of a professional Master's degree in digital communications and project management.

It began with two introductory sessions on the founding semiotic concepts, such as architext and computext. We placed these concepts within the broader context of a pragmatic approach that gives consideration to the context of production and reception of the websites we were going to study, particularly by examining the role of editorial units as modelers or anticipators of reception practices (Saemmer 2015; Tréhondart 2016). We used as a reference the works of Iser (1995) and Eco (1985) to arrive at the concept of the "model reader", and to make participants aware that we were going to consider each editorial unit not as invariable, but as the actualization of a potential which, within another context of reception, could give rise to other interpretations.

After sharing these tools, the participants were shown the BFM TV website.

Stage 1	Stage 2	Stage 3	Stage 4	Stage 5
Two short questionnaires on the methods of accessing information, and knowledge and points of view on the BFM TV website	Introduction to founding semiotic (architext, computext)	First viewing of the BFM TV website and collection of spontaneous impressions	Each participant fills out an individual table in order to identify the major units on the "front page" of the BFM TV website and to associate interpretative hypotheses with these	Work within two subgroups to prepare collective hypotheses based on the viewing of individual hypotheses. Results debated for about 60 min

Table 5.1. *Group 1 (21 students, average age: 23 years old, 80% female)*

5.3.2. *Spontaneous opinions and impressions from viewing BFM TV's website*

While very few students stated that they had visited the BFM TV website at any point previously (10%), the opinions of the site in 2017 remained linked to those of the channel, and especially its role during the 2015 terrorist attacks in France. The opinions were suspicious: "I don't like this channel very much, since it endangered the lives of the hostages during the attacks" – and emphasize its rush to provide an excess of information: "A channel that works to show that they are on the scene"; "A poorly thought-out channel, which gives 'hot takes'"; "On the edge of outright lies".

After viewing the site, the participants insisted on the presence of the editorial unit named News 24/7, which they associated with positive values (speed, staying current, immediacy), while making the connection with the main value associated with the channel, that of "specializing in live broadcasts". This unit was unanimously praised since it meets the need to save time. Highlighting this self-evident acceleration thus makes it possible to discuss both the apparent consent of students to these mechanisms of reading, and the responsibility of digital devices in reinforcing this desire for acceleration.

Conversely, none of the participants noted the presence of an editorial unit named "Focus", which provides reports backed by in-depth journalistic work, and which we ourselves had noticed as part of a close analysis of the site. By identifying these types of blind spots, in 2017, we attempted to make students aware of the way habits of thought weighed on the reception process. But revealing these blind spots would inevitably lead to the creation of a hierarchy between lay and expert interpretations, as if ignoring the presence of the focus division were not very legitimate. Now, it seems more relevant to us to take a closer look into the *reason* for this omission.

5.3.3. *Identification of editorial units and first interpretations*

5.3.3.1. *The menu: an essential markup*

All participants grouped the signifiers located at the top of the screen page (the keywords, "menu" button, BFM logo, magnifying glass icon) into a signifying unit, associating the signification of "menu" or "headline" with them. This first unit to be recognized would activate values of "categorization" and "structuring", "guidance" and "markup", following the "classic headings" of the press. The inclusion of a menu is presented as a necessity, a well-known grammar of production. According to the students, the identification of this unit was promoted by their knowledge in information-communication, and a habit of online media consumption.

5.3.3.2. *The front page as click bait*

Among the participants, 98% identified the frame below the menu, containing a bold title and a large image, as the second large meaningful unit. It was seen as a "headline", the information "happening now that we need to remember", reflecting an "editorial decision" by the channel, with the goal of "generating as many clicks as possible". "BFM puts whatever serves its interests on the front page!", exclaimed a student, thus reiterating his negative opinion of the channel while also evoking his knowledge of the political economy of the communications industry to justify his point of view.

5.3.3.3. *The news feed for news lovers*

The sequence of short titles on the right of the screen page was identified by 90% of the participants as a "news feed" that is directed toward "news lovers", a category with which most of the students identified themselves, citing their habits of checking updates on their mobile phones.

5.3.3.4. *Patchworks for "personalizing readings"*

The rest of the screen-page, consisting of titles, photographs and videos, was grouped by 80% of the students under the category of "thematic blocks" which would be addressed to readers wishing to choose information according to their personal interests. We asked if the presence of the menu was redundant in this case. One participant then stressed the strategic nature of the sequence of thematic blocks; she felt these were addressed to readers who were "in less of a hurry" than the one scrolling through the menu, a kind of "roaming reader".

5.3.3.5. *The "video blocks" as the "DNA of the channel"*

A quarter of the participants decided to consider the "video blocks" as a meaningful unit, arguing that moving images constituted the "DNA of the channel". Several of them then drew from their knowledge of the digital economy once again to decipher the strategic nature of this strong presence: "these are just chopped up replays that are easier to share", "this contributes to the visibility of BFM on social networks".

5.3.3.6. *The hit-list as a "click whore"*

Only a quarter of the participants noted the "list of the most read articles", a unit that nevertheless occupied an important place at the very top of the screen-page. First, they noted the strategic nature of this list: it served "to attract the reader's attention to the most popular topics", to "strengthen the buzz". Some qualified it as a "click whore", based again on the negative perception of the channel.

5.3.3.7. *Rarely mentioned units*

Few mentions were made of the block named Stories, the Eyewitness section, the slideshows, as well as the footer; the participants justified this by the fact that these parts were poorly classified on the front page, or that they were simply "banal". We received a surprised reaction when we pointed out two other units that no one had mentioned: the debate shows and the Focus block, offering a deeper look at a topic in the news. Noting that the Focus section was moderated by CELSA students, one student yelled, "Impressive!". This appears to be a guarantee of quality that seemed to him to be incompatible with the idea of "trash info" that he associated with the channel.

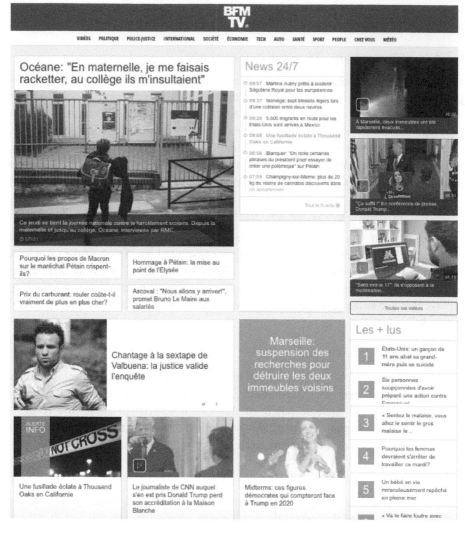

Figure 5.1. *Screenshot of the website BFMTV.com taken on November 8, 2018 at 10:30 a.m., to illustrate the different editorial units identified by the students. The layout of the site did not change between this date and that of the experiment. For a color version of this figure, see www.iste.co.uk/massou/analyzing.zip*

5.3.4. *Debating and choosing hypotheses*

During the last session, we formed smaller groups, which brought together about 10 participants for 1 h. We proposed to them to probe the strategic issues of the major units of meaning on the "front page" by asking them to imagine what they thought the "model reader" would be for each one. A vocabulary had to be created ad hoc to designate each unit according to this idea.

The first group has decided to focus on the issue of modeling reading practices: the headline was labeled "classificatory" because it was aimed at a reader wishing to access the classic categories of the press. The "headline" unit was called a "capture" feature because it would have the objective of capturing the reader's attention. The blocks of related titles were described as "in-depth" feature, intended for readers eager to "learn more". The news feed was called "instantaneity", aimed at readers in a rush. The thematic blocks were interpreted as "categorizing", allowing readers to look around by category. The lists of the most read articles have been described as "popularizing", modeling readers who let themselves be guided by trends. The stories were called "recreational", and the eyewitness unit "contributive". The Focus unit was described as "legitimizing": its goal would be to enhance the brand's image by offering practices of more in-depth readings. The point of view mobilized by this group was an interpretative scheme discussed in progress, inspired by a pragmatic approach to online press sites introduced upstream.

After a few minutes, the second group became literally inflamed about the idea that the BFM website was an "information supermarket". Each editorial unit was then characterized by a metaphor taken from mass distribution. The headline was the "shelving", a classification plan for consumers in a hurry. The "headline" was named the "head of the aisle", because its purpose is to showcase the flagship product of the moment. Logically, related products would surround the "head of the aisle" to retain consumers' attention. The news feed was called the "news shout": to keep up with competition, quality would be given a back seat. The thematic blocks were said to resemble the "shelves" of a supermarket: they would force readers to cross the page-screen in order to seduce them in passing. The most watched articles and videos would be the "top sellers", to help build more buzz. The blocks of videos would play the role of "samples", distributed to be shared. The stories would be the "extras", and the eyewitness part would be seen as "consumer experiences".

The point of view taken by this group seems to be based both on a negative opinion toward the channel formulated at the beginning of the experiment, a certain general pessimism toward the media, and critical approaches to digital communication.

For some, this site was merely a commercial outlet, created with the sole purpose of promoting shareable content on social networks: "Generating clicks and shares is generating revenue for the BFM brand", said one participant. For the others, BFM was trying to "restore its image" by presenting alternative content. At this point, we pointed out that some of the front pages of the publications *Le Monde* and *Libération*, media outlets declared by the participants to be much more reliable, contained similar units, such as a list of the most read or shared articles.

Should we then conclude that BFM was in fact using its website to position itself among the serious news sites by imitating their editorial design? Or should we instead conclude that most news websites were structured like news supermarkets? This is a dilemma, because both hypotheses could be supported by the identification of the editorial units recognized on the "front page", and their strategic distribution on the page-screen.

To summarize, our methodology used in 2017 consisted of identifying the major editorial units making up the site, and depending on the prioritization of a given unit by the participant, carrying out an analysis to decode the digital communication strategies of BFM. We had to give a central role within the experiment to the reflection on the interpretative filters that make a reader lean toward any one hypothesis. The collected transcripts certainly revealed differences in points of view on the object, as well as the way in which the participants assembled the building blocks of the design to constitute units of meaning, according to certain representations of the channel and the media, but did not probe the social depth of these semiotic decisions.

5.4. Second field: toward a social semiotic approach of websites

In 2020, the Master's students involved in a new co-interpretation workshop on the BFM site were familiarized with the specificities of our methodology, which had changed significantly since 2017. The group was also very close-knit. The situation of the university that year, between the teachers' strike at the beginning of the semester and then the Covid-19 pandemic crisis in the spring certainly, played a role in this relationship of mutual understanding and solidarity, which greatly facilitated the work of verbalization around the social motivations behind the points of view on the BFM TV website.

While the beginning of the semester had been marked by intense discussions around interpretative hypotheses sparked by images from the press, the closure of the university for health reasons forced us to carry out part of the interpretation of the BFM site remotely. We used a collaborative application, Framapad, to publish the questions we would have asked the students in person, asking them to answer in a way that was visible to all. This involved first listing their general opinions of BFM, then to state their first impressions of its website, to identify the major editorial units that make it up, and then to formulate an initial interpretative hypothesis.

Despite the complex situation of living through the lockdown, all the students were fully involved in this collective exercise. After a week, we had gathered plenty of material. We organized this material, consisting of about 20 pages of transcripts organized around five main interpretative hypotheses that we sent back to the group by asking each of them through a personal written document to summarize the results, then to elaborate a personal interpretation by probing as accurately as possible the interpretative filters motivating this personal choice.

Unlike the 2017 experiment, in 2020, we collectively identified the gender declared by the participants, as well as their nationality, in order to be able to take into account the possible role of these factors in semiosis.

Stage 1	Stage 2	Stage 3	Stage 4
In person: explanation of the research framework, introduction to the semiotics of websites, presentation of concepts and tools	On Framapad: collection of impressions of the television channel BFM TV. Collection of initial reactions to the site. Identification of the main editorial units of the site and their possible meanings	On Framapad: initial formulation of interpretative hypotheses argued from the site's production grammar. Between stages 3 and 4: summarizing of the researcher's writings around five main hypotheses. Publication of hypotheses on Framapad	Production of an individual writing revisiting interpretative hypotheses with a focus on the role of interpretative filters. Reasoned choice of an interpretative hypothesis, and in-depth self-analysis of personal interpretative filters

Table 5.2. *Group 2 (22 students in masters 1 professional digital communication and project management, ages 22–35 years old: four men, 17 women, one transgender person, one Italian student, one Russian student, one student from Burkina Faso, one student from Cameroon, one student from Mauritius. All other students were from France)*

Our presentation of the results of this second field study was no longer organized around the identified editorial units, model readers or the critical analysis of the communication strategies encoded in the BFM website, but instead focused on the interpretative filters. Indeed, it was no longer about identifying the blind spots of the subjects by juxtaposing more expert readings, or more ideological readings, but of analyzing with the participants the processes of social construction of the perceived reality of the site.

Of course, the analysis of the enunciative strategies of the site was always the starting point for reflection, but we insisted at all times on the fact that these strategies were not given or accessible "per se", as their perception and interpretation was inevitably guided by the personal or collectively shared interpretative filters.

5.5. Interpretative hypotheses and interpretative filters

5.5.1. *"BFM, the information supermarket", from the lens of an anti-capitalist viewpoint and professional habits*

As one student summarizes, a majority of the group (as well as the 2017 group) holds the idea that the BFM website has a "commercial purpose". Several editorial units common on media sites, such as the headline, the news feed or the patchwork, are interpreted as embodying this aim. As in the 2017 field study, the site was compared to a supermarket, "where the shelves are organized to help the visitors find what they are looking for, while doing everything possible to attract their attention to the other items in the store". The headline placed at the top of the patchwork is seen as being used to "generate clicks and promote reader engagement". The news feed, placed at the top at news 24/7, reflects the desire of "the BFM brand" to produce content based on hot news topics, bearing a passing resemblance to the American news channels like Fox News or CNN. The broadcast section, located a little further down on the patchwork and featuring portraits of "star journalists", also recalls the practices of American television.

The tab layout of the patchwork is associated with a "commercial strategy to please the greatest number of people". Several students also note the titles of the categories: "Politics, Economy, Tech, Auto, Sports, People... These categories reflect a group of values oriented towards liberal capitalism. For example, there is no mention of ecology, science, well-being". The scrolling necessary to navigate within this patchwork is compared to the gestures of social networks, and works to keep the readers on the site. The hit-lists of the most read articles and the most viewed videos also follow a "capitalist logic of profitability: to be productive, it is necessary to make time profitable, therefore it is better to be concise and factual". The videos contained throughout the patchwork also attest to BFM's desire to "create buzz": "Building buzz helps build a big audience, and having a big audience means more advertising". "With so many advertisements on this site, it appears to have completely turned into an e-shop".

Several students identified the fact they were enrolled in a professional Master's degree in digital communications as an important element of this interpretative filter: as one participant put it, "our studies allow us to see what is going on inside the machinery of the site". The belief that the media are companies pursuing primarily commercial objectives clearly influenced the analysis of the grammar of BFM's brand production. While the adjective "capitalist" appeared in several shared writings to describe the site's strategy, some participants identify it as a marker of a habit of thought: "When I read the word 'capitalist', I hear the voices of some of my comrades echoing in my head. I feel there is a general opposition and repudiation of capitalism there". One participant feels it reflects a habit characteristic of the students of the Paris 8 University, "left-leaning, and therefore socially oriented and anti-capitalist". In other words, he interprets it as a kind of interpretative reflexiveness with ideological overtones.

Another participant noted that he indeed knows many "leftists" with negative views of this TV channel, and he concludes, "This would probably push me to try to find something negative on the site". In the same self-reflexive impulse, the similarity between the editorial design of the site and American news channels such as CNN and Fox is deemed as being motivated not only by the highlighting of effigies of star presenters, but also by a shared "French-style" anti-Americanism: a "stereotypical vision of the United States", driving them to castigate the "stupidity of Americans who need simplified, easy-to-read information".

Many participants claimed to prefer other media outlets to get information about daily news: Arte and France Info are seen as being in opposition to private outlets like BFM. One student engaged in a deep examination about the reasons for his "hatred of BFM journalism". Working periodically with a public media outlet, he has heard many journalists criticize the channel "openly and blatantly". He then asks himself: "Are we able to analyze a media outlet with neutrality when we work for a competitor?" Fully aware of the fact that this means his point of view on BFM is also socially constructed, he feels the statements made by his fellow journalists take the view that "We are not BFM", as both a professional habitus and a reflexive class stance. This awareness of the patterns of belonging and belief which, in the face of the material realities of media industry production, may push the subject toward actions such as a semiotic decision of rejection, are precisely the objective of our social semiotics approach.

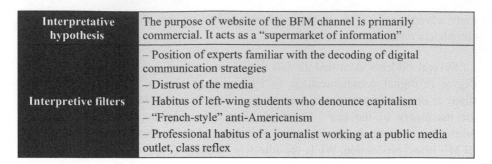

Interpretative hypothesis	The purpose of website of the BFM channel is primarily commercial. It acts as a "supermarket of information"
Interpretive filters	– Position of experts familiar with the decoding of digital communication strategies – Distrust of the media – Habitus of left-wing students who denounce capitalism – "French-style" anti-Americanism – Professional habitus of a journalist working at a public media outlet, class reflex

Table 5.3. *Hypothesis and interpretative filters*

5.5.2. The "sexist, right-wing BFM", through the prism of a feminist and intersectional perspective

Economics, sports, politics, etc.: For a group of students who were initially small in number, but whose entries included extensive commentary, the categories of the menu not only reflect the commercial objective of the site, but are also closely aligned with the "cisgender male" universe and, in turn, to the "dominant classes". The menu is seen as being targeted at a male reader, 40 years old or older, active, who could be placed on political spectrum as on the "neoliberal right". One student noted the inclusion of a "politics/justice" category in the menu, "which in practice is quite rare", but emblematic of the interests of the right. The blue color scheme that dominates the site is seen as being identified with both "the right-wing, and the man power" and is associated with authority. The news feed constitutes a pragmatic response to the need of a socio-professional class to quickly receive information on "what's going on in the world, and more specifically, in 'their' world". The same is the case for the hit-lists which, far from simply reflecting the preferences of the "customers", are alleged by some to be part of the world of social competition. The fact that there is a BFM Paris section confirms this targeted reader profile: "The dominant classes living in Paris".

Different personal lines of reasoning are given to explain the social construction of this perception of the BFM website as sexist and right-wing. One student cites her experience with a "typical" viewer of the channel, the father of one of her friends who was the director of commercial partnerships at a large firm, and a fan of BFM to the point of insisting on it as a kind of permanent background noise for his family. For several participants who held this hypothesis, it is above all the fact that they are female, which is seen as "opposed" to the identity forged by the grammar forged by production, which makes it easy for them recognize the sexist orientation of the site. One student considers that BFM and the traditional media more generally are "standardized, mostly gendered, and convey Western values" by their way of presenting information and prioritizing it on the media they publish.

Though only two women in the group had put forward this interpretative hypothesis at the start, it caused others to change their points of view. This conversion also prompted a reflection: why could this hypothesis not have been formulated at the outset by the majority of the group? For one participant, "the adherence to deeply gendered thoughts" explain that the sexism of the site has not been spontaneously recognized by everyone: this adherence runs so deep "that we no longer notice them because they simply seem 'normal', or even worse, insignificant". Therefore, in reality, the apparent neutrality of the BFM website is based on the incorporation of these mechanisms of domination, allowing them to be made invisible.

Conversely, one student who had defended this hypothesis from the start was quite aware of the fact that she was carrying out a "deconstruction of the binary system" to which she has voluntarily acculturated herself, as a member of the "LGBTQ+ community"; a way of doing things which, according to another participant, is maintained by a belief system consisting of "using morality as a figurehead, and denouncing capitalism as an institution and pure product of the patriarchy". The fact that the consideration of the working classes is excluded from BFM's site works perfectly to consolidate this point of view.

However, is the channel really watched mostly by upper social and professional categories (SPC+) men? One student asked about the regular consumption of the channel in her own family, one which, according to her, is "not part of the dominant class". In her view, watching the channel instead responds to the need to "be aware of what is happening in the world", "even though it is not necessarily 'our' world". This view reflects a comprehensive attitude toward the BFM viewers, and a certain distance from an anti-neoliberal belief pattern that is not necessarily held by working-class people. As one student put it: "One of the inherent features of the class system is not knowing which class you are in".

Interpretative hypothesis	BFMTV.com is a sexist, right-wing site
Interpretive filters	– Experience of political domination exercised by media outlets like BFM – Being female in gender – Holding feminist, anti-patriarchal, and anti-neoliberal beliefs

Table 5.4. *Hypothesis and interpretative filters*

5.5.3. *"BFM as a counter-power", through the lens of a complicit or critical adherence to the state media*

The participants characterizing the enunciative strategy of the BFM website as hostile, sexist or right-wing were the majority in the group, and were such a strong presence that during in-person discussions they may have drowned out all other points of view. However, since the experiment took place mainly in written form, first on a shared document and then by individual deliveries, these other points of view could be expressed. Some participants thus focused on the editorial units reflecting BFM's specialization in live broadcasting by associating it with positive values. The instant scrolling of the titles on the news feed reminded them of "the dispatches from major news agencies such as Agence France-Presse". The strong reactions to breaking news stories are seen as preventing abusive mediation and ultimately serve as a guarantee of neutrality and objectivity. For these students, the organized clear, and intuitive presentation, supported in particular by the inclusion of a classic menu, establishes BFM as an "independent media outlet" that has nothing to hide. The patchwork not only allows easier access to information, but also reflects the desire of the media to address "people of all classes".

This view, running contrary to the point of view of the majority in the group, nonetheless appealed to many participants, as evidenced by the final written descriptions. The pattern that provides the clearest explanation for this interpretative hypothesis is that of the "partisan" viewer of the channel. This was evidenced by statements such as one from a student who confirmed that she watches the channel and uses the site to meet her demand for live updates. Several other participants critical of the outlet recognized its "original" positioning, assuming that it meets the expectations of the contemporary public.

But is this point of view necessarily rooted in "right-wing" habits of thought, as one participant assumes? A look back at the chronology of the experiment shows that things are not so simple. It is remarkable to note that at first this point of view was defended by foreign students in particular. Is this fact explained, as one participant assumes, by a desire to adapt to the French system, that would prohibit them from holding a negative opinion of the site? One student from Burkina Faso had another reflection on the social construction from her point of view. Having worked as a journalist herself in her country, she recalls meeting frequently with colleagues working for private media companies similar to BFM. For her, the broadcasting of live news with "eyewitness" interviews and "on-the-scene" reports reflects an attempt to break free of the "crumbs" left by the official media outlets. Despite its commercial objectives, private media sources would thus serve as a power to counterbalance the state media.

A divide runs deep between the vision of BFM as a media "paid for by the French government", a view motivated by anti-sexist, anti-capitalist belief patterns or the habitus of public service journalism, and the vision of BFM as a potential counteracting power in the face of state media motivated by the experience of domination exercised by the state media, which is explained not only by political points of view, but also by patterns of belonging and individual experiences.

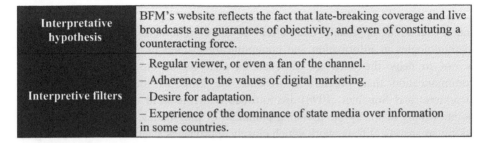

Interpretative hypothesis	BFM's website reflects the fact that late-breaking coverage and live broadcasts are guarantees of objectivity, and even of constituting a counteracting force.
Interpretive filters	– Regular viewer, or even a fan of the channel. – Adherence to the values of digital marketing. – Desire for adaptation. – Experience of the dominance of state media over information in some countries.

Table 5.5. *Hypothesis and interpretative filters*

5.6. Conclusion

Like some participants, we ourselves interpreted this site initially as an attempt by BFM to position itself as a "serious" media source. We recognized a traditional production grammar, composed of standardized editorial units, as well as a predominance of text elements that we found rather surprising for a TV channel website. Thus, we felt the challenge for BFM was, on the one hand, to build a presence on the Web, and on the other hand to restore the brand's image through media productions, anchoring it in a form of journalistic legitimacy. Having studied the design of other journalistic sites beforehand, in particular those of *Le Monde* and *Libération*, the enunciative strategy of BFM's website did not seem very different to us. The fact, for example, that the *hit-lists* are somewhat discreet on BFM's website, was for us an indicator of the channel's desire to distance itself from its commercially oriented reputation.

The assumption that the site's enunciative strategy is sexist destabilized our interpretative certainties. We had not observed a predominant role for the headings "economy, politics, sports" in the menu and in the hierarchy of the contents of the patchwork, nor did we associate the color blue with the image of stereotypical masculinity and spheres of power. The fact that we did not note these salient factors undoubtedly raises the question, as one student put it, of our own "deep assimilation of gender".

The assumption that a media outlet like BFM could represent a form of counteracting power also surprised us, questioning our personal belief in the value of public media. Moreover, after this experiment, we also became aware of the fact that our critical view of BFM is also a class reflex. Just as in the "serious" media outlets where some students who participated in our experiments work, the socio-professional environment of teaching and research, it is also not a "good look" to be a BFM viewer.

With this account of the genesis of our method, we hope to have shown what our social semiotic approach can offer as a complement to semio-pragmatic methodologies in information and communication sciences. Indeed, our objective is not to deny the need for an accurate analysis of the material realities of communication that structure a website: the tools of interpretative semiotics (Jeanneret and Souchier, 1998) are introduced in the field as a valuable starting point. Taking seriously the founding paradigm of pragmatics, our focus has shifted taking an analytical framework which closely approaches a semiotics of unveiling to a method attempting to analyze the social construction of the perceived and interpreted reality of cultural productions. In other words, we argue for a convergence between pragmatic semiotics and constructivist sociology, the first outlines of which we have drawn here.

We have performed this method on more than a dozen different fields and corpora (images, digital social networks, trailers for TV series, etc.), most frequently in an educational context. However, we observed that the approach had also begun to bear fruit with other audiences (Saemmer and Tréhondart 2020). We have made it evolve by adapting it to the prism of our teaching constraints (in attendance, at a distance), our audiences (Bachelor's degrees, Master's degrees) and different contexts (university institutions, Inspé, Paris, province, etc.). These various different experiments have allowed us in each instance to question the ways we do things and to raise new questions concerning, for example, the organization of debates, questions on the choice of vocabulary and language, the steps to be broken down, etc.

If we have now stabilized this approach in our teaching practices, the projects we are currently carrying out make it possible to open it up to new, stimulating perspectives. Thus, as part of the Crem-Inspé project at Lorraine, "Interpreting shocking images during pandemic times", funded by the Ministry of Culture, we have been working since September 2020 at transposing the method into classroom practices in primary and secondary schools, and in the field of social workers, by developing image education tools adapted to a younger audience. A new part of the reflection begins here, which will also be done in conjunction with implementation in non-pedagogical fields, as well as a forthcoming book which will provide a summary of the essentials of the approach (Saemmer et al. 2022).

5.7. Appendices

1. Choice of the site	The site to be analyzed is chosen by the organizers of the experiment, or selected from a corpus formed by the participants. A questionnaire asking about the cultural practices of press websites beforehand, for example, can be distributed and followed with a collective discussion of the results.
2. Collection of first impressions	After viewing the site, the participants note their first impressions in writing, then share them during a round table discussion.
3. Sharing of tools and concepts of interpretive semiotics	The organizers share the tools and concepts borrowed from the interpretive semiotics of websites.
4. Identification of the primary editorial units	Each of the participants individually lists the units on the site that make sense to them based on the tools and concepts that are shared. The results are put into perspective: how can we explain the individual focus on certain units, while others, despite being present, are not identified or recognized as important?
5. Production of an interpretative hypothesis of the site	An individual interpretative hypothesis of the site is produced in writing, using the formula of "This website means. ... to me, because..."
6. The individual hypotheses are put into perspective and discussed	–
7. Sharing of tools and concepts of interpretive semiotics	We introduce the tools and concepts of the semiotics of interpretation, shifting the focus from the results to the analysis of the interpretative process.
8. Production of an individual analysis of interpretative filters	The social motivations of the points of view on the site are analyzed using to the formula "This website means ... to me because I implement the following cultural knowledge ... and the following habits of thought ..."
9. The individual analyses of the interpretative filters are shared anonymously by the organizers and submitted to a final interpretative debate	–
10. Self-portrait/group portrait	Each of the participants writes a final interpretation argued both from the analysis of the editorial units chosen as important, and the analysis of their interpretative filters.

Table 5.6. *The main stages of an experiment in social semiotics of websites*

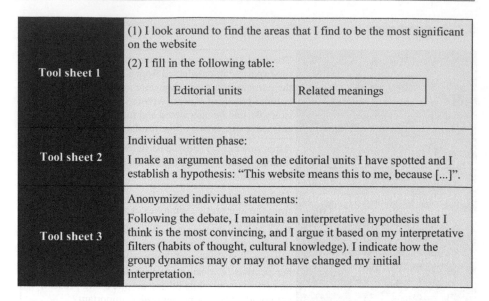

Tool sheet 1	(1) I look around to find the areas that I find to be the most significant on the website (2) I fill in the following table: | Editorial units	Related meanings	

Tool sheet 2	Individual written phase: I make an argument based on the editorial units I have spotted and I establish a hypothesis: "This website means this to me, because [...]".
Tool sheet 3	Anonymized individual statements: Following the debate, I maintain an interpretative hypothesis that I think is the most convincing, and I argue it based on my interpretative filters (habits of thought, cultural knowledge). I indicate how the group dynamics may or may not have changed my initial interpretation.

Table 5.7. *Tool sheets used in the educational context*

5.8. References

Althusser, L. (1965). *Pour Marx*. Maspero, Paris.

Berger, P. and Luckmann, T. (1997). *La construction sociale de la réalité*. Armand Colin, Paris.

Bourdieu, P. (1978). *La Distinction, critique sociale du jugement*. Le Seuil, Paris.

Eco, U. (1985). *Lector in fabula*. LGF-Livre de poche, Paris.

Fabbri, P. (2008). *Le Tournant sémiotique*. Hermès-Lavoisier, Paris.

Greimas, A.J. (ed.) (2016). Mythes et idéologies. In *Du sens en exil : chroniques lithuanienne*. Lambert-Lucas, Limoges.

Gomez-Mejia, G. (2016). *Les Fabriques de soi ? Identité et industrie sur le web*. MkF, Paris.

Hodge, R. and Kress, G. (1988). *Social Semiotics*. Polity, Cambridge.

Iser, W. (1995). *L'Acte de lecture – Théorie de l'effet esthétique*. Mardaga, Paris.

Jacobi, D. (2018). Veron (Eliseo). *Publictionnaire, dictionnaire encyclopédique et critique des publics* [Online]. Available at: http://publictionnaire.huma-num.fr/notice/veron-eliseo [Accessed 2 February 2021].

Jeanneret, Y. (2014). *Critique de la trivialité : les médiations de la communication, enjeu de pouvoir*. Éditions Non Standard, Paris.

Jeanneret, Y. and Souchier, E. (1998). Pour une poétique de l'écrit d'écran. *Xoana*, 6, 97–107.

Julliard, V. (2013). Éléments pour une sémiotique du genre. *Communication & Langages*, 17, 59–74.

Landowski, É. (1984). Les chantiers sociaux de la sémiotique. *Langage et société*, 28, 141–149.

Lloveria, V. (2015). De l'hypertexte au design monopage, une transition sémiotique. *CASA : Cadernos de Semiótica Aplicada*, 13(2), 57–87.

Lorusso, A.M. (2019). Sémiotique et culture. In *La Sémiotique et son autre*, Biglari, A. (ed.). Kimé, Paris.

Odin, R. (2011). *Les espaces de communication. Introduction à la sémio-pragmatique*. PUG, Grenoble.

Peirce, C.S. (1878). La Logique de la science. Comment se fixe la croyance. *Revue philosophique de la France et de l'étranger*, 4, 553–569.

Peirce, C.S. (1978). *Écrits sur le signe : textes choisis*. Le Seuil, Paris.

Saemmer, A. (2015). *Rhétorique du texte numérique*. Presses de l'ENSSIB, Villeurbanne.

Saemmer, A. (2017). Interpréter l'hyperlien en contexte pédagogique : éléments d'une sémiotique sociale. *Le Français Aujourd'hui*, 196, 25–34.

Saemmer, A. (2020). De l'architexte au computexte. Poétiques du texte numérique, face à l'évolution des dispositifs. *Communication et langages*, 203, 97–112.

Saemmer, A. and Tréhondart, N. (2020). Remonter aux motivations sociales et politiques du regard. *MEI*, 49, 101–113.

Saemmer, A., Tréhondart, N., Coquelin L. (2022). *Sur quoi se fondent nos interprétations ? Introduction à la sémiotique sociale appliquée aux images d'actualité, séries télés et sites web de médias*. Presses de l'Enssib, Villeurbanne.

Souchier, E., Candel, É., Gomez-Mejia, G. (2019). *Le numérique comme écriture : théories et méthode d'analyse*. Armand Colin, Paris.

Tréhondart, N. (2016). Le livre numérique enrichi : conception, modélisation de pratiques, réception. PhD Thesis, Université Paris 8 Vincennes – Saint-Denis, Paris.

Veron, E. (1978). Sémiosis de l'idéologie et du pouvoir. *Communications*, 28, 7–20.

Veron, E. (1995). *La Semiosis sociale : fragments d'une théorie de la discursivité*. Presses universitaires de Vincennes, Paris.

6

Analyzing the Mobilization Against the LPR on Twitter: Theoretical Issues and Methodological Challenges

Justine SIMON

ELLIADD, Université de Franche-Comté, Besançon, France

6.1. Introduction

Digital social networks have become prime locations for self-expression and interaction in times of protest. Faced with a growing feeling of distrust toward political activities, they have become essential places to criticize the decisions of leaders and to promote acts of protest.

Opposed to the future multiannual research programming law (LPPR) – which became the research programming law (LPR); approved on December 24, 2020[1] –

---

1 The draft "law on multiannual research programming" (LPPR: *"loi de programmation pluriannuelle de la recherché"*) was announced by Prime Minister Édouard Philippe on February 1, 2019. The Government's objective was to "resume the search for visibility, freedom and mechanisms", see : https://www.enseignementsup-recherche.gouv.fr/pid39124/loi-de-programmation-pluriannuelle-de-la-recherche.html. As early as October 2019, concerns began to be felt within the scientific community, leading to several forms of mobilization. More than a hundred academic journals declared themselves to have "joined the struggle". AGs were organized and motions were adopted. Despite the fact that the Covid-19 crisis slowed down social mobilization around the LPPR/LPR, many collective initiatives were put in place. Twitter

many representatives of higher education and research institutions (researchers, teacher/researchers, collectives, journals, unions, etc.) have seized on these networks in order to take a stand to defend the values of university professions with a public service vocation and promote their activist actions (AGMs, motions, demonstrations, flash mobs, collective HCERES candidatures [*Haut Conseil de l'évaluation de la recherche et de l'enseignement supérieur*], creativity challenges launched on the networks, "black screen" operations, etc.).

We know that the social-digital device of Twitter allows users to target different audiences at several levels of interaction: the connected general public (all Twitter users and non-registered Internet users), the circle of followers of the account and a particular account (in mentions, by adding the at-sign "@" followed by the account name). In the case of the university institution reform, Twitter allows users to directly address both the circles of political power and its scientific community[2]. Sharing content then becomes a way to criticize and challenge political leaders[3] and to mobilize the players inside the world of science.

Taking into account the subtleties specific to Twitter, this research aims to study the various online reactions of the scientific community to the news about the law in the year 2020. The objective of this research is to highlight and analyze the many different forms of mobilization on Twitter. The appropriation of Twitter device therefore questions the link between the technological dimension, the social practices (as a social experience within a community) and the semiodiscursive practice (taking into account the appropriation of the image, text and hyperlinks). In other words, we ask the following general question: how has the scientific community appropriated digital social spaces in response to the #LPPR/#LPR law?

In order to grasp the complexity of the communication logic implemented by Twitter users as well as the variety of semiodiscursive constructions, we have developed a theoretical and methodological model – which will be the subject of this article.

---

and other digital social networks spoke out against a neoliberal law going against the principles of public research. Faced with this unprecedented mobilization, the political agenda accelerated, and the law was adopted by the Senate on October 30, 2020 and then by the National Assembly on November 20, 2020, and finally entered into force at the beginning of 2021.

2 Or to be precise, to the followers of the account in question, playing a role in scientific life: accounts of fellow researchers, teacher-researchers, doctoral students, training and research support staff, laboratories, collectives, journals, unions, etc.

3 Particularly the representatives of MESRI: the Ministry of Higher Education, Research and Innovation.

The scientific approach is formed at the crossroads between information and communication sciences and digital discourse analysis.

It has a strong interest in hypertextual writing (Souchier et al. 2003; Saemmer 2015; Paveau 2017), in the questioning of "participatory culture" in the digital context (Jenkins 2013; Jenkins et al. 2017), the construction of identities – singular and collective – (Allard and Vanderberghe 2003; Gomez-Mejia 2016; Bigey 2018), as well as the conflicting logics present within the socio-digital arenas (Badouard et al. 2016; Granjon 2017).

From an epistemological point of view, on the one hand, it is necessary to explain the theoretical framework adopted by articulating three angles of approaches (interdiscursivity, narrativity and argumentativity) dependent on the theoretical framework formed by the information and communication sciences.

This framework raises the following questions:

– How have the reactions of this community been articulated to the political and social news of the year 2020 (especially in connection with the pension reform, the pandemic and the draft for the law on "global security")?

– How do the singular identities (of researchers or teacher/researchers) and the collective identities (of the scientific community) fit together?

– To what extent can breaking with codes (at the semiodiscursive and hypertextual levels) be considered as a new means of protest?

– What is the place of narration within the publications of the university community, and how does narration serve how arguments are made?

– And what are the relationships established between inter-iconic references (collective reference frames) narration, and argumentation?

On the other hand, again from an epistemological point of view, the problem also involves revisiting the choices made in terms of methodology, which are based on ethical considerations.

The first section of this article summarizes the theoretical framework. The second section highlights several ethical issues specific to this research, details the methodology used and presents a synthesis of the six sub-corpora of work constituted – supporting illustrations – in order to put some of the results into perspective.

6.2. Multidimensional approach to digital social networks

6.2.1. *Shedding light on the notion of hypertextualized discourse*

Several current research works can apply to the analysis of digital social networks, highlighting the reciprocal influence between the technological specificities of the device and its socio-discursive uses (Paveau 2017; Cervulle and Julliard 2018; Jackiewicz 2018; Pinède 2019). These approaches are intended to be mutually constructive and seek to highlight the interactions between the social realm and the discourse. In this context, the role of the device (Call et al. 2010) – representing a heterogeneous group that mixes discursive and non-discursive elements – is a prominent element. The challenge is thus to grasp what discourse – and the technological device intrinsically linked to it – does to society, and jointly, what society does to technicalized discourse.

The notional proposition of "hypertextualized discourse" (Simon 2016, Simon 2018a) enters into this reflexive concern. It shows that hypertext plays a role in the dynamic of writing/reading. For Pedro Barbosa (1992), the gestures of writing and reading come together, until the point where they merge, in what he calls "Wreading". We will see below that the hyper-contextualization of tweets complicates the approach that can be taken with narrativity. The notion of "hypertextualized discourse" makes it possible to analyze how the device creates a link between several discourses: on the one hand, with the idea of highlighting or reacting to a discourse already produced (example of the tweet quote or the response), and on the other hand, in relation to the potential for intrinsically anticipated or marked reactions to the discourse (typically through the use of hashtags and mentions; Bigey and Simon 2018). By introducing the concept of dialogism, to be described later, it is possible to explain these two levels of the relationship.

6.2.2. *Shared images and participatory culture*

One of the main challenges of this research is to test the notion of "participatory culture" (Jenkins 2013; Bourdaa 2015; Jenkins et al. 2017) with regard to the appropriation of digital social networks by the community of researchers fighting against the LPPR/LPR. This particular interest invites us to form a reflection that comes at the crossroads of an approach to the technological constraints of the Twitter platform (within the text space and as regards the possibilities of added elements to be inserted), creative potentials that mix different semiodiscursive materiality (among which images play a central role), the different degrees of visibility of the actors involved (anonymity versus displayed identity; individual, collective, institutional accounts, etc.) and socio-political issues thought out in a democratic ideal.

6.2.2.1. Constraints and creative potentials

First, we know that the Twitter platform has developed many functions that allow users to publish information. There are currently multiple possibilities for creating what we have called a "multimodal tweet" (Simon and Toullec 2018), which include the following:

– At the level of the text field (from 140 to 280 characters in 2017): the insertion of URL links, technosigns (hashtags and mentions), emoticons and emojis.

– At the level of the other elements to be inserted: the insertion of still images (up to four visuals), videos (with a maximum duration of 140 seconds), GIFs, automatic additions of Twitter cards while sharing links (allowing the linked discourse to be previewed), viewing a quoted tweet during a retweet with a comment (the "quote tweet" function), mixed configurations (quote and GIF insertion, for example), etc.

These possibilities (or constraints) offer a margin for users to maneuver in relation to the type of content shared, but also correspond to a framework that constrains writing in the broad sense. A truly complex relationship exists between usage and technology, and between freedom and restraint. Watching the semiodiscursive practices emerging within online protests yields interesting results. There are many different possibilities for offering original content: by uploading of photos or videos taken from wherever users are currently located (with or without filling in the text field), photos of artistic creations made from everyday objects (such as scenes staged with Playmobil characters), the creation of iconotexts[4] (visuals, posters, montages, etc.), inserting screenshots, sharing and commenting on a news article, direct reactions to a quoted tweet, photomontages or the repurposing of a well-known image, etc. The text report/image obviously offers a broad variety of perspectives on the creation of meaning. Among other things, it is necessary to note the rising power of the insertion of emoticons, emojis, and GIFs, keeping in mind that these images are "set" by the platform[5] because they only offer a limited number of them. We will return to this point in the last section of this chapter.

---

4 "Iconotext" is defined as "an indissoluble unit of text(s) and image(s) in which neither the text nor the image have an illustrative function" (Nierlich 1990, p. 268).

5 GIFs can also be associated with the emotions observed at the time of their use ("anger", "disgust", "slow applause" with a strong ironic value, "happy dance", "gross", "vomit", etc.) which influences the ways that feelings can be illustrated.

6.2.2.2. *Degrees of visibility*

In addition to these technological constraints, the criterion of visibility must be considered. The actors active in the dispute over the proposed bill do not all depend on the same degree of visibility.

We know that the Social Web (Millerand et al. 2010) makes it possible to facilitate many popular forms of expression, which are gaining visibility. The participation of different groups of the public is considered as a challenge for the "anonymous" users (Gunthert 2018) to use social-digital devices to shrink their social invisibility[6], claim their existence within a community, and in a broader sense, acquire social recognition from their peers (Voirol 2005; Riboni 2019). In the corpus studied, not all scientific actors enjoy the same degree of recognition, whether or not they use a pseudonym[7]. Some accounts are individual (personal or professional), others depend on collectives with varying degrees of institutionalization (collectives of doctoral students, accounts of laboratories, unions, etc.). However, regardless of this degree, the appropriation of the Twitter platform is used as a method to gain visibility. Indeed, for Fabien Granjon (2017), any form of digital mobilization is characterized by the challenge of highlighting the socio-political struggle[8].

6.2.2.3. *Digital democracy*

This quest obviously responds to the imperative need for certain demands made of the bill to be weighed in the public discourse and to be heard by the government. The appropriation of the Twitter platform can be considered as a form of distanced engagement (Granjon 2017). There are multiple objectives for this strategy: to influence the general public to get their support, and to build social ties with the scientific community to encourage them to take action and to go against the bill. The notion of participatory culture here is an account of the democratic ideal of the

---

6 The notion of "counterpublics", proposed by Nancy Fraser (1992) (cited by Badouard et al. (2016)) sheds light on this issue of social invisibility in a similar way.

7 The fact of not displaying or claiming the status of an institution can also be considered as a deliberate means used in the search for reaching a wider audience, and thus to expand one's audience.

8 The use of hashtags is one of the possible strategies users can take advantage of to make themselves visible: by falling back on formulas already set in the public debate (#Réforme DesRetraites [pension reform], #UrgenceClimatique [climate emergency], #Covid_19, #Distanciel, #PPLSecuritéGlobale [PPL global security], #TroisAnsDePrison three years of prison]), by creating forms similar to neologisms in order to create communities for sharing (#RevuesEnLutteEtConfinées [magazines fighting and restricted], #PayezLesVacataires [pay part-time workers]) or by reactivating old hashtags used for coordination (#ViedeMdC, #ESRenPeinture, used during the opposition to the LRU law of 2017; see Figures 6.8 and 6.9).

participation of researchers in the debate. This ideal – presented by Serge Proulx (2020)[9] – is articulated in three dimensions: the people and groups opposing the LPPR/LPR are considered contributors because they take part in the process of contesting ("forming part"), they have their say in the debate ("making a contribution") and they receive a benefit in return ("receiving a share")[10]. In this context, it becomes an issue of seizing the opportunities as well as the limits of the democratic arena that has formed on Twitter during the year 2020. Several works have analyzed digital social networks by putting their democratic power in context. For some of these, the expressions made by the counterpublics is not enough to act socially and politically. Political participation on the networks is only an "illusion of mobilization". Others highlight role of controversial statements in exchanges, characterized by an intrinsic impossibility that prevents any agreement from being reached (Angenot 2008; Amossy 2014; Mercier 2015).

Others have decried the rise in power and the turns these spaces have taken: the toxicity of the discourse; the proliferation of fake news, the appearance of narcissistic forms of exhibition influenced by the desire for positive attention (weighed down by the influence of metrics); the aggressiveness of the debates (the "dark side of force" according to the analysis by Mercier (2018b)) and the violence that emerge from them. Finally, some people have been direct victims of verbal attacks on Twitter, to the point where they chose to leave the network[11].

Does the multiplication and bursting of dissenting "bubbles" make sense to the point of tipping the balance of power with government representatives? Is the participatory creativity of the actors enough to tip the democratic balance? And to re-formulate one of the problems posed in the introduction, to what extent can breaking the codes be considered as the power to act collectively, or on the contrary, as an illusion of effective participation in the debate? Through analyzing multimodal tweets, this is an issue of questioning the process of image sharing (Gunthert 2015) from the perspective of democratization. Is the creation of multimodal content a new

---

9 For Serge Proulx, "participation presupposes that individuals take part in the situation in such a way that they can potentially modify this state of affairs through their contributory gestures" (2020, p. 22).

10 Especially in connection with the issue of online popularity; symbolic rewards such as subscriptions, retweets or "likes" represent rewards.

11 During the contact that we were able to make with several colleagues about the issue of anonymization of tweets for the presentation, during the study day on March 18 and for this chapter, a colleague told us about the difficulties she experienced recently because of these types of attacks. Arnaud Mercier (2019) also prevents his personal experience of harassment by far-right activists. The journalist Samuel Laurent was also a victim of such violence. He explains this in a recent book (2021).

way of thinking about activism? What power do images have to mobilize? How do images make it possible to express anger or criticism? How do they become a means of attacking an opponent while bringing a community together?

6.2.3. *Interdiscursivity, narrativity and argumentativity*

The framework of this research articulates three notions which then need to be explained: interdiscursivity, narrativity and argumentativity.

6.2.3.1. *Interdiscursivity and inter-iconicity*

The notion of interdiscursivity is present at two levels from a theoretical point of view; in connection with the two forms of dialogism (interlocutory and interdiscursive[12]) explained by many authors in discourse analysis (Volochinov 1977; Rabatel 2004; Lugrin 2006; Paveau 2006; Krieg-Planque 2012; Simon 2018a, 2018b).

As with memes (Bonenfant 2015; Simon, 2021a; Simon 2022), publications generated by Internet users constitute nodes within the vast expanse of the Web, with a strong potential for (re)productions. These creations implicitly register the possible reaction of the targeted community (through replication: shares, comments, likes; or by variation: publishing in turn, sharing and commenting on an image, making similar misappropriations, etc.). This is in line with the notion of "interlocutory dialogism".

Compared to a yarrow, all productions of discourse are also loaded with other discourses already there (myths, forms of speaking, narratives, ideologies, etc.). In this way, all discursive production is loaded with many things that have already been said, read, heard or seen. During the production and interpretation of a discourse, everyone uses collective and previous prediscursive data, referred to as "collective prediscursive frameworks" (Paveau 2006). All discourses more or less explicitly call on other discourses (this is interconnected with the notion of interdiscursive or inter-iconic dialogism), and this consideration is of course essential when talking about digital social networks.

6.2.3.2. *Narrativity*

The question of narrativity is put to use through three specific approaches in this work.

---

12 Here, we specify that we are talking about inter-iconicity (Arrivé 2015) when the expression cited is an image.

First, in the process of quoting (in connection with the previously introduced notion of inter-iconicity), it is often the case that an existing narration is exploited to increase a publication (a screenshot of a film or a series, or GIF). The narration that is quoted is a playful and creative way to talk about politics in the second degree. Fictional narration makes it possible to exaggerate a reality or to make "winks", all of which has the goal of creating a complicity. Concrete examples will be presented in the third section of this chapter.

Narrativity is then present as a process for creating a narrative in a restricted sense. The author of a tweet can take turns playing the role of narrator or actor. The events surrounding the bill are narrated as in a narrative: chronology, actors, quests, opponents, etc. And the author can take on a central role as a character. The staging of oneself and of one's intimate space forms part of the narrative (this point connects with the notion of *ethos* presented below, and will also be developed in section 3, with supporting examples).

The third approach in the broad sense, digital social networks are thought of as incomplete narratives, activated (or not) in a process of co-construction. For example, an incomplete story can be reactivated by an answer. To explore further, consider how a story is updated at the level of individual reception. This is in line with the theoretical proposal on "Wreading" presented at the beginning of this chapter. This broad perspective of narrativity, specific to socio-digital devices, is addressed in several works, starting from the notions of "interactive narratives" or "ghost narratives" (Campion 2008), which are based on the model of narrative possibilities proposed by Claude Bremond (1966); "micro-narratives" (Lits 2010), "hypernarrativity" (Boursier 2021) or "interactive visual narratives" (Simon 2018c).

6.2.3.3. *Argumentativity*

Finally, beginning from the notion of argumentativity two distinct axes emerge. An argumentative analysis of the discourse allows us to introduce the works of Ruth Amossy (2000, 2010), which differentiate, on the one hand, between "argumentative goals" (which openly seek to influence) and an "argumentative dimension" (which does not explicitly display the desire to persuade) and on the other hand, propose an analytical approach to the *ethos*. Our theoretical and methodological framework calls for these two approaches to be taken into account by analyzing all the publications of the scientific community, positioning themselves as a supra-discourse defended by Frédérique Vidal and by extension by the Government, which are therefore dependent on an argumentative purpose. A specific look at them will focus on the mechanisms of constructing the self-image for persuasive purposes.

In connection with the notion of argumentative goal, the objective is to analyze the discourses of the scientific community who are opposed to the LPPR/LPR, using the double axis of justification/positioning as the starting point (following Angenot (2008) and Micheli (2012)). The corpus that we will present in the next section, as we have noted previously, brings together a set of multimodal tweets made in opposition to a model favoring unequal and selective research to the detriment of academic freedom (a model considered as a counter-discourse overall). The issue of persuasion can clearly be observed in concrete form: researchers and student-researchers are unequivocally positioned against the bill, with the goal of having it withdrawn (positioning). In order to consolidate this position and strengthen the adhesion to their cause, these actors pursue various goals to justify their position: promoting joint activist events (AGMs, strikes, flash mobs, demonstrations, collective candidacies for the HCERES, black screen strikes, etc.), to encourage mobilization, to raise awareness of the difficulties encountered by the scientific community (by precarious workers in particular), to warn of an imminent danger to the scientific community, etc.

Analyzing the *ethos* is the second issue of our approach. The *ethos* is the representation of the image of ourselves that we put forward for others to see (whether strategically or not) and can be analyzed from the identification of markers of self-inscription in discourse (forms of subjectivity: the pronoun "I", expressions of feelings, the defense of a point of view, etc.). Every expression we make contains a self-representation that seeks to influence the audience we are addressing: a legitimate, credible self-image with a sense of distribution, having certain affinities, claiming a sense of belonging to a community, etc. Depending on the context in which we express ourselves and the issues of perception, this image can be adapted. In relation to our problem of multimodal tweets, the challenge is to be able to identify these "expressive" forms (Allard and Vanderberghe 2003) and positioning from the reappropriation of the technological device and the insertion of personalized multimodal content.

6.3. Ethical questions and methodological challenges

6.3.1. *Ethical concerns*

6.3.1.1. *Neutrality and objectivity of the researcher*

The first ethical question I faced upon[13] starting this work was that of neutrality, and the objectivity of the researcher. As a teacher myself whose livelihood depends

---

13 I will allow myself to use the word "I" in this section on ethics.

on the MESRI, this subject could be problematic. I am in a way part of my research topic and I am not neutral.

Angeliki Monnier (2018, p. 138) draws our attention to this difficult posture in these terms: "When [researchers] direct their gaze to one facet or another, they transcribe their own affinities and "worries", they "model" their subject in their own ways and construct a point of view. The very choice of the research topic has its importance and induces an axiological commitment. With Koren (2003), I think it is difficult not to speak out in favor of a "committed neutrality".

This question of the intimate relationship that the researcher establishes with his object has never been more of a factor than in this research. As a teacher-researcher, I worked together with many colleagues against this bill, and the question arose of whether I could legitimately engage in this research. That is why it is important to emphasize the distinction between neutrality and objectivity. Even if the orientation of research is subjective – or even ideological – this does not mean that it cannot be presented objectively. An objective presentation allows researchers to distance themselves. For this reason, the formation of a corpus and the analysis of data remain essential steps, carried out in the spirit of objectivity. The sociologist Boaventura de Sousa Santos summarizes this issue in the following way: "The attitude of the critical social scientist consists in maximizing objectivity and minimizing neutrality" (Pereira 2020).

6.3.1.2. *The issue of data anonymization*

The topic covered here is not only very close to my professional life, but it is also closely related to my use of Twitter. I happen to be an active user of this network, and therefore present in the corpus (publications and affective marking of publications around the LPPR/LPR). And many of the publications studied have been produced by colleagues with whom I have relatively strong ties (colleagues who I have been able to work with directly, who I have read or listened to, colleagues who I only know by name, etc.). So, I had to reflect on the practice of quoting tweets from my real and virtual community. From an ethical point of view, this is in line with the following more general question: "Do we have the right to work with materials that are available without the people who generate them being notified?" (Millette et al. 2020, p. 10). We know that publications on Twitter are viewable by the general public and that there are no fees for reproduction, but the displaying of the digital identities of colleagues preoccupied me in relation to the ideological dimension of the publications studied (during the study day on March 18, and for this publication). I therefore took the initiative to contact some of the colleagues who initially made the publications that are the subject of my analysis (by email, in a reply with notes or in a private message). During the study day, not all the accounts behind the tweets studied were able to be contacted. In the slideshow, all the account names of the tweets to which I had not received a reply or a negative reply had been hidden using a black screen (or alternatively, a black rectangle...). For this publication, the following have not been anonymized: the names of institutional collectives (not named) and of course those of colleagues who wished to appear using their name (thanks again to them for their feedback).

6.3.1.3. Methodological "tinkering"

Building a corpus from digital social networks is a crucial moment, and one that faces several major obstacles. Even within the ANR Obsweb (Simon et al. 2017) – who brought together oversight professionals and researchers specialized in different disciplines (computer science, statistics, CIS, etc.) on the same subject – we experienced many difficulties working on important databases. Without specific equipment, it was difficult to carry out the extraction and sampling of the data. However, I was able to accomplish this when I started this research (with neither sufficient financial resources nor technical skills, and facing time constraints). A collection of tweets dependent on the Twitter API – that is to say, a system which restricts the number of results to highlight the most popular publications (and therefore those most favored by the algorithm) - was carried out at the very beginning of this research and then developed through a "snowball effect" to arrive at the final result. And this corpus was then divided into sub-corpora dependent on separate issues (I will return to this in the next section). The gap between all the basic data (all the tweets that were published around the debate on the LPPR/LPR) and the tweets that are particularly the subject of my semiodiscursive analysis is therefore very strong[14]. However, the relationship between quantitative and qualitative approaches is essential for me (i.e. is the analyzed corpus representative enough?). Finally, I decided to abstract myself from these constraints, and above all to legitimize my approach. Conducting a fine-grained and exhaustive analysis of all publications is impossible. So, I made certain choices, and I now accept the imperfections of my corpus. With Lécossais and Quemener (2018), I therefore assume my "methodological tinkering", and I claim the fact that these are not contradictory with criteria of taking a scientific approach. The corpus that was

---

14 This article does not dig into the qualitative analysis of the sub-corpora of the work formed (except for the analysis of sub-corpus No. 5, presented during the study day), this will be the subject of future work.

ultimately constituted is part of a reflexive approach that questions and appropriates theories to answer various problems[15].

6.3.2. Methodological challenges

Conducting an epistemological reflection on a research work invites us to take into consideration the existing methodological approaches, describing in detail the steps taken and adopting a critical perspective that allows us to formulate different ways to make improvements compared to the ideal aimed at the beginning. Several stages were conducted one after the other to arrive at the final corpus and the six sub-corpora of work. This section addresses these different stages, summarizing the difficulties encountered and highlighting several challenges to be met in the future.

6.3.2.1. Data, corpus and sub-corpus of work: presentation of the stages

In February 2020, a survey of multimodal tweets containing the hash-tag #LPPR was carried out "by hand". We took screenshots of the 236 tweets collected between September 18, 2019 (first occurrence) and January 31, 2020. To compensate for the restrictive data update imposed by Twitter (the Twitter advanced search limits the times available), in February 2021, the continuation of the survey conducted "by hand" was carried out over the entire year of 2020 (through a search by the keywords #LPPR and #LPR). To obtain a corpus that is as representative as possible, a pre-analysis of the corpus constituted in February 2020 was carried out in order to uncover: the accounts whose activity was the majority (the most tweets), the most retweeted tweets (excluding replies and "likes") and the accounts that had the most followers. Additional data were collected based on these results. We carried out successive searches by cross-analyzing the account name and keywords (#LPPR and #LPR), paying attention to both original publications, replies and retweets with comments. Nine hundred twenty-eight multimodal tweets were collected between September 18, 2019 and December 31, 2020.

These research results were cross-referenced with data extractions collected by Loubère and Smyrnaios (2020) over the period from January 21, 2020 to February 23, 2021 (in this regard, I would like to thank them for their help). The query contained the keywords (and not just the hashtags): 5mars, FacsEtLabosEnLutte, LPPR and/or VidonsVidal (a play on sounds in French) (while not taking into account the keyword LPR).

---

15 In the field of discourse analysis, Sitri and Barats insist that the corpus is "formed according to research questions and hypotheses, or even according to the conception we have of discourse analysis, or even the tools or categories we use" (2017, p. 41).

There are several operations for cleaning and sorting that have been made from this new database: the deletion of tweets published in 2021 to keep the whole timeline of the year 2020; the removal of slavish retweets[16]; the removal of tweets that are unrelated to the draft law (an example of the results unrelated to the topic with keyword 5mars [March 5th]: "The last time I went to the hairdresser was on March 5th"). Out of a total of 98,866 subservient tweets and retweets, 15,414 tweets remain. In addition, a selection of tweets was made from the following elements: a selection made up exclusively of multimodal tweets (none that contained only text); a selection of tweets with a high degree of subjectivization and/or positioning and/or whose interlocutory dimension was explicit. It means that several publications corresponding to an "editorialization of informational content" (Simon et al. 2017) were not included in the final corpus. The following were excluded: informative publications (announcements or impersonal coverage of meetings, AGMs, demonstrations), presentations of flyers, communiqués and motions, objective tweets sharing traditional media publications and scientific or didactic analyses (forms of meta-discourse).

The corpus that was ultimately constructed contains a set of 1,370 multimedia tweets, gathered between September 18, 2019 and December 31, 2020. A word document was created for each month, bringing together the screenshots of the tweets together with a link to the tweets.

On the basis of this corpus, six sub-corpora were formed, demonstrating six specific problem sets. Not all of the 1,370 multimodal tweets are included in these six sub-corpora. These lines of analysis emerged as the collection progressed. They make it possible to focus on specific, distinct issues. The tweets that were set aside did not directly relate to the areas of focus raised. The question of the *ethos* was a significant concern in some tweets, while others focused on opposition discourse/counter-discourse. For other publications, the question of interdiscursivity stood out strongly.

These issues have been highlighted in another, more visually oriented document: a PowerPoint. This non-academic form was perceived as the most practical solution to create an overview of the various emerging issues. The difficulty here was to classify the publications into individual categories, because of course the three filters of interdiscursivity, narrativity and argumentativity could be present at the same time. At this stage of the work, six specific axes were selected corresponding to six distinct sub-corpora of work, representing a set of 424 multimodal tweets.

---

16 The "rslavish retweets" (Simon et al. 2017) refer to the simple shares made by clicking on the retweet button, which do not give the user the opportunity to modify the initial content.

Table 6.1 summarizes these work steps.

(a) Collection "by hand"		(d) Final corpus	(e) Six sub-corpora of the work
+ Additional successive searches (number of RT, influential accounts, # and @, etc.)		Screenshot + link of the tweet Distribution in monthly Word documents	Highlighting of six specific issues Sampling within a PowerPoint presentation A choice is made for classifying publications in a single category
(b) Data "extraction"	**(c) Operating**		
+ Extraction within an Excel database (Loubère and Smyrnaios 2020)	Several sorting operations (deletions and subservient RTs in 2021) and selection (multimodal tweets)	1,370 multimodal tweets	424 multimodal tweets

Table 6.1. *Stages of forming the corpus*

6.3.2.2. *Difficulties encountered*

The description of these "retooled" steps does not provide an adequate account of the difficulties that were encountered. We will briefly summarize the main obstacles we encountered.

As we have already noted, the collection of data by hand is limited because of the restrictions imposed by Twitter. The API restricts the number of results and does not resend posts from accounts that are not popular.

The data that relate to the draft law without referencing with hashtags and keywords cannot be taken into account. This difficulty forms part of what is one of the great challenges for researchers: how accurate can we make a corpus?

The research done using the so-called "snowball" method takes a long time but allows us to immerse ourselves in the corpus.

Due to the evolution over time of the content published on Twitter, we have been forced to delete accounts or tweets. The profiles of the account sending the tweet have often been modified, and the metrics collected have also changed over time.

Many tweets could not be found by copying/pasting the text of the tweet from the database, meaning it is to be assumed that they were deleted or that the Twitter search engine limits the results, which shows the importance of having access to the link to the tweet in the database.

Finally, we encountered difficulties in identifying multimodal content from the text of the tweet. A link to the uploaded image was given in the text, but these did not always represent multimodal content.

6.3.2.3. Challenges to consider

At the level of collection, it is important to make queries using keywords and not hashtags (to access both types of results). These keywords must not have multiple meanings (e.g. the term "5mars", or the acronym LPR leading to results related to a Portuguese aviation firm). It is essential to specify the date when the data were collected (so that changes over time can be noted).

The formalization of the corpus should make it easy to go back and forth between the collected data and the Twitter platform itself. To accomplish this, it is important to give the link to the tweet in the metadata. It would thus be ideal to be able to show whether a tweet is multimodal in the metadata as well. On the other hand, this point seems difficult given the diverse nature of these tweets (quote tweets, replies, Twitter cards, inserted images, etc.). The textual database is also not enough to soak up the corpus (even if it is important to have access to all the texts that can be used on Excel). We opted to make a presentation in PowerPoint format to directly demonstrate the particularities of multimodal tweets. And we are planning to routinely take screenshots to show the accounts of the Twitter users. Other metadata could be identified, such as the number of followers/follows (related to the issue of visibility), hashtags (excerpts from the text of the tweet), mentions (*idem*), the number of RTs/quote "tweets"/"likes", etc.

Date	Name	Number of followers	Number of follows	Text of the tweet	Multimodal content	Link to the tweet	Number of RTs/quote tweets/ "likes"

Table 6.2. *Blank template for visualizing metadata*

As for the analysis, it is useful to use data visualization software to show the most influential accounts or the most used hashtags. It would be important to be able to analyze the results on the popularity over time to analyze the references against socio-political news events. Using word processing software to automate lexicological research (pragmatic, argumentative and emotional properties of discourse) is another possible alternative. Finally, for the last challenge, it is necessary to be able to automate the image processing as well (finding similarities with other images, from image databases) for comparative purposes. From the point of view of the evaluation of the results, it is ultimately conceivable to apply a structured system for the anonymization of publications.

6.4. Presentation of the six sub-corpora

Some 424 unique multimodal tweets were classified into different sub-corpora using criterion that we considered the most relevant. As we recently noted, this ranking is not self-evident, as some publications may fall into different categories. Here is the general view of this distribution in Table 6.3.

Sub-corpus 1	Sub-corpus 2	Sub-corpus 3	Sub-corpus 4	Sub-corpus 5	Sub-corpus 6
92 tweets where the account administrators play the role of narrator	66 tweets whose accounts play the role of narrator-character (telling a lived experience): interweaving individual identities and collective identities (39 tweets using "I" and 27 using "we")	33 performative tweets (making calls to action)	111 shares of visual gags, press drawings or aestheticized images featuring objects, animals or impersonal fictional characters (50 images showing a variety of things; 11 self-images in specific scenes, and 50 GIFs): interactive mini-stories	74 visual shares made from collective cultural references (inter-iconicity): double narratives (31 inter-iconic GIFs; 22 quotations from references; 11 transformations, and 10 imitations)	48 tweets marked by a discourse-counterdiscourse opposition (juxtaposed on the same visual space; often as a quote tweet)

Table 6.3. *Synoptic view on the six sub-corpora of the work*

6.4.1. *Sub-corpus 1: the narrating Twitter user*

Figure 6.1. *The narrative coverage of the news. For a color version of this figure, see www.iste.co.uk/massou/analyzing.zip*

The forms of protest from the scientific community have been varied, and much of the coverage of the events has taken a creative approach. A narrative style of covering the news was used by some Twitter users to promote group actions or to denounce the catastrophic situation of the precarious workers. In these cases, the Twitter users assume the role of the narrator, choose an angle of attack, present the main players from the news as characters and present the news as a narrative. Figure 6.1 gives a characteristic example, showing the ironic hashtags #engraandepompe ("with great pomp") and #requiem[17].

6.4.2. Sub-corpus 2: the narrator-character Twitter user

Twitter users can also represent themselves as the narrator-character in the action. The individual identity, most often constructed with the help of the "I", has an important place in this sub-corpus. For example, the thesis corpus serves as a symbolic illustration of the high-anxiety situation experienced by doctoral students. It envisions their uncertain future with ironic humor. The day-to-day practice of "doing the best with what you have" (*démerdentiel*) is illustrated by demonstrations of scenes from the private lives of teacher-researchers. According to the principle of extimity, chats allow you to talk about yourself in a personified way. A chat is also a euphemism for talking about a difficult situation[18]. And the use of the pronoun "I" also often co-exists with that of "we"[19]. Talking about yourself is a way to talk about the community in general. The unifying hashtags such as #FacsEtLabosEnLutte (universities and labs taking up the fight), #RevuesEnLutte (magazines taking up the fight) or #NousSommesCandidat (we are the candidates) play an important role in how this is configured. Mentions are also important because they strengthen alliances between accounts sharing the same goals.

---

17 Studies on the use of hashtags (Mercier 2018a) show that they are tools for social coordination. Hashtags make it possible to connect people who do not know each other, even temporarily, to build a critical conversation on a specific theme. Here, the hashtags used are polemical, ironic and narrative at the same time.

18 The sharing of humorous images can also shed light on the idea of resilience, in the sense that it offers the ability to make fun of a difficult situation in order for that situation to be overcome. The different types of humor given with a comic tone (light winks and nods, benevolent tones, ridiculousness, absurdity, etc.) or a cynical one (black humor, irony, satire) allow for taking a distanced look at a stressful situation, seeking to transform the dramatic emotions into positive emotions.

19 On digital social networks, the representation of the self-image is intimately linked to that of the other, through the interactive dynamics linking accounts to each other (virtual communities, the role of hashtags and mentions). In the context of collective mobilizations, this interweaving between the individual and the collective is reinforced through an adaptation to the common values of the defense of the public university. The interlocutory dimension, which invites the others to publish similar elements (such as memes), may remain implicit, but there are also discursive traces allowing for a more direct analysis of this identity construction (personal pronouns and other techno-discursive demonstratives such as mentions that can designate communication partners).

Isa Garcin-Marrou
@IGarcinMarrou   ...

Je ne sais pas si c'est la pluie, la LPPR, le démerdentiel...
j'ai du mal à bosser. Et suis pas trop trop aidée on va
dire !

2:54 PM · 22 sept. 2020 · Twitter for iPhone

25 J'aime

Figure 6.2. *Interweaving of individual identity. The tweet says: "I don't know if it's the rain, the LPPR, or having to cope with so much. I'm having trouble working. And it looks like I'm not getting a lot of help!". For a color version of this figure, see www.iste.co.uk/massou/analyzing.zip*

Mikaël Chambru
@mchambru   ...

 Message de service
Nous sommes finalement 1360 à avoir officiellement
déposé notre candidature collective à la présidence du
@Hceres_ 🤍
🔽 Il n'y pas désormais plus qu'à croiser le doigts pour
que nous soyons nommé-e-s 🌿 👌
#LPPR #NousSommesCandidat @rogueESR

Mikaël Chambru @mchambru · 23 janv. 2020
Et voilà, c'est envoyé 🍺
📬 Dossier de candidature posté ce matin par courrier avec CV et profession de
foi pour la présidence du @Hceres_
👉 J'invite tous mes collègues @UGrenobleAlpes à en faire de même, marche à
suivre : rogueesr.fr/procedure-de-c...
#NousSommesCandidat @rogueESR

Afficher cette discussion

10:18 AM · 27 janv. 2020 · Twitter Web App

1 Retweet   **1** Citer le Tweet   **8** J'aime

Figure 6.3. *Interweaving of collective identity. The top part of the post references the 1360 people who have submitted their candidacy for the presidency of @Hceres. The original tweet urges colleagues to follow the same course of action. For a color version of this figure, see www.iste.co.uk/massou/analyzing.zip*

6.4.3. *Sub-corpus 3: calls to action*

The publication of multimodal tweets is also a way to encourage action. Sharing an image thus becomes a "performative act" (Lambert 2014) promoting social cohesion within the community. Performative hashtags, discourse and speech formulas are given with the goal of inciting strikes or mobilizations in a broader sense: "#VidonsVidal, Warm up the AG, Send us your photos", etc. The challenge also has an important role in joining together the community, as shown in Figure 6.4.

 Revues en lutte @RevuesEnLutte · 22 mars 2020   ···
Ami.e.s des @RevuesEnLutte, on vous lance un défi ! Principe : chacun.e se prend en photo sur son balcon/fenêtre le visage masqué par sa revue préférée et tweete avec le hashtag #RevuesEnLutteEtConfinées en désignant les collègues de son choix. C'est parti.
@ChRabier @bibiapavard

Annabelle Allouch et 3 autres personnes

◯ 4   ↻ 12   ♥ 27   ⬆

Figure 6.4. *The challenge, a performative dimension. Followers of the page are invited to take a picture of themselves on their balconies or by the window, covering their faces with their favorite magazine. For a color version of this figure, see www.iste.co.uk/massou/analyzing.zip*

6.4.4. *Sub-corpus 4: sharing visual gags and interactive mini-stories*

The publications of researchers, teacher-researchers and other collectives show real imagination from the point of view of the variety of images inserted (unusual photographs, parody videos, newspaper caricatures, etc.). Eleven of the visuals are representations that use staged scenes to raise awareness of the alarming situation at the university. These include the use of Playmobils or Legos, used extensively during the lockdown more broadly, as in the example below which praises the value of fighting while in lockdown[20]. The text report/image is important in most shared publications, both with regard to the text added to the image (montages) or in the comment space. These iconotexts are often used to make absurd or light-hearted jokes. They also make use of a playful mode or double meanings through the use of GIFs (exaggerated or ironic emotions, humorous mimicry of the situation, particular gestures, images of babies or cute cats to represent doctoral students – or nasty snakes to attack the CNRS). Images embedded in tweets can also have autonomy in the sense that their meaning remains ambiguous while waiting to be placed (almost anywhere).

 PrécaireESR @PrecaireESR · 1 mai 2020   ...
#1Mai Manif au temps du numérique (détail) #LoiRecherche #Precarite #LPPR #ServicePublic #JoursHeureux

Q   ⟲ 18   ♡ 25   ↑

Figure 6.5. *Images demonstrating a playful form of communication. The tweet references a protest during digital times. For a color version of this figure, see www.iste.co.uk/massou/analyzing.zip*

20 This visual representation using photographs featuring Playmobils is still very active to this day on the recent account @LprNon.

6.4.5. *Sub-corpus 5: sharing of inter-iconic images and double narratives*

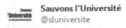
Sauvons l'Université
@sluniversite

Vidal 1, Vidal 2? sa #LPPR on s'en savonne. #StopLPPR

Traduire le Tweet

3:00 PM · 8 juil. 2020 · Twitter Web App

6 Retweets   **1** Citer le Tweet   **11** J'aime

Figure 6.6. *Visual gags. Here is a play on words in French but can be translated as "I'm washing my hands of the issue". For a color version of this figure, see www.iste.co.uk/massou/analyzing.zip*

GIFs and images can also be found at an inter-iconic level. The emotions or actions represented have a double meaning since in these cases, the posts "awaken" the encyclopedic knowledge of the public, or at least the memory they have of the work quoted (whether an artistic work, a TV series, a film, a musical work, or a reference to popular literature, etc.). The representation of the new action staged in the publication is updated at the time of receipt, that is why it is important to update the notion of interactive narratives given in first section of this article. The GIF below shows the character from "Halloween" in a phase of the "actualization" of a process of degradation, that of murdering someone (to use the term established by Claude Bremond). The interpretation of the new narrative remains open to the reader in relation to the current events of the LPPR (will the scientific community actually be elected?).

 Olivier Le Deuff @neuromancien · 25 juin 2020   ···

#lppr La Putain de Pire Rentrée qui s'annonce (c'est pour faire un titre à la @Affordanceinfo2) On est déjà dans le scénario d'Halloween mixé avec celui du jour sans fin

Figure 6.7. *Inter-iconic GIF. The tweet strongly references living out a plot of Halloween mixed with Groundhog Day. For a color version of this figure, see www.iste.co.uk/massou/analyzing.zip*

From the point of view of inter-iconicity, several lines of analysis can be identified and should obviously be explored. We just discussed the degree of recognition of quoted references, this depends both on its level of stereotyping (ultra well-known references) and the degree of knowledge and recognition by the public. In terms of the nature of the reappropriation, it is also possible to differentiate between reappropriations that fall under "intertextuality" in the restricted sense, or "hypertextuality" (according to the distinction proposed by Lugrin (2016)). In relation to the nature of the cultural reference, there is also an issue of making the link with current events (such as a publication that blurs the faces of police security inspectors to criticize the draft law on "global security"). And finally, of course, it is necessary to describe the semiological nature of the reference (quoted or transformed images, imitations or reappropriations of words for musical references).

Sauvons l'Université @sluniversite · 20 août 2020   ...

EC prêts à défendre l'université contre la #LPPR
#ESRenPeinture

♡ 2   ⟲ 9   ♡ 38   ⬆

Figure 6.8. *Inter-iconicity: quotes. The tweet references the institution being ready to defend the university against the LPPR. For a color version of this figure, see www.iste.co.uk/massou/analyzing.zip*

Bibia Pavard
@bibiapavard

Rétention des fèves #LPPR #greve24janvier
#ESRenLutte

1:26 PM · 29 janv. 2020 · Twitter for Android

8 Retweets   **1** Citer le Tweet   **31** J'aime

Figure 6.9. *Inter-iconicity: transformation. The tweet references the iconic French pies joining the fight, guiding researchers. For a color version of this figure, see www.iste.co.uk/massou/analyzing.zip*

6.4.6. *Sub-corpus 6: oppositions of discourse/counter-discourse*

The last sub-corpus has a special status because it brings together publications that always place an instance of discourse (quoted through the "quote tweet" function) and a counter-discourse (in the restricted sense, because it is directly opposed to a co-presented speech) against each other. Here, researchers and teacher-researchers strongly position themselves against the bill and against the main players who created it. In each case, the account that is criticized receives a notification indicating that its tweet is quoted, and the use is often done to address someone directly: the enunciative and argumentative engagement is increased to guarantee a stronger confrontation.

Figure 6.10. *Discourse/counter-discourse. The tweet references how the LPPR is being portrayed as the rope and stool to hang the EST from the beam of precarious work. Reference is also made to the multi-annual research programming bill. For a color version of this figure, see www.iste.co.uk/massou/analyzing.zip*

6.5. Outlook and analytical perspectives

Naturally, this first analytical approach must be further developed along each of the axes presented. It allows us to re-examine key concepts by comparing them against the specificities of a technodiscursive device in the form of Twitter.

The conversational dimension must be taken into account in the context of the conflictive dialogue with the government, since the posts, whether directly (through mentions) or indirectly, respond to previous speech instances (the counter-speech made in opposition) and also anticipate the reactions to them in order to better disqualify them. The chain reactions on Twitter also bring to mind the interactive functioning of memes, where the reappropriation of certain writing patterns generates collective participation (some examples of formulations using the phrase "in a GIF" are "The effects of the #LPPR in a GIF", "The #LPPR in a GIF").

At the interdiscursive (or again, depending on the context, inter-iconic) level, the notion of participatory culture is central to the popular references cited. Whether from textual (or hypertext) formulas, images or GIFs, publications opposing the LPPR/LPR often make use of other well-known discourse instances (slogans, popular personalities, fiction from popular culture, references to current events, etc.). This notion is essential for us, and raises the question of the different configurations of representation of the other discourse on the social-digital device Twitter (taking into account the role of hypertextuality).

The narrative dimension is itself sometimes correlated with this inter-iconic dimension since the quoted discourse can be a narrative or an excerpt from a narrative, allowing it to make a statement on current effects by comparing it to fiction. Twitter users can also represent themselves as characters. Creating staged scenes featuring users themselves, their homes or their pets is a playful way of talking about current events. It is also a way to create social bonds through building an *ethos* of sincerity and authenticity.

These fabrications of self-image are part of semiodiscursive, prohibitive and narrative strategies that are closely linked to the argumentative project of the scientific community, that of causing the LPR to be withdrawn.

6.6. Conclusion

In conclusion, several characteristics specific to the digital participation of the scientific community against the LPPR/LPR bill have been brought to light. These have a specific relationship to political news, since they denounce the excesses of the managerialization of the public service more broadly. The construction of collective identity also transcends that of individual identity, with the aim of building solidarity. The digital participation of the scientific community is also characterized through the diversity and vitality of semiodiscursive expression. The technodiscursive potential offered by the Twitter platform (retweets, quotes, replies, technodiscourses, the "like" button, etc.) are used for the benefit of strengthening social ties and mobilization. The creativity of narrative and interdiscursive experiments goes beyond the constraints imposed by the device. Humor in all its forms (jokes, double meanings, irony, etc.) plays a crucial role in these argumentative productions, and these forms of new writing are a perfect example of what Granjon and Cardon call "creative activism"[21].

At the end of this reflection, multiple analytical perspectives emerge. The methodological progress has highlighted several major challenges. It has led to the observation of the extent to which the act of combining different methods makes it possible to enrich the works, and that it is necessary to share skill sets to the goal of producing collaborative work. If we also want to gain an idea of the challenges of the appropriation of sociotechnical devices in a political and social context, we must always make sure to put into perspective the gap existing between the quantitative elements of the initial data and the qualitative approach of the applications. The constitution of "very small corpora" makes sense from the moment a specific problem is examined. Working on a small number of examples is legitimate as long as they are placed in relation to the entire corpus and are the subject of a fine level of analysis.

The article can also be a source of inspiration in relation to the theoretical framework formed at the crossroads of information and communication sciences and the analysis of digital discourse. The dialogue that is proposed between concepts from different conceptual approaches deserves to be expanded further. In particular, we have in mind the commonalities that can be tied together between the following notional pairs: "interlocutory dialogism" and "participatory culture", "interactive visual narratives" and "cultural convergence", "argumentative controversy" and the "democratic arena".

Analyzing the specificities of hypertext writing entering into different possibilities of interaction (tweets, replies, quote tweets) and making use of different forms of technological discourse (hashtags, mentions) also responds to the challenges of corpus studies carried out using digital social networks. The question of the interdependence of technology and the culture of sharing thus remains to be

---

21 In their work on media activism (2010), two forms of online activism have come to light: first, "counter-hegemonic activism", referring to the old forms of criticism of powers, as well as "creative activism", meaning contemporary forms of struggle that point to the emergence of play, light-hearted parody, art or celebration.

explored: how does the device constrain writing and reading? And conversely, how do uses reconfigure devices?

Finally, the analysis – based on a cross-analysis with other ongoing research (Bigey and Simon 2021) – has led us to note how crucial the issue of reception is in the process of interpretation[22]. The multimodal tweets studied could be compared against the subjectivity of other receivers, who use their own imaginations to interpret the frames of reference implemented, which in turn would give another dimension to this work.

The theoretical comparisons as well as the methods that have been developed are therefore intended to evolve in an approach seeking to continuously improve the research.

6.7. References

Allard, L. and Vanderberghe, F. (2003). Express Yourself ! Les pages perso entre légitimation technopolitique de l'individualisme expressif et authenticité réflexive peer-to-peer. *Réseaux*, 117, 191–219 [Online]. Available at: https://www.cairn.info/revue-reseaux1-2003-1-page-191.htm [Accessed 13 October 2022].

Amossy, R. (2000). *L'argumentation dans le discours. Discours politique, Littérature d'idées, Fiction*. Nathan, Paris.

Amossy, R. (2010). *La présentation de soi. Ethos et identité verbale*. Presses Universitaires de France, Paris.

Amossy, R. (2014). *Apologie de la polémique*. Presses universitaires de France, Paris.

Angenot, M. (2008). *Dialogue de sourds. Traité de rhétorique antilogique*. Mille et Une Nuits, Paris.

Appel, V., Boulanger, H., Massou, L. (eds) (2010). *Les dispositifs d'information et de communication : concept, usages et objets*. De Boeck, Brussels.

Arrivé, M. (2015). L'intelligence des images – l'intericonicité, enjeux et méthodes. *E-rea*, 13(1) [Online]. Available at: http://journals.openedition.org/erea/4620 [Accessed 13 October 2022].

---

22 This is in line with the sociosemiotic framework developed among others by Saemmer (2015). And the example of the recent current of intersectional discourse analysis (Paveau 2020) also shows the interest of integrating anthropological and ethnographic methods to analyze the conditions of the production and reception of instances of discourse.

Badouard, R., Mabi, C., Monnoyer-Smith, L. (2016). Le débat et ses arènes. *Questions de communication*, 30, 7–23 [Online]. Available at: https://journals.openedition.org/questionsdecommunication/10700 [Accessed 13 October 2022].

Barats, C. and Sitri, F. (2017). Constituer un corpus en analyse du discours, un moment crucial. In *Méthodes et outils informatiques pour l'analyse des discours*, Née, E. (ed.). Presses universitaires de Rennes, Rennes.

Barbosa, P. (1992). Metamorfoses do real. Criaçâo literaria e computador. Universidade nova de Lisboa, Lisbon.

Bigey, M. (2018). Twitter et l'inscription de soi dans le discours. L'Ethos pris au piège (ou pas) de la frontière sphère privée/sphère publique. *Les Cahiers du numérique*, 14, 55–75 [Online]. Available at: https://www.cairn.info/revue-les-cahiers-du-numerique-2018-3-page-55.htm [Accessed 13 October 2022].

Bigey, M. and Simon, J. (2018). Analyse des discours d'escorte de communication sur Twitter : essai de typologie des tactiques d'accroches et de mentions. In *#Info. Commenter et partager l'actualité sur Twitter et Facebook*, Mercier, A., Pignard-Cheynel, N. (eds). Éditions de la MSH, Paris.

Bigey, M. and Simon, J. (2021). Désinfoxiquer les images sur les réseaux socionumériques. Vers une démarche empirique d'éducation à l'image. In *Actes du Colloque International TICEMED – L'éducation aux médias tout au long de la vie : des nouveaux enjeux pédagogiques à l'accompagnement du citoyen*, Bonfils, P., Dumas, P., Remond, É., Stassin, B., Vovou, I. (eds). Association internationale Ticemed, Athens.

Bonenfant, M. (2015). Le même numérique : étude sémiotique des réseaux à partir des concepts de trace et d'indice. *RISCP*, 12, 27–42 [Online]. Available at: https://journals.openedition.org/communiquer/1295 [Accessed 13 October 2022].

Bourdaa, M. (2015). Les fans studies en question : perspectives et enjeux. *Revue française des sciences de l'information et de la communication*, 7 [Online]. Available at: http://journals.openedition.org/rfsic/1644 [Accessed 13 October 2022].

Boursier, A. (2021). Notice "Hypernarrativité", Publictionnaire. Dictionnaire encyclopédique et critique des publics [Online]. Available at: http://publictionnaire.huma-num.fr/notice/hypernarrativite [Accessed 13 October 2022].

Bremond, C. (1966). La logique des possibles narratifs. *Communications*, 8, 60–76.

Campion, B. (2008). Vers l'actualisation d'un "récit fantôme" ? *Communication*, 26 [Online]. Available at: http://journals.openedition.org/communication/824 [Accessed 13 October 2022].

Cervulle, M. and Julliard, V. (2018). Le genre des controverses : approches féministes et queer. *Questions de communication*, 33, 7–22 [Online]. Available at: http://journals.openedition.org/questionsdecommunication/12076 [Accessed 13 October 2022].

Gomez-Mejia, G. (2016). *Les fabriques de soi. Identité et industrie sur le web*. Mkf Éditions, Paris.

Granjon, F. (2017). *Mobilisations numériques. Politiques du conflit et technologies médiatiques*. Presses des Mines, Paris.

Granjon, F. and Cardon, D. (2010). *Médiactivistes*. Presses de Sciences Po, Paris.

Gunthert, A. (2015). *L'image partagée : la photographie numérique*. Textuel, Paris.

Gunthert, A. (2018). La visibilité des anonymes. Les images conversationnelles colonisent l'espace public. *Questions de communication*, 34, 133–154.

Jackiewicz, A. (2018). De l'hypertextualité dans des tweets polémiques. In *Le discours hypertextualisé : espace énonciatifs mosaïques*, Simon, J. (ed.). Presses Universitaires de Franche-Comté, Besançon.

Jenkins, H. (2013). *La Culture de la convergence : des médias au transmédia*. Armand Colin, Paris.

Jenkins, H., Ito, M., Boyd, D. (2017). *Culture participative. Une conversation sur la jeunesse, l'éducation et l'action dans un monde connecté*. C&F Éditions, Caen.

Koren, R. (2003). L'engagement de l'Un dans le regard de l'Autre. Point de vue d'une linguiste. *Questions de communication*, 4, 271–277 [Online]. Available at: https://journals.openedition. org/questionsdecommunication/5581#text.

Krieg-Planque, A. (2012). *Analyser les discours institutionnels*. Armand Colin, Paris.

Lambert, F. (2014). Performances et performativité des images, L'agir image et les nouveaux territoires médiatiques. In *Nouveaux territoires médiatiques*, Ballarini, L., Delavaud, G. (eds). Mare et Martin Éditions, Paris.

Laurent, S. (2021). *J'ai vu naître le monstre. Twitter va-t-il tuer la #démocratie ?* Les Arènes, Paris.

Lits, M. (2010), L'impossible clôture des récits multimédiatiques. *A contrario*, 13, 113–124 [Online]. Available at: https://www.cairn.info/revue-a-contrario-2010-1-page-113.htm [Accessed 13 October 2022].

Loubère, L. and Smyrnaios, N. (2020). De la LRU à la LPPR: l'opposition des universitaires aux réformes néolibérales sur les réseaux socio-numériques. Communication lors du séminaire du 13 mars 2020, Axe "Médias et médiations socionumériques". LERASS, Toulouse.

Lugrin, G. (2006). *Généricité et intertextualité dans le discours publicitaire de presse écrite*. Peter Lang, Bern.

Mercier, A. (2015). Twitter, espace politique, espace polémique. L'exemple des tweet-campagnes municipales en France (janvier-mars 2014). *Les Cahiers du numérique*, 11, 145–168 [Online]. Available at: https://www-cairn-info.scd1.univ-fcomte.fr/revue-les-cahiers-du-numerique-2015-4-page-145.htm [Accessed 13 October 2022].

Mercier, A. (2018a). Hashtags : tactiques de partages et de commentaires d'informations. In *#Info. Commenter et partager l'actualité sur Twitter et Facebook*, Mercier A., Pignard-Cheynel, N. (eds). Éditions de la MSH, Paris.

Mercier, A. (2018b). L'ensauvagement du web. *TheConversation.com* [Online]. Available at: https://theconversation.com/lensauvagement-du-web-95190 [Accessed 13 October 2022].

Mercier, A. (2019). Stratégie de harcèlement et d'intimidation de militants d'extrême droite sur Twitter (retour d'expérience personnelle). In *Violences et radicalités militantes dans l'espace public*, Fleury, B., Walter, J. (eds). Riveneuve, Paris.

Micheli, R. (2012). Les visées de l'argumentation et leurs corrélats langagiers : une approche discursive. *Argumentation et Analyse du Discours*, 9 [Online]. Available at: http://journals. openedition.org/aad/1406 [Accessed 13 October 2022].

Millerand, F., Proulx, S., Rueff, J. (eds) (2010). *Web social, Mutation de la communication*. Presses de l'Université du Québec, Quebec.

Millette, M., Millerand, F., Myles, D., Latzko-Toth, G. (eds) (2020). *Méthodes de recherche en contexte numérique. Une orientation qualitative*. Les Presses de l'Université de Montréal, Montreal.

Monnier, A. (2018), *Diasporas en réseaux. Pour une lecture socioculturelle des usages numériques*. Le Bord de L'eau Éditions, Lormont.

Nerlich, M. (1990). Qu'est-ce qu'un iconotexte ? Réflexions sur le rapport texte-image photographique dans La Femme se découvre d'Evelyne Sinnassamy. In *Iconotextes*, Montandon, A. (ed.). Ophrys, Paris.

Paveau, M.-A. (2006). *Les Prédiscours. Sens, mémoire, cognition*. Presses Sorbonne Nouvelle, Paris.

Paveau, M.-A. (2017). *L'analyse du discours numérique. Dictionnaire des formes et des pratiques*. Hermann, Paris.

Paveau, M.-A. (2020). Analyse du discours intersectionnelle. Carnet de recherche [Online]. Available at: https://adi.hypotheses.org/310 [Accessed 13 October 2022].

Pereira, I. (2021). Maximiser l'objectivité et minimiser la neutralité : du militantisme en sciences sociales. *The Conversation France* [Online]. Available at: https://theconversation.com/ maximiser-lobjectivite-et-minimiser-la-neutralite-du-militantisme-en-sciences-sociales-1561 59.

Proulx, S. (2020), *La participation numérique : une injonction paradoxale*. Presses des Mines, Paris.

Pinède, N. (2019). Introduction. Dispositifs numériques et organisations. Entre permanences, tensions et changements. *Les Cahiers du numérique*, 15, 9–16 [Online]. Available at: https://www.cairn.info/revue-les-cahiers-du-numerique-2019-4-page-9.htm   [Accessed   13 October 2022].

Rabatel, A. (2004). *Argumenter en racontant. (Re)lire et (ré)écrire les textes littéraires*. De Boeck, Brussels.

Riboni, U.L. (2019). Images anonymes, registres de visibilité et espace(s) public(s). *Questions de communication*, 35, 153–169 [Online]. Available at: https://www-cairn-info.scd1.univ-fcomte.fr/revue-questions-de-communication-2019-1-page-153.htm [Accessed   13   October 2022].

Saemmer, A. (2015). *Rhétorique du texte numérique : figures de la lecture, anticipations de pratiques*. Presses de l'Enssib, Villeurbanne.

Simon, J. (ed.) (2016). Le discours hypertextualisé : problématique de renouvellement des pratiques d'écriture et de lecture. *Semen – Revue de sémio-linguistique des textes et discours*, 42 [Online]. Available at: https://journals.openedition.org/semen/10603 [Accessed   13 October 2022].

Simon, J. (ed.) (2018a). *Le discours hypertextualisé : espace énonciatifs mosaïques*. Presses Universitaires de Franche-Comté, Besançon.

Simon, J. (2018b). Appropriation, reformulation et circulation de La Liberté guidant le peuple sur les réseaux socionumériques durant les événements de Paris. *Interstudia*, 24, 48–60.

Simon, J. (2018c). Analyse de narrations visuelles interactives sur les réseaux socionumériques. In *Conférence invitée au Colloque International Jeunes Chercheur.e.s "Mettre en récit. Enjeux des formes contemporaines de narration"*. AJC CREM, Université de Lorraine, Metz.

Simon, J. (2021a). Partage social des mèmes : un remède en situation de crise sanitaire ? Analyse sémiodiscursive de détournements humoristiques en contexte numérique. In *Pour que tu mèmes encore. Penser nos identités au prisme des mèmes numériques*, Bédard, M., Girard, S. (eds). Éditions Somme Toute, Montreal.

Simon, J. (2021b). Inventivités narratives en opposition à la future #LPPR / #LPR sur Twitter. In *Journée d'études Communication des organisations et narrations en ligne*, Falgas, J., Massou, L. (eds). Université de Lorraine, Metz [Online]. Available at https://videos.univ-lorraine.fr/index.php?act=view&id=14307 [Accessed 13 October 2022].

Simon, J. (2022). *Républigram* fever. Rencontre passionnée entre technologie et culture du partage. In Mitropoulou, E., Wilhelm, C. (eds), Culture.s du technique, de l'innovation et de la communication : imaginaires, potentialités, utopies, *Interfaces Numériques*, No. 11. Available at: https://www.unilim.fr/interfaces-numeriques/4742 [Accessed   13   October 2022].

Simon, J. and Toullec, B. (2018). Quand les tweets avec images renouvellent le partage d'informations. In *#Info. Commenter et partager l'actualité sur Twitter et Facebook*, Mercier A., Pignard-Cheynel, N. (eds). Éditions de la MSH, Paris.

Simon, J., Toullec, B., Badouard, R., Bigey, M., Compagno, D., Mercier, A., Pignard-Cheynel, N., Sebbah, B. (2017). L'influence des discours d'accompagnement sur le partage social. Identifier et analyser les discours d'escorte sur Twitter. In *Corpus de communication médiée par les réseaux : construction, structuration, analyse*, Ledegen, G., Wigham, C. (eds). L'Harmattan, Paris.

Souchier, E., Jeanneret, Y., Le Marec, J. (eds) (2003). *Lire, écrire, récrire. Objets, signes et pratiques des médias informatisés*. BPI-Centre Pompidou, Paris.

Volochinov, V.N. (1977). *Le Marxisme et la philosophie du langage*. Minuit, Paris.

7

Metaphor and Analysis of Websites: Transformations of a Media Object

Pergia GKOUSKOU

GRIPIC, Université Clermont Auvergne, Vichy, France

7.1. Introduction

In this chapter, we will study the relevance of the concept of the metaphor in the epistemological analysis of the "website" object, while at the same time attempting to define this object in the context of the continuous transformation of the digital landscape.

Following a thesis on the media composition of the "website" and then on the works regarding the websites of open data projects, here we will look at the evolution of the Web from playing an advisory and documentary role to becoming a Web of direct interaction and manipulation of visualized content that causes a feeling of immediacy among Internet users.

In this environment of immediate and ephemeral communication, would there be relevance in an analysis of display-pages as "display writings" endowed with an intrinsic metaphorical meaning? Can new media objects such as interactive open data visualization devices be approached as document spaces that have the goal of transmitting messages at several sociocultural levels, and not simply sharing information? And if so, can the metaphorical approach be implemented to analyze them?

Analyzing Websites,
coordinated by Luc MASSOU, Patrick MPONDO-DICKA and Nathalie PINÈDE.
© ISTE Ltd 2023.

First of all, we will reflect on the notion of the "website": what is a website? What are the nature and the functions of this object? In particular, we will explore the object of the "website" in its documentary, media and technological dimensions of human action.

Next, we will approach this object from within a context of visual textualizations. Here, we will examine the mechanisms of metaphor that emerge between the strategies of the creators, the practices of the users and the properties of the medium. As an analytical approach, the metaphor will be taken into account in its socio-cognitive dimension, that is to say, as a generator of a communications framework between old and new media experiences.

First, we will analyze the metaphorical process in the case of institutional websites, in other words, the official websites of public institutions. Next, we will observe the evolution of this metaphorical process in the techno-semiotic structure of open data visualization websites.

7.2. Uses of metaphors for analyzing websites and digital communications

7.2.1. The "website" object: between documents, media and devices

Since its appearance, the object of the "website" has been treated as a document with unique properties. These special features, which have been constantly evolving, have impacted the perception of the documentary nature of objects in general.

According to Pédauque (2007), the historical investigation shows that what is considered to constitute a document, regardless of its medium (printed, silver plates, film, magnetic tape, etc.), is its functionalities, and in particular those of evidence (piece of conviction) and intelligence (representation of the world or testimony). The document is then given a system of signs (text) inscribed on a medium and intended to be communicated within a social environment.

In this context, the group proposes a method of studying documents based on the traditional three-way intersection between all communicating objects: their distinction as form (materiality), signs (a meaningful system that has been given intentionality) and a medium (the social function).

According to Jean-Michel Salaün, the digital document, for its part, crosses the boundaries between mass media and interpersonal communication media by being both a medium for recording traces of exchanges between actors and a large-scale broadcaster of content through a network of interconnections at the same time[1].

This revised notion of the document led the Roger T. Pédauque collective to the idea to redocumentarize the world. Indeed, beyond the fundamental transformation of the nature of the document that the transition to digital media implies, the system of the Web induces an even deeper transformation of the different collections of documents and the possible ways to organize them, which acts in reverse on the nature of the document. As the authors note:

> To shed light on the relationship between the digital and social realms, we can draw a parallel between the role of printed paper documents in the emergence of modern societies and that of the digital document in the social transformations we are witnessing. (Pedauque 2007, p. 15)

A system of signs implies an organization or reorganization of meaning between subjects and actors, and this activity of the creation and communication of meaning is used by the semiologist Eliseo Veron as the basis for his definition of media. According to Veron, a media outlet is "a support of meaning, a place for the production (and therefore manifestation) of meaning" (Veron and Levasseur 1983, p. 27).

In terms of communication, websites are part of what we refer to as "digital media", or until recently "new media". In the CIS literature, the media are sometimes identified with a system of memorization, transmission and/or information processing, that is to say, with what could be called a writing system. For example, Jean-Pierre Meunier and Daniel Peraya note:

> During the history of mankind, communication has become mediatized. Images and writings were the first instruments of this media, and in fact are much older than our current interest in a media society, which we consider as dependent on modern technologies, would lead us to believe. (Miller and Peraya 2004, p. 297)

---

1 According to Jean-Michel Salaün, there are two very "normalized" social practices that are changing through the Web. On the one hand, the "floating" border or public border between private correspondence and advertising shifts, and all social codes and organizational forms related to it are then shaken up. On the other hand, as illustrated by the prefix "hyper" (hypertext, hypermedia), the relationships between documents are distributed differently between sharing and links, between posting online and networking (Salaun 2004).

Other researchers instead focus on the representation of information. This is the case for Anderson, who defines the media as an organized activity that intervenes to transform socio-cognitive practices: "A media is a distinct human activity that organizes reality into readable texts intended for an action" (Anderson 1988).

As far as we are concerned, we consider the notion of media in its initial sense, that is to say, a technical medium, a technological materiality that occurs through and within human activity, and imposes more or less precise forms on communication exchanges by inducing particular writing practices. Indeed, the media are characterized by a transformative power in the communication exchanges between the actors, thus being a cultural and social power. As technical objects, they constitute sets and prostheses[2] which prolong and increase human action[3]. Nevertheless, they are distinguished from other technical objects since they are not built to take actions on nature but on the way people meet, create meaning and communicate. As Yves Jeanneret notes:

> If it is true that every technical project is inhabited by a desire to act on the human condition, the intent of the media engages what people do when they communicate, what they cannot do, or what they would like or should be able to do: it expresses a project that is anthropological in nature, to transform the *homo communicans*. (Jeanneret 2000, p. 66)

Websites are media, that is to say, technical objects with a social function. They intervene in the social process by transforming it through their symbolic and cultural forms. As digital media, websites incorporate multiple media forms. The content (information) is transported onto a complex medium consisting of several pre-existing digital media (texts, images, videos, etc.) linked together by hypertext and hypermedia links. The amount of text accessible on this complex medium is greater than on any other medium and the user/reader perceives the information through an interactive cultural interface (Manovich 2001). As we have seen over the history of the media, each new media form integrates the previous media, and this gives rise to cultural transformations.

This observation led us to consider digital media as a device in the Benjaminian sense of the word. Walter Benjamin talks about a technical device that intervenes in and reformulates human perception by inducing a new relationship between the

---

2 A term used by Divina Frau-Meigs (2010) to refer to the media as cultural objects that allow for the balancing of individual and collective identities.

3 According to Sarah Labelle (2007, p. 22), a panoply "makes it possible to highlight a set of devices that are both heterogeneous and convergent".

human body and the world around it. By studying the socio-cognitive impact of the techno-artistic and urbanist inventions of the industrial era, and photography and cinema in particular, Benjamin notices that each artifact conforms the representation of the world to the formulation of reality by the artifact itself; he then went on to speak of an artificialization[4] of human perception.

For the philosopher Jean-Louis Déotte, "within the principle of the mechanical device, there is the function of 'making things the same', of 'matching': of comparing what had been heterogeneous up to that time" (Déotte 2007, p. 18). Indeed, we can note that each new cultural technology is characterized by this visibility and common representation of elements that seem separate and/or invisible to the eye and human sensations. This transformation of human perception that accompanies each new technology has been highlighted by several researchers, creators and media theorists such as Eisenstein (1970) who demonstrates how film editing creates objects to be perceived through unreal antitheses or juxtapositions or by Bolter and Grusin (1998) who introduce the concept of "hypermediacy" to describe the presentation of a media reality that transcends the boundaries of time and space.

We consider that the website in the broadest sense goes beyond the limits of the definitions of a documentary or media device and is instead closer to what we could describe as an *apparatus*. As Jean-Louis Déotte notes, the crucial point of distinction between an apparatus and any other device is that the latter induces a new temporality, a new relationship between social subjectivity and reality, which "creates an era" (Déotte 2004).

In this context, the question that arises is as follows: "Is the Web an era?" First of all, is there a temporality induced by the Web that differs from that introduced by previous cultural devices? In fact, the Web consists of three types of temporalities that result from different parts that make up the system. These operations take place in asynchronous times, regularities and rhythms: the temporality of the terminal, which is a "loop" or "computable" temporality; that of the network, which is a synchronization temporality; and that of the server, which is governed by the updates made to the site. It is interesting to note that these three distinct temporality mechanisms are found when we attempt to consider the technical system of the Web no longer as an assembly of the three separable components noted above, but as a superimposition of layers of a network, each corresponding to a different level of abstraction.

---

4 For example, regarding cinema, Benjamin writes, "The characteristics of the film lie not only in the manner in which man presents himself to mechanical equipment but also in the manner in which, by means of this apparatus, man can represent his environment" (Benjamin 2000, p. 303).

The limitations and complementary nature of these three ways of viewing websites – as documents, media and devices – suggest to us that we cannot be satisfied with extending pre-established concepts to include the characteristics of the Internet that are not covered within an analysis done with the help of these concepts, and that, conversely, it is necessary to organize a more careful observation of these characteristics in order to grasp the theoretical conclusions that they may bring about. In this context, we will then ask the question of meaning through metaphor as an axis of observation of the multiple mediations that revolve around the "website" object.

7.2.2. The place of metaphor in the analysis of the "website" object

Throughout our research work, we study the role of the metaphor in the process of creating meaning, in relation to the intermediary relationships that develop between the functions and social roles of the Web and those of other media. We consider that the metaphor forms the explanation of the frames of experience (Goffman 1974) that emerge from the different media universes and hybridize with each other to produce new ways of perceiving and communicating.

According to Erving Goffman, frames of experience represent the way human and social activity is organized. They consist of the mobilization of organizational premises that help participants to interpret the new data and to act in their environment. Through these frames, we appeal to our convictions to understand how things happen, that is to say, how they are modeled and manufactured. However, the process of anchoring the action in reality presupposes the mobilization of patterns of interpretation of data from the real world that have already been acquired. The use of frames of experience causes them to be transformed. The perception of new things arises from the difficulty of perfectly applying the patterns that have been acquired in new situations that emerge. Thus, a continuous comparison occurs between the old and the new, a game of continuity based on rupture.

Indeed, we approach the notion of the metaphor using the sociolinguistic approach, that is to say, as a conceptual process. In their book *Metaphors We Live By*, sociolinguists George Lakoff and Mark Johnson study the metaphor from everyday linguistic experience. The authors give many examples of conventional metaphors in which primitive experiential gestalten (forms) builds a general model of understanding[5]. From this angle, the metaphor is identified each time with a metaphorical concept that is based not only on the development of people's

---

5 A characteristic example is that of the human body ("medical body", "teaching body", "corporation", etc.).

discursive argumentation but also on their non-discursive practices (actions). A metaphorical concept structures what we do when we discuss, as well as how we understand what we are doing.

> The essence of a metaphor is understanding and experiencing one kind
> thing in terms of another. (Lakoff and Johnson 1985, p. 8)

For George Lakoff and Mark Johnson, objects of reality can only be appreciated in situations of interaction with the subject. The nature of the objects is not defined objectively, but rather in accordance with the activity of the subject. The properties of objects are therefore not inherent to objects but are defined in relation to the functional role of objects in situations of action.

The implementation of a metaphor gives rise to the creation of a conventional environment of action, with rules and benchmarks that guide the behavior of the actors and leave their traces on the medium. However, these conventional universes have an ephemeral status: the rules and identifiers that temporarily reduce strategic uncertainty will also necessarily include a degree of ambiguity that leads them to be questioned. The rules apply in such a way as to transform and give way to new patterns of action.

7.2.3. Metaphor and intermediality

We consider that this interplay between old and new is expressed in the speech of participants as well as in the vocabulary and design of the websites. The metaphor, both verbal and visual, reflects the displacement and transformation of the organizational frameworks of the experience. Indeed, the metaphor constitutes the explanation of the frames of experience that emerge from the different media universes and hybridize with each other to produce new ways of perceiving and communicating.

In this context, we may connect the notion of metaphor to that of intermediality which refers to the interactions between the different media universes, as well as the question of remediatization, which describes the ways in which a medium reconfigures itself in another media. As far as the Web is concerned, the previous media are integrated into the technosemiotic materiality of the interface and appear in the mental representations of the actors.

The metaphorical processes develop between the constraints induced by the technosemiotic nature of the medium, the communicational practices of the participants and the promotional and/or cultural strategies of the site owners as they have taken shape on their sites. Metaphors are explained iconically (on the interface) or linguistically (in the participants' speech) through interactions that can be analyzed from a semio-pragmatic point of view.

We believe that interactions between the media are expressed on two levels:

– The semio-cognitive level concerning the development of experience frameworks emerging from the hybridization of action and apprehension patterns in the communication universes created by pre-existing media on the Web.

– The rhetorical level in which the metaphor is loaded with a symbolic value. This level instead concerns the image signifying the institution's identity that the institution seeks to convey on the screen.

As an integrator and transformer of the traditions and practices induced by previous media, digital media evolves through the intermediatic metaphor. It is within this issue that we will examine the concept of intermediality. Indeed, intermediality systematizes studies on the connections between the different media. Posed as an extension of the notion of intertextuality[6], it specializes in the field of media interaction analysis for the production of meaning.

Intermediality studies are relatively recent. However, the idea that the evolution of communication modes is marked by the process of integrating old media into new ones is the subject of general acceptance in the works of several theorists whose works cover art, cinema or television[7]. In the same way, the coexistence of several types of writing within the same surfaces has always been an important point of analysis in the field of aesthetics and the semiology of the image[8].

Media studies from the point of view of the mixing of sign systems have developed over the past two centuries. In fact, the appearance of technically and

---

6 We recall that, in her book *Revolution in Poetic Language* (1974), Julia Kristeva defines intertextuality as "the transition from one system of signs to another".

7 As Jürgen Ernst Müller notes, "If what we mean by 'intermediality' is that there are variable media relations between the media and that their function arises, among other things, from the historical evolution of these relations, this implies that the conception of 'monads' or of types of 'isolated' media is inadmissible [...]" (Müller 1994, p. 213).

8 For example, we note the analysis of the epigraphs of the painting *Ex-Voto* of Philippe de Champaigne by Louis Marin, or the analysis of the significant system of medals by the same author: "Which amounts to saying that the meaning of these objects can only be discovered outside of them by a global decryption, but that this is possible only on the condition of exploring very precisely the metaphorical and metonymic relationships of reciprocal transformation of textual elements and visual elements of the object" (Marin 1971, p. 115).

semiotically complex media such as cinema has created questions around the evolution of the communicational process carried out around and through media that carry multiple codes and languages from pre-existing media universes. The mutational mixing of the different codes has been considered a very important point in the study of the history of these media. In the same sense, the aspect of the genealogy of media forms and the mixing of genres has been studied in the analysis of television[9].

The continuously evolving nature of websites is largely due to the progressive mutation of dynamic structures from other media universes, but that is integrated and reshaped within the world of the Web. The analysis of this hybridization process requires the use of observation methods that emphasize the continuous circulation of forms and practices between players and media. Epistemologically and methodologically, we believe that the notion of metaphor is proving to be a very important entry point into this process. More specifically, we believe that the metaphorical expression constitutes the visual or linguistic explanation of the media universes that are used in the form of communication unique to the Web and the way they progressively mutate. These include both the forms on the screen as well as the representations of the participants that bring them to life. It is through these representations that forms and practices evolve and continually hybridize with the new medium. Metaphors constitute the tool for observing the process of concretization and materialization of these representations in the techno-semiotic forms of the medium.

7.2.4. Metaphors, remediatization and strategies of digital communications

During our studies of institutional websites, we noticed that intermediary metaphors are always inherent in the institution's communication strategies. By using metaphors, designers designate the thematic categories of their site or the style of communication that they wish to establish. In metaphorical terms, they also present the prospects for the evolution of their site, the new frameworks of action that they would like to introduce through modifying the existing ones.

For Internet users, the metaphorical process reflects the interactive adaptation of their patterns of apprehension and action. Carrying on the traditions of the media universes in which they were trained, Internet users interpret the forms on the screen, seeking to adapt their previous patterns of experience.

---

9 As Bernard Leconte notes, cinema is made up of "five subjects of expression: photographic images, movement, noises, music, sound, and written texts" (Leconte 2004, p. 78).

Through their websites, institutions transmit the image of their identity either by displaying the environment of the institution's physical space on the site or by using the site as an information or transaction document (Gkouskou-Giannakou 2007b; Gkouskou-Giannakou 2012). The use of the institution's website thus generates frames of perception and action explained by the metaphors that circulate between the participants and the medium.

The metaphor is an essential element in the process of Web communication in both cases. Metaphoric expression, closely linked to the phenomenon of re-mediatization, appears in the discourse of designers and users, as well as in the interface and architecture of a website. These metaphors appear in the materiality of the medium and the iconicity of its forms (Gkouskou-Giannakou 2007b).

We use the term remediatizaion to mean the phenomenon of the configuration of forces and practices induced by one media in another media. Remediatization does not mean the simple visualization of forms that evoke another media, but rather the transfer of the generative data of the other media, everything that can be included in its architext[10] or its control panel. It is thus from the point of view of generating a framework for action that the phenomenon of remediatization is of interest to us, and not from the point of view of simple evocation.

The presence of one media in another media was studied in the 1990s by Jay David Bolter and Richard Grusin. Jay David Bolter and Richard Grusin use the term *remediation* to refer to "the representation of one medium in another remediation, and will argue that remediation is a defining characteristic of new digital media" (Bolter and Grusin 2001, p. 45). For Jay David Bolter and Richard Grusin, *remediation* can be explained using two processes: *hypermediacy* and *immediacy*.

What the authors call *hypermediacy* is "a type of visual representation that aims to remind the viewer of the presence of the media". In all its manifestations, *hypermediacy* reminds the viewer/user of the presence of the media. This type of representation reveals the fascination of the viewer/user with the media. It is a visual style that, according to the authors, favors fragmentation and indeterminacy. By provoking strong emotions through the multiplication of signs recalling the various media, he creates the illusion of a real experience in the sense of "grasping reality"[11]. On the other hand, the notion of *immediacy* applies to a certain type of

---

10 A term originally used by Gerard Genette and adopted by Yves Jeanneret and Emmanuel Souchier to refer to any tool that allows the existence of "display writings".

11 As the authors note, "Hypermediacy offers a heterogeneous space, in which representation is conceived of not as a window on to the world, but rather as 'windowed' itself – with windows that open on to other representations or other media" (Bolter and Grusin 2001, p. 35).

visual representation that seeks to cause viewers to forget the presence of the media, attempting to make them believe that they are in direct contact with the objects represented[12]. Their analyses were carried out on media using different technologies, particularly television and digital technologies[13].

Our first analysis of websites from the perspective of the metaphor of remediation was carried out in 2007, which we conducted on the websites of three scientific and technical institutions (Gkouskou-Giannakou, 2007a). We found that the dynamic image of a site is the ideal medium to represent a physical space. Indeed, the notion of immediacy is of particular importance in the identity representation of an institution and in particular of a pedagogical institution that wishes to convey a sense of identity. The site functions essentially as a virtual tool to insert Internet users inside the institution, where they can see objects, check documents, or explore informative media. For example, during our study, we found that in the thematic category "Laboratory Notebooks" from the website www.onera.fr, access to educational content is made through a tree structure of links. The final text takes the form of a briefly formulated statement (which can be classified as an observation or conclusion), which is always signed by a researcher from the laboratory. A link on the page leads to a video document (a simulated image) with very small dimensions and that lasts a few seconds. For some of the Internet users who were interviewed, this video document gives the sensation of peeping through a keyhole to look at a secret scientific experiment within the institution. This tiny simulation image accompanied by a fragmentary speech is not shown, but it is seen. The Internet users notice excerpts of a communication between participants, as if they had secretly sneaked inside the institution.

It is often through visual clues that the user is given the feeling of entering into the space of the institution. Through the simple image of an institution's exhibits to much more hypermediatized forms of representation, with the online posting of complex multimedia or content pages which go beyond the elements seen during a physical visit of the premises[14], the metaphor of space is related to that of the metonymic illusion of "being there" inside the institution.

---

12 "A style of visual representation whose goal is to make the viewer forget the presence of the medium (canvas, photographic film, cinema, and so on) and believe that he is in the presence of the objects of representation" (Bolter and Grusin 2001, p. 273).

13 One characteristic example of their analysis are television "windows", developed in particular in the 1990s under the influence of digital forms of representation, which transmit a sense of panoramic immediacy of an event from a process of "hypermediacy".

14 This is the case for the "Laboratory" page of the website for the Cité des Sciences et de l'Industrie (City of Sciences and Industry), as we show in the same study (Gkouskou 2007).

In addition, we note that the metaphorical process among the actors is identical to a transition and a displacement of the frames of a documentary experience. One characteristic example is the qualification of an animated homepage as a "brochure" by Internet users. Indeed, they metonymically link the animated visual form of a page to an advertising strategy, which is unmistakeably that of a printed brochure. The search for words in pre-existing digital cultural universes to characterize online hypermedia presentation formats is a common practice among designers and users of digital media, and is also manifested in the interfaces[15].

In this context, we ask the question of the place of metaphor in the analysis of new types of interfaces, and more particularly on interfaces for the interactive visualization of open data.

7.3. Websites that visualize open data: making sense using the metaphor as inquiry

We believe that the metaphorical processes of "making meaning" and simulation are becoming increasingly present on the Web as it evolves. Within the logic of "user-centered design", these metaphors place the Internet user at the core of not only the consultation process, but also of data processing and dissemination, through procedures that are rather playful in nature. Websites for data visualization, Web documentaries, games or information or fiction multimedia are based on this idea of a simulative metaphor.

Using the example of open data visualization websites in particular, the creation of a metaphorical universe personalizes the presentation by attracting the user. Open Data has allowed citizens direct access to data in the public domain. However, the continuous and abundant flows of this raw data are often considered difficult to decipher, understand, or use by non-specialists in statistical methodologies. The goal of their visualizations is thus to adapt this data to the reader.

Abstract data visualizations are not only intended to reveal information, but also to facilitate the reading of that information through metaphors.

---

15 Regarding the metaphorization of previous cultural universes in the digital world, we also recall the work of Yves Jeanneret on the term "page", taken from the world of print and transferred to the digital world (Jeanneret 2007), the work of Lev Manovich on the presence of the cultural traditions of print and audiovisual in the digital interface (Manovich 2001) and especially the work of Annette Béguin-Verbrugge on the metaphorization of these universes in the jargon of designers (Béguin-Verbrugge 2014).

As an example, we present here some metaphorical formats of visualization and the framing of interaction. These formats are maps, mosaics, and that of the internet users as "interlocutors" or "researchers". These formats function as frames of experience by involving the Internet user in different phases of the media project.

7.3.1. *Hypermedia maps in data visualization*

A very common data visualization format is the interactive map. This format was used in projects such as "New York City: 1836 vs. Today"[16], which allows viewers to see the evolution of the city of New York between the 19th century and today (see Figure 7.1).

Figure 7.1. *"New York City: 1836 vs. Today". For a color version of this figure, see www.iste.co.uk/massou/analyzing.zip*

It consists of two images superimposed on each other: a digitized map from 1836 and a satellite image. This interface is based on the metaphor of the magnifying glass, giving the impression to the user of an autonomous search. Through the magnifying glass, the user can "zoom in" across space and time. Here, the magnifying glass constitutes the graphic visualization of the control panel (Manovich 2001), and users thus have the feeling of using a space that is available to them alone. In this way, the interactive map, inherent to the development of the

---

16 Available at: www.smithsonianmag.com/history/interactive-map-compares-new-york-city-1836-today-180947939/.

Web, is used in this case to convey to the user the illusion of dominance over space and time. The screen becomes a true instrument of control and monitoring. It is therefore a hypermediated reading that provokes a feeling of immediacy and dominance.

By also incorporating visual media (photos or videos), cartographic visualizations of the data can even simulate the presence of the users in a geographical space. This is the case for the project "Nor: a paranoid cartography"[17], which brings to light and visualizes the various surveillance systems around the world (Figure 7.2). Within a map-based website, users can navigate through different geographical regions, read textual information related to their location and see the photos of the monitoring systems registered there.

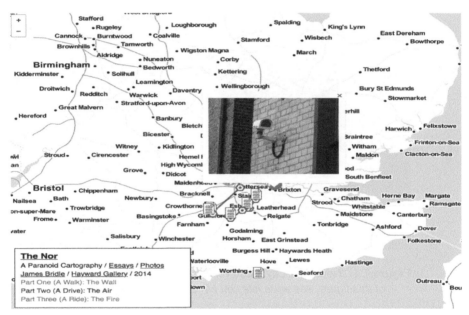

Figure 7.2. *"Nor: a paranoid cartography". For a color version of this figure, see www.iste.co.uk/massou/analyzing.zip*

In their abstraction, interactive maps can also have the form of a metaphorical diagram (Brunet 1987), as is the case of the project "Top secret America"[18], where

---

17 Available at: www.shorttermmemoryloss.com/nor/map.

18 A project designed and uploaded to the internet by Dana Priest and William M. Arkin on the website of the *Washington Post* in 2011.

the information is presented in the form of a reconfigured "radar" (Joannès 2010, p. 134), which can be manipulated by the reader/users. This project reveals the different collaborations of the US secret services with private companies for the production of counterterrorism technologies. The user can "navigate" through these projects by selecting colors that represent the different military and industrial sectors. The project is an interactive graphic abstraction created from geometric shapes and colors that gives the user the impression of a panorama of information complemented by a control panel. Thus, the user can select the different parts of this information using the graphical variables (Figure 7.3).

Figure 7.3. *"Top Secret America". For a color version of this figure, see www.iste.co.uk/massou/analyzing.zip*

A graphic image is made up of colored pieces that are called visual variables[19]. For Bertin (1973), the father of graphic semiology, a stain is a visible trace that has a meaning. Following the logic of the semiology of Saussuri, a stain is considered as a sign, since it participates in a system where "knowledge of the meaning of each sign precedes the observation of the assembly of signs" (Bertin 1973, p. 6). Graphic images, which come from the printed tradition, are transformed on the Web to become interactive infographics that reduce information into ergonomic visual variables while simulating tangible space through objects and interactive practices.

---

19 According to Bertin (1973), these variables are size, value, grain, color, orientation and shape.

7.3.2. *The metaphor of the mosaic in data visualization*

Another type of metaphorical visualization is that of the "mosaic" of images. This type of graphic metaphor is suitable for data representation projects that contain objects or media, and in particular for websites for the public provision of visual or documentary archives. This format, which comes from the world of images, is an exploratory reading, which is to say to a free-form journey by Internet users on the site, without the intention of searching for a specific content or document.

One very creative mosaic-type visualization project is "Cinema Redux"[20], which allows a moving image to be spatialized. The project essentially seeks to distill an entire film into a single image. Moving images are processed through software that allows for the sampling and generation of images every second. Each line of images corresponds to 1 min of film. At the synoptic level, the image of each film gives an overall idea of the color shades, as well as the pace of the editing process (Figure 7.4).

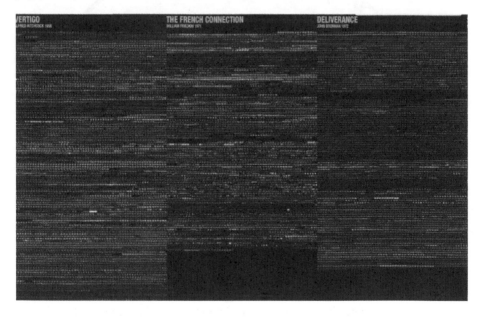

Figure 7.4. *"Cinema Redux". For a color version of this figure, see www.iste.co.uk/massou/analyzing.zip*

20 Available at: www.processing.org/exhibition/works/redux/index.html.

The mosaic visualization can be formatted as a map, a cloud or a timeline. The timeline is suitable for visualizing data that have a temporal dimension. This format is used for the website called "The preservation of favoured traces"[21], which demonstrates the evolution of the work *The Origin of Species* by Charles Darwin through the various editions that were released.

Starting from a moving chronological frieze that is gradually filled with tiny interactive squares in different colors, the user has access to excerpts of the text that differ in each edition (Figure 7.5). The idea of the evolution of species is combined with that of the evolution of a scientific work over the course of a thorough investigation, using a logic of continuous movement.

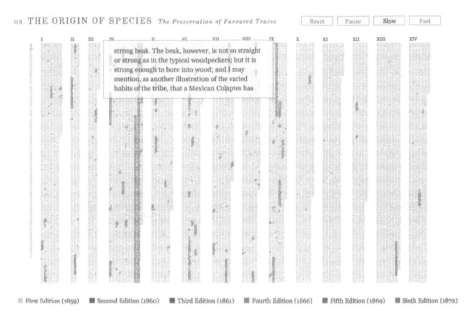

Figure 7.5. *"The preservation of favored traces". For a color version of this figure, see www.iste.co.uk/massou/analyzing.zip*

7.3.3. *Metaphor as a framework for action: involvement of the Internet user and a sense of transparency*

In observing these Open Data websites, we can note that the visualizations very often transform into the role of an interlocutor who immediately answers the reader's questions. These questions often concern major social, economic or

21 Available at: www.fathom.info/traces/.

political topics, but through interfaces that simulate a situation of direct interpersonal communication. One example of this type is the project "The Equalizer" (Le Pariteur)[22] in which the preface offers readers a form to fill out to compare their own salaries with the salary of a person of the opposite sex (Figure 7.6).

The anthromorphized design transforms into a situation of a verbal exchange, aided by a graphic that parodies an old-fashioned stereotypical representation of men and women. Through this parody of playful dialogue, the visualized project reveals its critical point of view to the Internet users on the inequality of men's and women's wages.

Figure 7.6. *"Le Pariteur"[23]. For a color version of this figure, see www.iste.co.uk/massou/analyzing.zip*

As data visualization projects develop, the model of a user-centered interactive consultation is evolving toward the conceptual integration of users and their

---

22 Available at: www.francetelevisions.fr/lab/le-pariteur.

23 Translation: You are a WOMAN. You earn as much as a MAN?

THE EQUALIZER

Change the gender of your pay stub

Slide the cursor to the right or the left.

transformation into co-authors: the reader participates in the construction of the media, either through feedback actions on a document that has already been created or through practices of crowdsourcing or collective knowledge management.

The interfaces that call on users to contribute to the production of content often use the format of a form to be filled out. This is a regularized process that is guided by the device. Examples of readers' participation in the analysis of expense reports of British parliamentarians during the realization of the "MPs' expenses" project launched by the newspaper *The Guardian* in 2009, we can see a strong research activity supervised and formatted by the online interactive content processing system. In Figure 7.7, we can see that the process the readers/survey participants of the newspaper *The Guardian* need to follow to analyze the expense reports of British parliamentarians that are digitized and published online is fully demonstrated by the device.

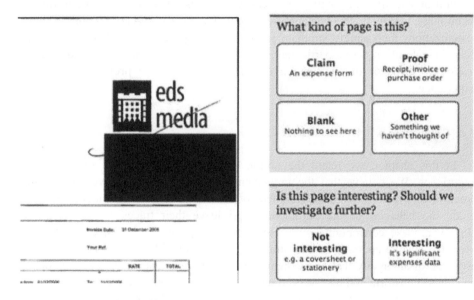

Figure 7.7. *"MPs' expenses". For a color version of this figure, see www.iste.co.uk/massou/analyzing.zip*

More precisely, as we can see above, the reader must complete a series of tasks step by step: first, characterize the type of document according to certain categories ("expense report", "receipt", "empty document", "other") and then evaluate the importance of the document to be analyzed by answering the question: "Is this page interesting? Should we analyze it further?", by clicking on the "not interesting" or "interesting" button. Thus, the device provides the readers with steps to be respected by clearly setting the confines of their investigation.

Drawing from the analysis of Jeanne-Perrier (2012) on the convergence between scientific writing and journalistic writing that is induced by the formatting of online content management systems (CMS), we can notice that through the media of the device, precise methodological rules are formulated to be followed at all times by the Internet users, who turn into a researcher or investigative journalist. The data processing and management system thus plays the role of a real research management system. It is an active metaphorization in the sense of a process that puts users in a real situation through a simulation process.

The visualization of data through graphic or pictorial and photo-graphic images is increasingly used for the representation and communication of journalistic, cultural or scientific information on websites. This is a language specific to digital technology, even if the metaphorical remediations are very obvious. These visualizations increasingly simulate situations and spaces in which Internet users play the role of an active participant, which can be that of an explorer, detective, reader or spectator of an interactive film, following these previous frames of experience.

7.4. Conclusion

In this chapter, we relate the notion of the metaphor to that of frames of experience. We believe that the implementation of a metaphor gives rise to the creation of a conventional environment of action, with rules and identifiers that guide the behavior of the participants and leave their traces on the medium. However, these conventional universes have an ephemeral status: the rules and identifiers that temporarily reduce strategic uncertainty will also necessarily include a degree of ambiguity that leads them to be questioned. The rules apply in such a way as to transform and give way to new patterns of action. The metaphor is thus a rhetorical process, part of the cognitive process that allows the users to create meaning and act.

In the context of a transitory Web, where all presence is fluid, a website can no longer be thought of as a place (space), media or document, but rather as an environment. Even more so than the notion of media, the concept of the apparatus as a system for the "preparation of phenomena" is the best expression of this enormous and heterogeneous field of action that "makes eras". Indeed, what characterizes the apparatus is the mixture of different temporalities and spatialities. In the case of the Web, the interweaving of three types of temporalities (the terminal [operation of the navigation software], the network [data transmission] and the server [content on-line]) constitute a unique phenomenon in the history of socio-technical systems. From this point of view, the Web can be seen as an immense apparatus integrating and normalizing all human interaction, or in other words, a "grammatological machine"[24] which reformats the writing of human expression.

With regard to the metaphorization of open data, we continue the quest for a sense of immediacy through hypermediated processes. The use often simulates the reading of a personalized "story" from interactive procedures and reaches the actual participation of the user in the design and distribution of these contents.

The transformation of the writing of the "website" object in a context of metaphorization and hypermedia simulation is continuously evolving. We believe that this transformation impacts the modes of visualization and narration not only of the interfaces of websites that describe or represent reality, but also of websites that present fiction, digital art or video games. Furthermore, the evolution of the "website" object in a world of ubiquity and transmedia relations will also be a very important epistemological issue for the coming years.

7.5. References

Béguin-Verbrugge, A. (2004). Métaphores et intégration sociale des technologies nouvelles. *Communication & langages*, 141, 83–93.

Benjamin, W. (2000). *Œuvres (Tome III)*. Gallimard, Paris.

Bertin, J. (1973). *Sémiologie graphique : les diagrammes, les réseaux, les cartes*. Mouton, Paris.

Bolter, J.-D. and Grusin, R. (2001). *Remediation, Understanding New Media*. The MIT Press, Cambridge.

Brunet, R. (1987). *La Carte, mode d'emploi*. Fayard/Reclus, Paris/Montpellier.

Charbonneaux, J. and Gkouskou-Giannakou, P. (2015). Data journalism: an investigation practice? A glance at the German and Greek cases. *Brazilian Journalism Research*, (11)2 [Online]. Available at: http://bjr.sbpjor.org.br/bjr/article/view/855 [Accessed 25 November 2022].

Cooper, A. (1999). *The Inmates Are Running the Asylum: Why High Tech Products Drive Us Crazy and How to Restore the Sanity*. Sams Publishing, Indianapolis.

Déotte, J.-L. (2004). *L'époque des appareils*. Manifeste, Paris.

Déotte, J.-L. (2006). *Qu'est-ce qu'un appareil ? Benjamin, Lyotard, Rancière*. L'Harmattan, Paris.

---

24 A term introduced by Jacques Derrida in 1967 and used by Henri Hudrisier (2000).

Doueihi, M. (2011). *Pour un humanisme numérique*. Le Seuil, Paris.

Eisenstein, S. (1970). *Le film : sa forme, son sens*. C. Bourgois, Paris.

Frau-Meigs, D. (2010). La panique médiatique entre déviance et problème social : vers une modélisation sociocognitive du risque. *Questions de communication*, 17, 223–252.

Gkouskou-Giannakou, P. (2007a). Les productions audiovisuelles dans les sites web des institutions de diffusion de la culture scientifique et technique : esquisse d'une analyse des médiations. *Spirale*, 40, 81–94.

Gkouskou-Giannakou, P. (2007b). Composition médiatique des objets sites web. Le cas des sites web des institutions de la culture scientifique et technique. PhD thesis, Université de Technologie de Compiègne, Compiègne.

Gkouskou-Giannakou, P. (2012). Mutations médiatiques et métaphorisations numériques : transformations entre concepteurs et usagers du Web. In *Communication numérique et lien social*, Prouxl, S., Klein, A. (eds). Presses Universitaire de Namur, Namur.

Goffman, E. (1991). *Les Cadres de l'expérience*. Éditions de Minuit, Paris.

Hudrisier, H. (2000). L'Ère des machines grammatologiques : la normalisation des technologies de l'information comme attracteur de leur convergence. HDR Thesis, Université Paris 8, Paris.

Jeanne-Perrier, V. (2012). Les pratiques éditoriales comme moyen d'action sociale sur des corps de métiers : les journalistes soumis aux outils des medias sociaux. *Connexions*, 101–118.

Jeanneret, Y. (2000). *Y a-t-il (vraiment) des technologies de l'information ?* Presses Universitaires du Septentrion, Lille.

Jeanneret, Y. (2007), La page à l'écran, entre filiations et filières. *Visible*, 3, 153–172.

Jeanneret, Y. and Souchier, E. (2005). L'énonciation éditoriale dans les écrits d'écran. *Communication & Langages*, 145, 3–15.

Joannès, A. (2010). *Data journalism. Bases de données et visualisation de l'information*. CFPJ, Paris.

Kling, R. (1977). The organizational context of user-centered software designs. *MIS Quarterly*, 4(1), 41–52.

Labelle, S. (2007). La ville inscrite dans "la société de l'information" : formes d'investissement d'un objet symbolique. PhD Thesis, Université Paris 4, Paris.

Manovich, L. (2001). *The Language of New Media*. The MIT Press, Cambridge.

Marin, L. (1971). *Études sémiologiques : écritures, peintures*. Klincksieck, Paris.

Marin, L. (1995). *Philippe de Champaigne ou la présence cachée*. Hazan, Paris.

Meunier, J.-P. and Peraya, D. (2004). *Introduction aux théories de la Communication*. De Boeck, Brussels.

Muller J.E. (1994). Top Hat et l'intermédialité de la comédie musicale. *Cinémas*, 5(1–2), 211–220.

Nielsen, J. and Tahir, M. (2002). *Homepage Usability. 50 Websites Deconstructed*. New Riders, Syracuse.

Norman, D. (1986). *User-Centered System Design: New Perspectives on Human-Computer Interaction*. CRC Press, Roca Baton.

Norman, D. (2005). *Emotional Design: Why We Love (or Hate) Everyday Things*. Basic Books, New York.

Pédauque, T.R. (2007). *La redocumentarisation du monde*. Cépaduès, Toulouse.

Salaun, J.-M. (2004). Chronique inachevée d'une réflexion collective sur le document. *Communication & Langages*, 140, 9–17.

Veron, E. and Levasseur, M. (1983). *Ethnographie de l'exposition. L'espace, le corps et le sens*. Centre Georges Pompidou, Paris.

PART 3

The Website as a Communication Device

8

Thematic Analysis of Hyperlinks: A Taxonomic Approach

Nathalie PINÈDE

MICA, Université Bordeaux Montaigne, Pessac, France

8.1. Introduction

The French academic world has been undergoing profound changes over several decades, especially since the 2000s (Barats 2020). In this way, in the field of research, the rules of the game for how financing is provided have changed considerably, with the strengthening of the programmatic dimension of research (Algava et al. 2016). The widespread search for external sources of funding requires an intensification of this activity and a cultural shift – one that has created a great deal of turbulence for certain disciplines in the humanities and social sciences – toward other methods for the "production" of research (Musselin 2014). In addition, university rankings, such as the emblematic Academic Ranking Word Universities (better known as the "Shanghai Rankings"[1]), impose their performative logic on the entirety of French higher education and place themselves as instruments for the evaluation, prioritization and even management of institutions (Bouchard 2013; Mercier 2013; Barats et al. 2018). The issue of the digital transformation of university organizations (pedagogy, administration, research), or even its platformization (Bullich 2018), considerably increased in the context of a pandemic that has since subsided, is also at the heart of governance forms today.

---

1 Available at: www.shanghairanking.com.

Analyzing Websites,
coordinated by Luc MASSOU, Patrick MPONDO-DICKA and Nathalie PINÈDE.
© ISTE Ltd 2023.

In this complex environment where limits to visibility, performance and often contrasting realities in the field are common, even under tensions (particularly financial ones), the issues involving the digital presence of the university are becoming ever more urgent and are also subject to procedures of evaluation[2]. In this perspective, we would like to focus on university websites, considering that, as with any organization, they retain a true legitimacy, in parallel other dynamics that are a factor in this digital presence, such as social networks (Pinède 2018). To describe this type of website, we also proposed the expression "organizational website" (OWS) so as to highlight the enunciating authority embodied by an organization (Pinède and Reymond 2013). Within the perspective of an analysis of this strategic dimension of the OWSs of the academic world, we had also established a taxonomy of the contents observed on the home pages on the basis of the textual anchors of the hyperlinks (Pinewood et al. 2011; Pinède and Reymond 2013).

In this chapter, we propose an updated version of our research work on academic websites for the purpose of both testing the stability and interest of the methodology of classification that has been developed, but also in order to analyze in this light certain current trends in terms of communication profiles. How are the contents presented and how have they evolved in terms of how they are seen on the interfaces of the home pages of the websites within a corpus of universities? What do they tell us about certain choices that are made? What effects leading to normalization, as well as those of a site seeking to distinguish itself, can we spot?

First, we will recall the main general principles structuring our analysis framework before presenting the methodological approach used for this investigation at a finer level, along with the adjustments we have made. We will then present the corpus on which we have worked, before giving the main results and the elements of discussion that follow from them.

8.2. Analytical framework for an info-communicational reading of websites

Within the framework of enunciation constituted by the so-called OWS, the analysis framework mobilized comprises two elements (Figure 8.1): the home page of the site, as a singular space for strategic structuring of information and the

---

2 An international ranking of university websites, using the "model" used by Shanghai, also exists. Available at: www.webometrics.info/en.

hyperlink, apprehended from its textual facet, as it is given to the user to read. We called it a hypertext lexical unit (HLU)[3].

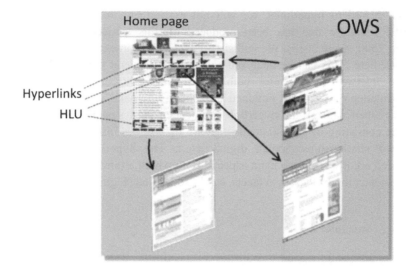

Figure 8.1. *Framework for the analysis of hyperlinks in the context of an organization. For a color version of this figure, see www.iste.co.uk/massou/analyzing.zip*

The home pages of websites constitute their own "micro-genre", because "not only do they form a complex hyperstructure reflecting both the global and detailed organization of the site, but they act as a kind of business card that is in many cases decisive for the success of its operation" (Bonhomme and Stalder 2006, p. 12). Since 2002, Jakob Nielsen and Marie Tahir have insisted on the role of an organization's home page in showcasing its identity, helping it to stand out as compared to the competition or to offer a selective showcase of products or services. In this sense, the home page is a hybridized place that naturally acts to highlight the main axes of information carried by the organization, but also reflects choices, by valuing certain dimensions over others, essentially by producing a certain discourse for certain users. As such, the home page is not intended to be the same as the site map, and therefore to represent all the content that is present in the site. By constituting a gateway to the website, by orienting the user to the main contents of the site while inscribing the organization in its environment (institutional, social, economic, etc.),

3 We will return more specifically to this concept of HLU in the rest of this section.

it contains a real strategic dimension, in that it provides a certain orchestration and valuation of dimensions deemed important to or representative of the organization.

With regard to hyperlinks, we will not expand any further on the abundant scientific literature that has been produced on this subject (Balpe et al. 1995; Clément 2000; Angé 2015). We will simply recall the context in which we enter the hyperlink here. This can be analyzed according to several contextualization maps that are interwoven and refer both to the materiality, spatialization and the implementation of the link. Contained at the heart of a page, a screen or a document (whatever their nature), the hyperlink is extended by a gesture, using information practices consisting of user strategies that are themselves inscribed within complex spaces of relationships (social, digital, etc.). The hyperlink can therefore be subdivided according to two main aspects, from which a third dimension, correlated to the instantiation of these two facets, can be identified (Figure 8.2).

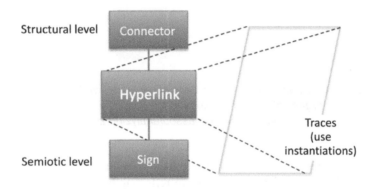

Figure 8.2. *Facets and instantiation of the hyperlink. For a color version of this figure, see www.iste.co.uk/massou/analyzing.zip*

In a first, almost immediate level of perception, the hyperlink is understood in terms of its function as a "connector", one that is encoded into the functionality of the Web at its most basic level. This immediately refers us to this vision of the Web, its enmeshed connections and the paths that result from it, but also to a principle of reality: the first layer of Web is made up of hypertext. This representation of the net and the hyperlinks from which it is "woven" leads us to topological approaches and logics of flow. Nevertheless, it would be wrong to reduce the hyperlink to this dimension of connection alone. Beyond this "false evidence of the hyperlink", Davallon and Jeanneret (2004) highlight the fact that the hyperlink has a density that transcends this illusion of neutrality. They also propose substituting the notion of "sign" for the notion of "link", and the expression "passing sign" instead of that of "hyperlink". This unwavering coupling of connector and sign, which by its implementation gives rise to the production of a digital trace, makes it possible to obtain an overview of the multidimensionality and the different facets of the hyperlink.

As per our understanding, we will concern ourselves with one of the aspects of the hyperlink, considering it as a "sign" located in a particular context, that of an OWS. Two principles of focus are adopted. First, we target *internal* hyperlinks from the home page. In the field of Web metrics, there are three types of hyperlinks that can be distinguished (*hyperlinks*) as "connectors": the incoming links (inlinks), the outgoing links (outlinks) and internal links (selflinks) (Björneborn and Ingwersen 2004). If we consider the website A as the main site, the outgoing links correspond to the bibliographic reference principle and go from site A to site C, the incoming links correspond to the citation principle and direct from site B to site A, and for the internal links, they correspond to a link from one page of site A to another page of site A (Figure 8.3).

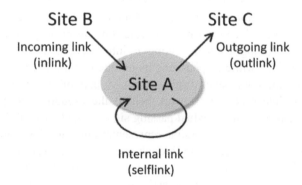

Figure 8.3. *Hyperlinks and websites. For a color version of this figure, see www.iste.co.uk/massou/analyzing.zip*

With regard to this typology, we can exclude the outgoing links (outlinks) and the incoming links (inlinks), retaining only the internal links (selflinks) which provide the function of directing users to specific informational areas on the site in question from the home page, that is, a physically performative function as identified by Brügger (2009). Outgoing links are of course part of the organization's external communication strategies, while incoming links are important indicators of the reputation of the site (as used particularly in Google's PageRank algorithm), but here we have chosen to restrict the scope of our study to the staging of its content and services, focusing only on internal links.

Moreover, these involve mobilizing the hyperlink as a "sign", though by using the textual form of the hypertext sign that is visible and can be activated since it is visible on a screen, in this case that of the home page. By text, we mean an "autonomous linguistic suite (oral or written) constituting an empirical unit, and produced by one or more enunciators in an attested social practice" (Rastier 2001, p. 302). We called this clickable textual fragment a "hypertext lexical unit". This approach to the hyperlink therefore leads us to consider it as an utterance produced by a speaker who is given the "voice" of the organization in question. There is a will, an intentionality, that inscribes a first level of meaning at the heart of the statement and marks a positioning through the lexical materialization of the hyperlink. Its visible, tangible form (design) stems from intentional, even strategic choices, while inducing effects and behaviors on the users' side.

Concentrating on the textual dimension of the hyperlink naturally reduces its semiotic depth but makes it possible to understand it from an original point of view, allowing other registers of understanding and analysis to emerge. This reading that places the hyperlink at the core of the organizational website is very much in line with the process of "editorial enunciation" (Souchier 1998; Jeanneret and Souchier 2005), even if it takes place on a modest scale. Giving priority to the form of the hypertext as a signifying element, taking it into account as an element of the structure of the artifact while emphasizing its unique materiality, within a space that is itself singular (the homepage, display page), is part of an approach seeking to updating the multiple processes at work behind the pseudo-banality of this link. Indeed, this dimension of the "textual passing sign" (Souchier et al. 2003; Davallon and Jeanneret 2004) brings two possible representations into play, and possibly into tension: those of the designers, who through these signs translates their intentions; and those of the users, who will interpret and appropriate these elements of information. As Maingueneau (2013) reminds us, it would obviously be wrong to consider that the inscription of a semantic orientation through the statement prescribes the way it is read: "whoever interprets the utterance reconstructs its meaning from indications given in the utterance produced, but there is no guarantee that what they reconstruct coincides with the representations of the enunciator" (p. 8). The contextual dimension, which is extremely malleable in this case (the context of the link inscribed in the environment of a Web page, the context of reception, prior intentions, representations of the user, etc.), models and influences the conditions for understanding a statement of any kind, and the wording of hyperlinks in particular.

This triangulation around three elements (an organizational website, the home page, the text component of internal hyperlinks) contributes to generating an analytical framework from which it is possible to perform an info-communicational reading of the websites considered.

8.3. The interest of a taxonomic reading grid for websites

Marked at the same time by publishing constraints and Web structuring, by the strategic objectives of information valorization, as well as by the editorial capacities of the authors, the HLUs of the home page produce an info-communicational "signature" for the home page and, by extension, of the website in question itself. The HLUs of a site homepage can therefore be considered as representative of the set of information contained by the site, and characteristic of what is put forward in terms of its communication strategy. But we can see that these internal HLUs also offer access to features, tools and content profiling depending on the type of user visiting the site. Moreover, the processing and interpretation of HLUs on a home page makes perfect sense when working on the scale of an organizational domain. In this perspective, the HLUs represent not only the most emblematic activities, but also structural information or information related to the current state and the day-to-day activity of the organization they represent; they also provide access to functionalities made possible by the Web media (software tools, RSS feeds, etc.), as well as selective approaches to content according to the categories of the target audience.

On the basis of the principles established above, the study of the textual forms of hyperlinks contained on organizational websites in the academic field (universities) was based on a taxonomy-type classification making it possible to highlight the information and discursive dominants from which an organization makes itself visible. The hypothesis can therefore be seen to emerge from this taxonomy:

– similarities and regularities in terms of types of information, content valorization, communication strategies and similarities that make it possible to broadly characterize the organizational field considered (academic, healthcare, local authorities, etc.);

– differences in the qualification of information, or strategic priorities highlighted on the home page.

Before detailing the methodological approach that was developed, it is necessary to give some additional elements of contextualization. First, we will focus on the issue of classifications and taxonomies, especially in the digital and Web era. Second, we will situate our approach in relation to other classificatory approaches to hyperlinks in order to better understand their unique features.

In terms of content organization, the act of classification is an ancient act, and it constitutes in particular an emblematic form as a system for organizing documentary knowledge. We have chosen the term "taxonomy"[4] rather than "classification", referring in particular to the current use of this term to designate the organization of the content of digital resources (see, for example, Chu (2005)). Originally, the term "taxonomy" was dedicated to describing the classification of biological organisms, such as the *Systema Naturae* by Linnaeus (1768), which proposes a taxonomy of plant and animal life. While this foundational understanding of the term "taxonomy" continues to be used, and is even currently seeing a renewed interest[5], the field in which this term has been applied has significantly expanded (see, for example, Parrochia and Neuville (2014)). Generally speaking, Warner (2004) defines taxonomy as a system of labels constituting a hierarchical navigation system. Its specificity lies in the use of labels familiar to users so that they can find information by browsing the structured hierarchies. The structure also implies that the information is found in contexts or categories. Categorization is the process of dividing the world into groups of entities in which each is in some way similar to the others (Jacob 2004).

Nevertheless, there is not necessarily a consensus on what is behind the use of the term taxonomy, and a variety of divergent definitions have been given to it. Bruno Menon proposes an extensive definition, characterizing a taxonomy as "an organizational framework for digital resources of all kinds (and not only documentary [...]) intended to allow an orderly presentation and giving access to them by hypertext navigation" (Menon 2007, p. 23). In addition to the renewal of the taxonomic approach in one of its more appropriate fields of application, the systematics of life, it is important to note that the term taxonomy has gradually broadened considerably, first evoking the notion of a hierarchical classification system, then to any classificatory system, and finally to be regularly used to apply to digital content or in professional contexts. This is of particular interest to us here.

Another relevant differentiating element can be established in terms of the approach as such. In the configurational approaches developed in organization theory, notably under the impetus of Mintzberg (1982), the objective is to rely on methods of classification to grasp the complexity of the phenomena being studied.

---

4 Note that the two spellings "taxonomy" and "taxonomy" are admissible in the French. Here, we have chosen to use "taxonomy".

5 The file named "The renewal of taxonomy: modalities, effects, and practical issues" from the *Revue d'anthropologie des connaissances* 2013/2 (vol. 7, No. 2) uses a series of articles to illustrate the challenges and limits of the science of taxonomy and the initiatives taken since the end of the 1990s to overcome a "taxonomic handicap" in terms of knowledge and the surveying of biodiversity.

As such, we can distinguish between "typology" and "taxonomy": the former applies conceptual configurations a priori, while the latter applies empirical configurations a posteriori. In other words, "unlike typologies, taxonomies are based on an inductive approach, since the classes emerge from the data" (Borgès Da Silva 2013, p. 635). While here we do not take this approach proposed in organization theory literally, it nevertheless resonates quite well with the approach we have developed for a taxonomy of hyperlinks.

In general, taxonomy, as it is used today in many contexts, and in particular within business contexts, has become a relevant and effective content organization tool for several reasons: because it has been able to gain flexibility in terms of the notions of classes and relationships, because it has extracted itself from a relatively rigid hierarchical model, and finally because it emerges from contexts that it strives to order, as close as possible to the realities that form them. As Liquète and Kovacs (2013) note, classification is an "orderly arrangement of documents or content related to a space for making them available and accessing them"; classification is a "reference tool for a field, a science, a sector of activity [...] based on an intellectual activity of information processing", while "taxonomic approaches" involve the search for overall coherence, through gradually developing a partial and negotiated consensus between the actors representing the observed domain" (p. 18). This flexibility of content arrangements in relation to a localized approach to the content is perfectly suited to our problem of OWS hyperlinks.

Of course, the distortions that come with such an approach are real. Each classification approach is the result of a form of simplification that is carried out according to a series of objectives and criteria which are duly chosen. This is indeed an operation of translation (Goody 1977). The proposed taxonomic structure is therefore part of a given context and a given space-time, without being able to claim any universality.

In addition to these elements of generic framing on the issue of taxonomies and classifications, we will now look more specifically at what is happening in the works on the classification of hyperlinks, most of which are in English.

Since the late 1990s, web page classification studies have been developed (Almind and Ingwersen 1997; Cronin et al. 1998; Kleinberg 1999). At the beginning of the 2000s, hyperlink ranking methods emerged in a more specific way, which would mainly address the ranking of these links based on reasons for it to be placed between two websites. This process thus involved categorizing the links on the basis of the motivation, either explicit or assumed, for why a hyperlink would be placed. This motivation was then updated in two ways. Interviews with the authors of the web pages in question make it possible to identify and then codify their explicit motivation, that is to say, the reasons why they created a link (Park et al. 2002). Another way is to identify the supposed motivation, that is to say, the apparent intentions that can be identified for a corpus of links between sites, from the text of the link/target of the link.

On this basis, a good deal of research has been carried out on the websites of universities, which is of particular interest to us because of our field of application. In the academic field, and as part of an a posteriori categorization of motivations (supposed motivations), we may note in particular the works of Wilkinson et al. (2003) and Bar-Ilan (2004, 2005). These authors created an elaborate, multifaceted classification around the study of hyperlinks, considering that in the study of the possible reasons for links to be made between different academic websites, it is necessary to take into account not only the source and the target of the link, but also the link itself, as well as the environment of the link. This classification was later utilized by Payne and Thelwall (2008) as part of a broad and far-reaching study analyzing changes in the structure of academic links between universities in Great Britain, Australia and New Zealand.

In general, the works studying hyperlinks that use classificatory methods are interested in external links as well as inbound links (which act as citations). However, it should be noted that these classificatory approaches have declined to a certain extent in the last decade, being replaced in particular with approaches oriented toward big data to understand and visualize the dynamics of hyperlinks.

8.4. Presentation of the methodological approach

Our taxonomy-based approach to hyperlink classification has both similarities and significant differences to the methodologies mentioned above. To recall, the approach to classifying hyperlinks in the form of a taxonomy is part of the previously defined analysis framework, which we intend to apply to the academic field:

– OWS;

– home page of the OWS;

– lexical facet of internal hyperlinks (HLUs).

8.4.1. *Corpus of university websites*

To form our corpus initially, we relied on the list offered by the Ministry of Higher Education and Research, in XLS format[6]. This list offers 24 major institutions and 67 universities for which a certain amount of information is given (location, GPS coordinates, postal and telephone contact information, contractual group of membership, decree of creation, social media accounts, website URL address, etc.).

We made our first selection by selecting only the 67 universities as the reference corpus. This subset of 67 universities is associated with a typology that makes it possible to classify universities using an approach by discipline. In this case, the 67 universities are divided as follows:

– 18 multidisciplinary universities with no healthcare department;

– 26 multidisciplinary universities with a healthcare department;

– three scientific and/or medical universities;

– four tertiary and economics universities;

– eight tertiary universities in the letters and humanities;

– eight undefined universities.

To make up our sample, we opted for a random draw at first, in order to extract a sub-corpus of 14 universities, or about one-fifth of the initial corpus (specifically, 20.9%).

However, compared to this initial random draw, we have made some corrections in the margins in order to ensure the various categories presented above are represented to a certain degree. Thus, the final sample of 14 universities[7] contains:

– three multidisciplinary universities with no healthcare department;

– six multidisciplinary universities with a healthcare department;

– one tertiary and economics university;

---

6 Available at: www.enseignementsup-recherche.gouv.fr/cid88022/les-universites-francaises-et-les-grands-etablissements.html.

7 The final sample does not include a representative of scientific or medical universities, because their number was too small (3) compared to the percentage of universities that we selected (from 20% to 25%).

– two tertiary universities in the letters and humanities;

– two undefined universities.

The sample that has been formed (see Table 8.5 in the appendices in section 8.7) thus proves to be relatively balanced, without blatant over-representation of any one type of university with regard to the ministerial nomenclature[8].

8.4.2. *A semiodiscursive and taxonomic analysis of web pages*

Our methodological approach was based on two lines of exploration. First, we took screenshots of each of the home pages of the websites in our sample so as to determine the most notable elements, not only in terms of the HLUs that appeared to be dominant, but also in order to identify certain elements specific to the design of these home pages. This first corpus will then be the subject of a semiodiscursive analysis. For our second step, we proposed a taxonomic reading of home pages from a collection of HLUs on our sample of websites. The first analysis therefore aims to provide first contextualization elements at the scale of the screen-page. In practice, a taxonomic approach tends to "crush" certain semiotic characteristics related to the design of the link or through the prioritization of the elements on the screen. This first semiodiscursive analysis therefore has a function of supporting and highlighting prior to the taxonomic analysis. With this in mind, we have focused our attention on elements related to the logical organization and appropriation of the content of the home page, as suggested by Stockinger (2005).

As the second step, we have compiled a corpus of HLUs of the home pages of the corpus of websites. This collection was carried out using the WebtoolHub Link Extractor tool[9], specifying "Inbound" for the type of link. The links extracted have been retrieved in CSV format, and the text titles used as the anchors have been isolated, to form corpora of HLUs for each of the universities[10]. A manual verification process was also created, consisting of a comparison with the homepage of the website concerned, in order to verify the compliance of the collection with the identifiables of the HLU on the web page. The use of an automatic software tool effectively makes the detection of HLUs dependent on the technical structuring of

8 In the rest of the article, for the sake of objectivity and avoiding personal influence, we have chosen not to refer to universities by name. These universities have been numbered, and referenced by the numbers they are given.

9 Available at: https://www.webtoolhub.com/tn561364-link-extractor.aspx.

10 This collection procedure voluntarily excludes hypermedia-type links. Our initial methodological stance leads us to consider only the textual fragments immediately perceptible by the user of the site. We will return to the limits of this method in our conclusion.

the elements on the page, and significant differences can be found between one website to another. This manual verification phase therefore made it possible to possibly adjust the corpus to the scope of our approach.

Once the corpora were created, the HLUs were classified for each website by reviewing the structure of the taxonomy as it was previously established. As we will see in the discussion, this classification phase also made it possible to carry out some adaptations at the level of the classificatory structure, particularly with the goal of simplification. Finally, the taxonomy consists of 14 classes, presented in Table 8.1.

Classes	Definition
Research	Research-related activities
Education	Education-related activities
Partnerships/transfer/valorization	University public partnerships (excluding internationally)
International	International relations and politics of the university
Student and campus life	Miscellaneous information related to student life on campus
Organization	Operations, strategy, components, presentation, etc.
News	Content of a time-sensitive or temporary nature
Digital services	Access to identified services accessible online (directory, etc.)
Recruiting	Job offers, recruiting method (excluding education)
Access	Geographical or Web access notices (navigation)
Contact	Forwarding to a contact
Regulatory aspects	Reference to regulatory notices or legal information
Web access	Authentication procedure (without mention of the associated service)
User profiles	Referral to a specific user profile (category or language)

Table 8.1. *List of classes in the HLU taxonomy*

This taxonomy was then used to classify the different HLUs collected on the fourteen home pages of our sample of websites. Note that during this classification process, for each HLU, its occurrence of presence was also recorded (from 1 to n) on the home page under analysis. The systematic consideration of the occurrence of each HLU makes it possible, among other things, to bring to light HLU redundancy strategies on the same page, which are related to choices made for highlighting certain topics.

The classification was carried out using a relatively fluid approach, first due to our experience with this taxonomy and this field of academic websites, and also due to a certain form of standardization of digital discourse through the HLU. We will come back to this during the presentation and discussion of the results. Finally, very few HLUs were unable to be classified, and the corpus that was formed, initially segmented by university and then assessed comprehensively, was the subject of quantitative processing in Excel, in particular to generate profiles of infocommunication. A qualitative look was also taken at the textual statements in order to highlight original choices or the use of interesting stylistic effects.

8.5. Primary results

As previously noted, two types of results will be given. First, we will provide the elements of the results after an analysis of the design of the home page of the sites in our corpus, particularly targeting the main menu bars proposed. In a second step, we will propose a series of results after the study of the HLU corpora collected on these same home pages.

8.5.1. *Analysis of the main menus of the home pages*

The home pages of the websites of our sample of universities have a number of similarities in their composition and structuring of content. For instance, an image carousel was used on 11 websites, which is almost 80% of our corpus. Three to seven types of current events are displayed in this carousel, the vast majority of which follow a horizontal reading format (only one university chose vertical scrolling). As for the other presentation choices (the minority), two universities opted for a still image, another for a looped video. Only one university did not use a strong iconic presentation. We can therefore see the place that the image holds in these home pages, and in particular, the use of the carousel format.

Moving on to the main menu bar (i.e. the one providing access to the most important content of the site), we can make a number of observations. First, what we identify as the main menu bar is always located in the upper half of the home page, and usually quite near the top. It also uses a horizontal and left-to-right reading direction. This main menu bar can be supplemented by secondary menu bars, providing additional navigation options for users, to information specific to user profiles (type of user – high school student, professional – or to change language), to tools (directories, digital workspace, internal search engines, etc.), etc. Figure 8.4 gives an illustration of a spatialized hierarchy of menus.

In this case, it is the menu bar "Home – Education – Research – Student life – International – University – Libraries" that we consider as the main menu bar.

Figure 8.4. *Example of menu bars (main/secondary). For a color version of this figure, see www.iste.co.uk/massou/analyzing.zip*

The number of text entries included on these menu bars varies between four and eight (with an average of six terms). On the menu bars of the 14 home pages of our sample, unsurprisingly, a triptych emerges recurrently: these are the terms "*Formation*" (Education), "*Recherche*" (Research) and "*Université*" (University) (with the variant "The University"). Looking at the order in which these terms appear, the "University" entry is most frequently the top ranked (in eight out of 14 cases), with the "Education" entry receiving the top ranking in four out of 14 cases. The "Education" entry most frequently receives the second place ranking (in seven out of 14 cases), while "Research" is ranked second in four out of 14 cases. Without spending too long on this quick analysis, we should note two additional elements: "Research" is never ranked at the first place; if "University" does not rank at the top, it will then be near the end of the menu bar. Inside this classic configuration of the information given through these three entries, the ordering choices can nonetheless be indicative of certain prioritizations. In addition to these three most common terms, others are also in frequent use among these menu bars: the terms "International" (10 cases out of 14) and "Campus" – or "*Vie des campus*" (Campus Life) – (eight cases out of 14).

These five terms alone represent 68% of the corpus containing all the terms collected on the menu bar[11], but which vary in terms of the order in which they appear. Figure 8.5 summarizes the positioning variations of these five key themes (from the left – first place ranking – TO right – *n*th place ranking).

This "standard" configuration, formed around these five terms, thus applies to an overwhelming majority (13 out of 14 universities), with only one having chosen a different type of access to the primary content. In this particular case, the menu bar is located on the left, vertically, and is structured around the following keywords: "*Explorez...*" (Explore...)/"*Vous êtes...*" "(You are)..."/"*Accès directs...*" (Direct access...)/"FR-EN", and the magnifying glass symbol to represent the search function. These text entries, opened by using an ellipsis, allow for a more classic structuring to take place in the second step: under the term "Explore ...", for example, we find the categories "*Université*" (University), "*Formation*" (Education), "*Recherche et valorisation*" (Research and valorization), "International", "Campus" and "*Patrimoine et culture*" (Heritage and culture). This therefore includes the (original) choice of an ellipsis, an initial mystery that is revealed as soon as we hover over the item in question.

Finally, we will focus on one last element: references to social networks. All the universities in our sample offer a list of social networks (between four and eight). The four-star entries among these links, offered almost methodically, are Facebook, Twitter, Instagram and YouTube. LinkedIn is mentioned in eight out of 14 pages, and the option to subscribe to RSS feeds is given in five pages. Much less frequently (with one occurrence each), ResearchGate, Flickr and DailyMotion are mentioned. Only one university offers a link to its own social network, one for its Alumni. However, aside from this widespread inclusion of social networks, there is an important difference in the positioning of the corresponding logos. For half of the pages in our sample, these logos are located at the top of the page, so they are visible right away. The others are positioned at the bottom of the page, which requires scrolling down the page to reach them. Thus, their visibility is not identical.

Obviously, these few elements for analysis only provide a summarial overview, which does not represent the semiotic breadth of the home page, and beyond that, of the website for which it is a key element.

---

11 Others appear much less frequently in this main menu bar: for example, "Libraries" (three cases out of 14 cases) or "Orientation" (three cases out of 14 cases). Finally, in isolated cases, terms such as "Covid-19" (related to current events), "Foundation"/"Make a donation", "Company", etc., may appear.

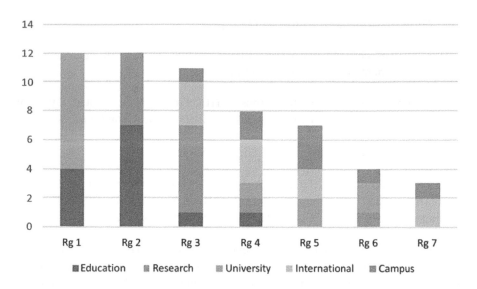

Figure 8.5. *Classification of themes in order of appearance in the main menu bar. For a color version of this figure, see www.iste.co.uk/massou/analyzing.zip*

Nevertheless, this first level of reading makes it possible to bring to light certain trends in the communication strategies of universities, which vary between standardization and attempts to stand out. For all universities, the use of an image carousel on many home pages provides very important placement in practice to current events, treated here in visual form, but also presented through textual and illustrated sections, which are usually found later on the page.

In addition to these dynamic and well-anchored elements on the home pages, the main menu bar positions the university's missions and the organization itself through its HLU, thus primarily enhancing its paratextual and textual functions (Stockinger 2005). Finally, the rebound effect toward social networks (especially with the recurrence of the four most popular ones) now appears to have been activated for all the sites. Here, we can observe very similar communication strategies on all the sites within our corpus. However, at a finer level, it is interesting to also note peculiarities in the design choices or in the order of the menu bar elements, thus making for subtle differences and positioning effects, beyond the observable similarities. We will explore this further with an analysis of the HLUs extracted from these different pages.

8.5.2. *Generic approach to the HLU corpus*

This involves carrying out a second-level reading through the aggregation of information elements scattered throughout the page.

Let us first briefly describe the corpus of HLUs that was constituted: a total of 1,615 HLUs (a figure which increases to 2,106 when combined with the occurrences) were collected on all the sites of our sample and classified, which corresponds to an average of about 115 HLUs per homepage.

There are significant differences from one university to another. In fact, the minimum recorded on a homepage is 75 HLUs with occurrences, while the maximum recorded for a page is 246 HLUs with occurrences (Table 8.2).

This choice to take into account two levels of uses of the HLUs (singular flexing and weighted flexing by occurrences) thus makes it possible to note two types of editorial choices, and consequently, Web communications that emerge. Indeed, some home pages have a very low HLU redundancy rate on their home page (the minimum HLU redundancy rate is 1.01, which for the page analyzed – university 8 – is 90 HLUs without occurrences and 91 HLUs with occurrences). On the contrary, others would broadly increase the presence of their HLUs using a principle of repetition, such as by repeating the elements of the main menus at the top of the page and at the bottom of the page (a maximum HLU redundancy rate of 1.76, which for the page analyzed – page 12 – is 75 HLUs without occurrences and 132 HLUs with occurrences).

Between these two extremes, intermediate repetition rates can be found which correspond to a valuation of certain classes or of certain terms. In total, five out of 14 universities (which is about one-third of our sample) have a repetition rate of more than 50% of their HLU corpus (a repetition rate of more than 1.5); moreover, four out of 14 universities have a repetition rate for their HLUs of less than 10% (i.e. a repetition rate of less than 1.1). We will come back to this during our discussion on these effects of the redundancy or non-redundancy of information.

The entirety of this corpus of HLUs is of course very diverse with regard to the terms from which it is made. Nevertheless, some HLUs stand out as being "standardized", present on almost all the home pages examined. These HLUs may be connected to the primary missions of the university (Education, Research, International), the institutional aspects (University, Foundation), current situations or ongoing events (such as Covid-19), or they may provide practical functionalities (Contact, Access). In light of this reading, the "education" HLU (with this wording, or given in many other ways: "continuing education", "work-linked training", "initial training", "lifelong learning", but also "our training offer", "training catalogue", etc.) appears as the dominant meta-HLU in this corpus (91 occurrences, if we take into account the multiple HLUs formed from "education"). The HLUs derived from the term "Research", while well represented, nevertheless remain below this figure (19 occurrences for the HLU "Research" and 29 for HLU formed around the term "research" – such as "Valorization of research", "Research teams", etc.).

The term "News" (mostly in the plural in French, *actualités*) that is used for forming different HLUs (*"Actualités"* [News], *"Actualités internationales"* [International news], *"Toutes nos actualités"* [All our news], etc.) is listed 41 times, which makes it the second most frequent keyword of the corpus. We note that in this register of current events, the relatively high presence of a contextual keyword: "Covid-19" identified nine times (for its part, the term "Coronavirus" has one single occurrence). In the HLUs in connection with functionalities, which could be called HLU "tools", we note the term "Access", noted 17 times in reuses (primarily the HLUs *"Accs"* [Access], *"Plan d'accès"* [Access Plan] or *"Plans d'accès"* [Access Plans] or the term "Contact", with 21 occurrences covering different types of HLUs ["Contact"/"Contacts", *"Nous contacter"* [Contact us], *"Contactez-nous"* [How to contact us], etc.).

Finally, to close this quick overview of this corpus of HLUs, we may note the significant presence of HLUs built around certain terms, also referring to a particular position of the university in relation to its environment. These are the HLUs derived from the term *"Entreprise"* (Company) (*"Entreprise"*, Company, *"Entreprises partenaires"*, Partner companies, *"Entrepreneuriat étudiant"*, Student entrepreneurship, etc.) for which 25 occurrences can be identified. The term "Foundation" is also present in HLUs, with 13 occurrences. Finally, even though the term "Alumni" has a relatively low occurrence rate (nine times), the term appears on a number of home pages of our corpus.

In addition, more in-depth textual analyses[12] could be conducted on this corpus, but this first reading of the HLU corpus nevertheless offers some noteworthy trends within the dominant HLUs.

---

12 Detailed processing is being carried out on this corpus.

	U1	U2	U3	U4	U5	U6	U7	U8	U9	U10	U11	U12	U13	U14	Total
HLUs without occurrences	174	173	107	88	125	97	67	90	85	74	225	75	70	165	1,615
HLUs with occurrences	220	218	181	116	142	170	104	91	93	126	246	132	75	192	2,106
Repetition rate	1.26	1.26	1.69	1.32	1.14	1.75	1.55	1.01	1.09	1.70	1.09	1.76	1.07	1.16	–

Table 8.2. *Distribution of HLUs by university*

8.5.3. *Informational profiles from the taxonomy of the HLUs*

Turning our interest to a reading of Web interfaces made based on the taxonomy classifications, several observations can be highlighted. Table 8.3 gives the overall distribution of HLUs (with and without occurrences) by class.

Table 8.6 in appendix 2 (section 8.7) gives the detailed distribution by university, of the HLUs within the different classes of the taxonomy.

From these elements, we can focus on the dominant classes at rank 1 (Figure 8.6), as emerges from the positions identified on each university and based on the number of HLUs with occurrences[13].

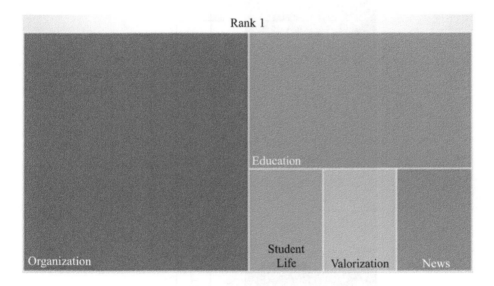

Figure 8.6. *Presentation of the dominant classes of HLU with rank 1 (in percentage of inclusion). For a color version of this figure, see www.iste.co.uk/massou/analyzing.zip*

---

13 We choose to give preference to HLUs with occurrences because we consider that the repetitions of HLUs are significant in determining the importance that is given to them. However, we note that there are relatively few differences in classification if we observe the dominant classes with the HLUs without occurrences (e.g. three inversions/14 between ranks 1 and 2).

	HLUs without occurrences	HLUs with occurrences
Total	1,615	2,106
User profiles	109	138
Regulatory aspects	43	46
Contact	33	39
Access	102	115
Recruiting	35	53
Digital services	56	85
News	225	287
Organization	284	382
Student life/campus	162	226
International	84	113
Transfer/valorization	98	114
Education	220	289
Research	164	219

Table 8.3. *Distribution of all HLUs by class*

The "Organization" class is the most represented class in HLUs for half of the university sites, and it also retains a very strong presence in rank 2 where it still represents almost a third of universities. The "Education" class, on the other hand, is dominant in almost one third of the sites in our sample. Finally, the classes "Student life", "Valorization" and "News" are dominant each time only in a university case, which can also be the marker of different communicational choices. Finally, it should be noted that the "Research" class, which is absent in this ranking, is not a majority class in the top 3 of the dominant classes, regardless of the university, which is consistent with what we have observed in the main menu bars.

We find the weight of this institutional-type communication in the radar representations made for each of the university sites and on all HLU classes (with occurrences). A number of pages present similar profiles, where we see the dominant place occupied by the class "Organization", and the other themes that appear are more marginal (Figure 8.7).

Other profiles have also emerged, profiles in which the placement of the "Education" class is important, next to other dimensions ("Organization" and "News", in the cases of Figure 8.8). We classify these profiles as "mixed", though they provide an important representation of educational aspects in all cases. It should also be noted that only one university (out of the 14 studied) shows the "Research" class in a relatively prominent light.

Finally, we will mention two relatively atypical profiles compared to all the visualizations (Figure 8.9). The first one, next to conventionally represented dimensions ("Organization" and "News"), emphasizes the "Access" part. In this case, the home page of this site offers many HLUs related to the navigation features of the site, geographical access points, as well as accessibility. A second page proves to be atypical, proposing a largely dominant class oriented toward valorization and openness to society. The enunciation made on the homepage through the many HLUs that make it up (this university also has the largest number of HLUs) is quite different with regard to the content structuring generally observed in our sample set.

These visualizations in the form of radar displays, based on weighting the different classes of the taxonomy for each university, make it possible to create "silhouettes" for each university and to highlight overall trends: the role of the website in the "corporate" communication of the institution, the importance communications oriented toward education and therefore toward students (or future students), the "research" positioning of non-dominant universities through the institutional website. Nevertheless, alongside these relatively consensual approaches, some editorial choices also emerge, which can be read through the taxonomy, and which stand out from these general trends and mark unique strategies, as in the case of university 11.

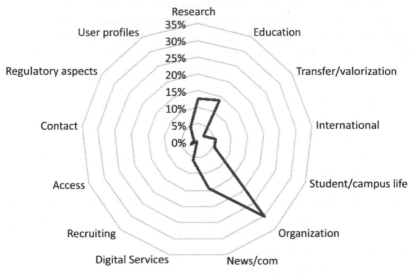

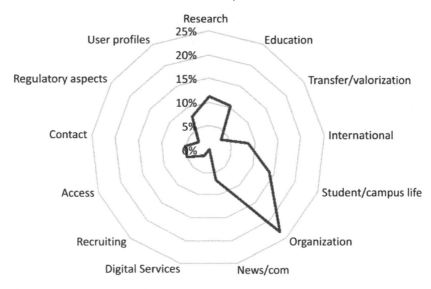

Figure 8.7. *"Institutional communication" profile from two universities. For a color version of this figure, see www.iste.co.uk/massou/analyzing.zip*

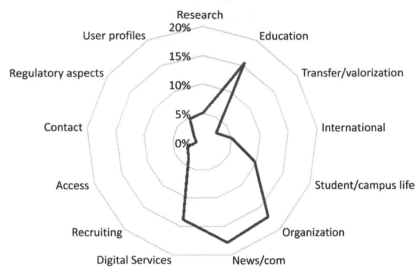

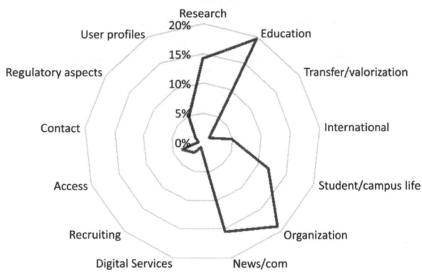

Figure 8.8. *Mixed profiles with "Education". For a color version of this figure, see www.iste.co.uk/massou/analyzing.zip*

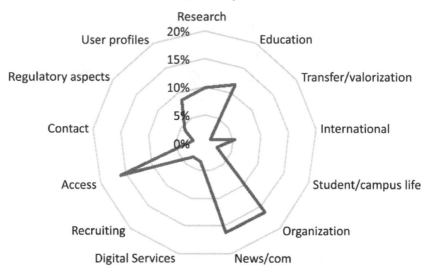

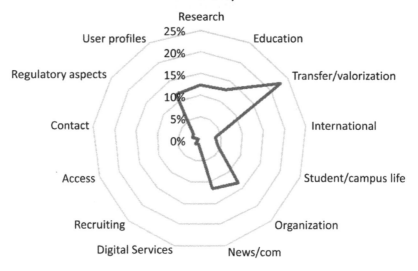

Figure 8.9. *Atypical profiles. For a color version of this figure, see www.iste.co.uk/massou/analyzing.zip*

8.5.4. *A closer look at a class: "User profiles"*

Finally, we will end with a focus on one of the classes of the taxonomy, the "User Profiles" class. In the limited space of this chapter, we cannot give a complete overview of the composition and representation of the 14 classes of the taxonomy. We have chosen to focus our attention on the "User Profiles" class, because it is emblematic of one of the notable developments that we have identified on the home pages of universities: the near universal targeting of content toward user profiles which, conversely, have become very significantly diversified.

We identified that content profiling on the basis of user types was done on the home pages of 13 out of 14 universities, whether in the form of a language profile or a profile related to the user's situation (students, companies, journalists, etc.). In this class, which contains 130 HLUs with occurrences, we performed a grouping of HLUs in order to see the typical user profiles more clearly. These re-groupings allow for the formal variations used to be smoothed to a certain extent, using elements such as the choice of whether or not to use inclusive language, the management of singular/plural inflections[14], personalized and unique forms of addressing the user[15] ("You are a high school student" versus "I am a high school student"), etc. This segmentation into 18 profiles, produced by bringing together semantically similar HLUs, brings out a variety of situations encountered, and beyond this diversity, the types of users who are favored the most (Figure 8.10).

Three user profiles stand out in particular: the profiles of "*Étudiant*" (Student) (13.8%), "*Langues*" (Languages) (13.8%) and "*Entreprise*" (Company) (12.3%). We have chosen to treat the "Foreign student" profile separately (8.5%), so as to highlight the consideration for the international, but if we aggregate these elements with the general "Student" profile, we obtain 22% of our corpus of HLUs, which makes it the most represented category of user. The linguistic area is also widely present, which is not surprising; perhaps more surprising is the communication oriented toward companies and partnerships, which are well represented in our corpus.

Beyond these somewhat more dominant profiles, we can also note the diversity of the profiles of targeted users (journalists, high school students, alumni, adults returning to study, etc.). On the other hand, there does not appear to be a particularly strong presence for researchers and teacher-researchers, including internationally.

---

14 These examples correspond to specific aspects of the French language.

15 We have therefore chosen to keep "You are" as a full subcategory, as a "tool" profile, thus allowing it to point to a type of user.

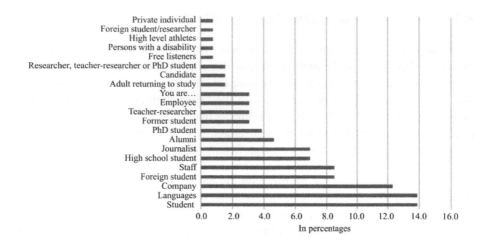

Figure 8.10. *Distribution of types of targeted users. For a color version of this figure, see www.iste.co.uk/massou/analyzing.zip*

Beyond this comprehensive reading of the entire corpus of HLUs of this class, it is also interesting to propose a university view, that is, a view that identifies the number of universities mentioning the user profile identified in one form or another. Table 8.4 echoes this other reading.

	Number of HLUs (with occurrences)	Number of universities involved
Student	18	11
Languages	18	9
Company	16	10
Foreign student	11	7
Personnel	11	9
High school student	9	6
Journalist	9	6
Alumni	6	4
PhD student	5	4
Former student	4	3
Teacher-researcher	4	4

Employee	4	3
You are...	4	4
Adult returning to study	2	2
Candidate	2	1
Researcher, teacher-researcher or doctoral student	2	1
Auditing students	1	1
Disabled persons	1	1
High-level athletes	1	1
Foreign students/researchers	1	1
Individual	1	1

Table 8.4. *User profiles by HLU and by university*

This reading generally confirms the trends observed with the analysis of the HLUs, namely a trend toward the generalization of certain profiles (students, companies, languages, as well as staff) and in addition, a greater diversity and dispersion of other, more varied user profiles (such as the mixed profile of "researcher, research teacher or doctoral student"), or more marginal ("free editors", "private individual").

8.6. Conclusion

We cannot present the entirety of the results generated from the exploitation of these data here, whether in their original form (as HLUs) or through the classification made. Nevertheless, several aspects stand out as prime subjects for discussion.

Thus, from a methodological point of view, we used a pre-defined and previously used approach. The work carried out here has allowed us to highlight the relative stability of the structure of the taxonomy. The most significant modification that had to be made was a decrease in the number of classes (from 24 to 14 classes), through the merging of separate classes into single classes. This simplification makes it possible to reduce the dispersion of HLUs during classification, and therefore to cause the trends appear more clearly in the construction of info-communication strategies. However, all classification approaches come with some distortion, and our approach is no exception: we had to make certain trade-offs to link certain HLUs to one class and not to another (e.g. should an HLU named

"Research News" be classified in "Research" or "News"?). These difficulties and potential distortions owe to the situational and pragmatic approach that was taken.

The proposed taxonomy makes it possible to carry out a thematic analysis of content on the basis of the visible text element of hyperlinks and, from this reading, to examine certain communicational choices that can be found on the home pages of university websites. As we have noted previously, a number of trends are emerging, in the form of the smoothing of interfaces and standardization, and on the other hand, through the emergence (in a minority of cases) of strategies intended to stand out. Whether in the design of interfaces, in the structuring of information or in the choice of terms as embodied through the HLUs, the home pages of university websites have become homogenized (or even professionalized...), and often offer similar "ways of doing things", while fitting in with the institution's graphic universe but also with the current era (place of social networks). For some, this can almost be seen as a form of digital marketing. These normalization effects can also be observed in the choice of HLUs. These have come to include textual smoothing effects and a consensus on terminology, which represent a significant change compared to the case studies that we conducted in the early 2010s (Pine Forest et al. 2011; Pinède and Reymond 2016). Many HLUs are common among all the pages of our sample ("education", "research", "contact", to name just a few). These normalization effects need to be quantified and analyzed more precisely in order to better measure the extent and the reasons behind this smoothing of information. Of course, we should not underestimate the weight of the technical configuration (the use of CMS software that is the same among several universities in these normalization effects, especially in terms of page design). The choice to examine the same organizational sphere with a cultural anchor (the French academic world) also partly explains the similarities that were observed.

However, beyond these visible trends toward standardization, the analysis of the classes and their weighting, the projection of these with a visualization in the form of radar allows for thematic profiles to emerge (profiles oriented toward "Institutional Communication", mixed profiles with a strong "Education" dimension or atypical profile focused on an opening oriented toward valorization and dissemination). These profiles can reveal trends in communication strategies, but this requires additional investigations. An analysis that only covers interfaces and uses a narrow and incomplete frame of analysis does not allow us to determine whether such constructions are deliberate or more accidental. It would therefore be necessary to confront these elements with an in-depth study of the organizational contexts concerned, as well as with the designers of the sites, the communication managers or the political decision-makers of the university.

The reading of Web interfaces that we propose here thus offers original semantic elements of readability on the thematic profiles identifiable on the homepage of organizations, such as universities. By integrating them into a contextualized and hybrid analysis framework (e.g. interface design, speeches of key stakeholders – designers, politicians, users), it will be able to acquire the depth needed to allow for an analysis that spans quantitative and qualitative considerations, to be applied to the Web communication strategies of universities.

8.7. Appendices

Universities used in the corpus	Type of university
University 1 (U1)	Multidisciplinary university with a healthcare department
University 2 (U2)	Tertiary university – letters and humanities
University 3 (U3)	Not defined
University 4 (U4)	Multidisciplinary university with a healthcare department
University 5 (U5)	Tertiary university – letters and humanities
University 6 (U6)	Multidisciplinary university with no healthcare department
University 7 (U7)	Multidisciplinary university with a healthcare department
University 8 (U8)	Multidisciplinary university with a healthcare department
University 9 (U9)	Multidisciplinary university with no healthcare department
University 10 (U10)	Not defined
University 11 (U11)	Multidisciplinary university with a healthcare department
University 12 (U12)	Multidisciplinary university with no healthcare department
University 13 (U13)	Tertiary university – law and economy

Table 8.5. *Appendix 1 – profile of universities from the corpus*

	U1	U1	U2	U2	U3	U3	U4	U4	U5	U5
	HLU without occurrences	HLU with occurrences	HLU without occurrences	HLU with occurrences	HLU without occurrences	HLU with occurrences	HLU without occurrences	HLU with occurrences	HLU without occurrences	HLU with occurrences
User profiles	10	10	5	10	11	20	7	9	7	7
Regulatory aspects	4	4	4	4	5	5	3	3	2	2
Contact	2	2	2	2	4	5	3	6	1	1
Access	6	6	5	5	7	15	6	6	5	5
Recruiting	6	8	1	1	1	2	2	2	2	3
Digital services	15	30	9	13	7	10	0	0	1	1
News	35	39	27	32	24	27	7	8	13	22
Organization	34	38	40	66	14	30	19	27	25	27
Student/campus life	17	21	11	11	10	18	12	16	16	17
International	8	11	11	12	2	4	7	10	7	7
Transfer/valorization	6	6	4	5	4	8	4	4	2	2
Education	22	34	29	30	9	20	8	12	25	28
Research	9	11	25	27	9	17	10	13	19	20

	U6 HLU without occurrences	U6 HLU with occurrences	U7 HLU without occurrences	U7 HLU with occurrences	U8 HLU without occurrences	U8 HLU with occurrences	U9 HLU without occurrences	U9 HLU with occurrences	U10 HLU without occurrences	U10 HLU with occurrences
User profiles	7	7	6	6	6	6	8	8	0	0
Regulatory aspects	1	1	3	3	5	5	4	4	3	4
Contact	1	1	2	3	5	5	2	2	3	3
Access	13	13	11	11	10	10	12	15	2	3
Recruiting	4	7	2	4	2	2	2	3	2	4
Digital services	4	8	0	0	2	2	3	3	2	3
News	13	26	5	5	3	4	11	15	19	23
Organization	10	17	12	23	16	16	15	15	13	26
Student/campus life	12	26	5	9	6	6	2	2	11	22
International	7	14	5	8	11	11	5	5	1	2
Transfer/valorization	3	5	0	0	0	0	1	1	2	4
Education	13	26	7	13	16	16	11	11	8	16
Research	9	19	9	19	8	8	9	9	8	16

		Research	Education	Transfer/ valorization	International	Student/ campus life	Organization	News	Digital services	Recruiting	Access	Contact	Regulatory aspects	User profiles
U11	HLU without occurrences	29	32	55	6	11	31	28	3	4	1	4	4	17
	HLU with occurrences	31	32	56	9	11	33	29	3	4	1	4	4	29
U12	HLU without occurrences	7	8	5	5	12	5	13	2	3	12	1	1	1
	HLU without occurrences	14	18	10	10	24	10	17	4	6	13	2	2	2
U13	HLU with occurrences	6	12	1	6	10	6	10	4	1	3	2	2	7
	HLU with occurrences	6	12	1	6	12	7	10	4	2	3	2	3	7
U14	HLU without occurrences	7	20	11	3	27	44	17	4	3	9	1	2	17
	HLU with occurrences	9	21	12	4	31	47	30	4	5	9	1	2	17

Table 8.6. Appendix 2 – HLUs classified by university

8.8. References

Algava E., Belghith F., Bideault M., Calmand J., Corre F., Dalous J-P., David C., Demongeot A., Dixte C., Enock Levi T. (2016). L'état de l'Enseignement supérieur et de la Recherche en France. 50 indicateurs, no. 9, juin [Online]. Available at: http://www.epsilon.insee.fr/jspui/bitstream/1/54197/1/SIES_Etat_2016_9.pdf.

Almind, T.C. and Ingwersen, P. (1997). Informetric analyses on the World Wide Web: Methodological approaches to Webometrics. *Journal of Documentation*, 53(4), 404–426.

Angé, C. (ed.) (2015). *Les objets hypertextuels. Pratiques et usages hypermédiatiques*. ISTE Editions, London.

Balpe, J.-P., Lelu, A., Saleh, I. (1995). *Hypertextes et hypermédias*. Hermès, Paris.

BarIlan, J. (2004). A microscopic link analysis of academic institutions within a country – The case of Israel. *Scientometrics*, 59(3), 391–403.

BarIlan, J. (2005). What do we know about links and linking? A framework for studying links in academic environments. *Information Processing and Management*, 41(4), 973–986.

Barats, C. (2020). Management et évaluation de l'enseignement supérieur dans les années 2000. *Quaderni*, 99–100, 69–80.

Barats, C., Bouchard, J., Haakenstaad, A. (eds) (2018). *Faire et dire l'évaluation. L'enseignement supérieur et la recherche conquis par la performance*. Presses des Mines, Paris.

Björneborn, L. and Ingwersen, P. (2004). Toward a basic framework for Webometrics. *Journal of the American Society for Information Science and Technology*, 55(14), 1216–1227.

Bonhomme, M. and Stalder, P. (2006). Analyse sémiolinguistique des pages d'accueil des sites politiques suisses sur Internet. *Mots. Les langages du politique*, 80, 11–23.

Borgès Da Silva, R. (2013). Taxonomie et typologie : est-ce vraiment des synonymes ? *Santé Publique*, 25(5), 633–637.

Bouchard, J. (2013). Les classements d'établissements d'enseignement supérieur et de recherche : des miroirs déformants aux instruments de régulation. *Questions de communication*, 23, 175–196.

Brügger, N. (2009). Website history and the website as an object of study. *New Media & Society*, 11(1–2), 115–132.

Bullich, V. (2018). La "plateformisation" de la formation. *Distances et médiations des savoirs* [Online]. Available on https://journals.openedition.org/dms/2096.

Chu, H. (2005). Taxonomy of in linking Web entities: What does it imply for web metric research? *Library & Information Sciences Research*, 27, 8–27.

Clément, J. (2000). Hypertexte et complexité. *Études françaises*, 36(2), 39–57.

Cronin, B., Snyder, H.W., Rosenbaum, H., Martinson, A., Callahan, E. (1998). Invoked on the web. *Journal of the American Society of Information Science*, 49(14), 1319–1328.

Davallon, J. and Jeanneret, Y. (2004). La fausse évidence du lien hypertexte. *Communication et langages*, 140, 43–54.

Goody, J. (1977). *La raison graphique. La domestication de la pensée sauvage*. Éditions de Minuit, Paris.

Jacob, E.K. (2004). Classification and categorization: A difference that makes a difference. *Library Trends*, 52, 515–540.

Jeanneret, Y. and Souchier, E. (2005). L'énonciation éditoriale dans les écrits d'écran. *Communication et Langages*, 145, 3–15.

Kleinberg, J. (1999). Authorative sources in a hyperlinked environment. *Journal of the ACM*, 46(5), 604–632.

Linnaeus (1768). *Systema naturae per regna tria naturae, secundum classes, ordines, genera, species, cum characteribus, differentiis, synonymis, locis* (12 ed.). Laurentius Salvius, Stockholm.

Liquète, V. and Kovacs, S. (eds) (2013). Classer, penser, contrôler. *Hermès, La Revue*, 66.

Maingueneau, D. (2013). *Analyser les textes de communication*. Armand Colin, Paris.

Menon, B. (2007). Les langages documentaires. *Documentaliste – Sciences de l'information*, 44(1), 18–28.

Mercier, A. (2013). Classer, marchandiser et manager : quel idéal de l'Université opposer aux dérives en cours ? *Questions de communication*, 24, 125–144.

Mintzberg, H. (1982). *Structure et dynamique des organisations*. Eyrolles, Paris.

Musselin, C. (2014). Le changement dans les organisations : l'évolution des universités. *Administration & Éducation*, 143(3), 43–51.

Nielsen, J. and Tahir, M. (2002). *L'art de la page d'accueil*. Eyrolles, Paris.

Park, H.W., Barnett, G.A., Nam, I. (2002). Hyperlink affiliation network structure of top web sites: Examining affiliates with hyperlink in Korea. *Journal of American Society for Information Science and Technology*, 53(7), 592–601.

Parrochia, D. and Neuville, P. (2014). *Taxinomie et réalité*. ISTE Editions, London.

Payne, N. and Thelwall, M. (2008). Do academic link types change over time? *Journal of Documentation*, 64(5), 707–720.

Pinède, N. (2018). Du site web aux identités numériques organisationnelles : proposition d'un modèle d'analyse. *Questions de communication*, 34, 75–94.

Pinède N. and Reymond, D. (2013). Classer les sites web organisationnels. Une approche taxonomique des liens hypertextes. *Hermès, La revue*, 66, 181–188.

Pinède N. and Reymond, D. (2016). Améliorer la lecture du Web : synthèse informationnelle des interfaces web. In *Des usages aux pratiques : le web a-t-il un sens ?*, Riccio, P.-M., Vidal, G., Bautier, R. (eds). Presses universitaires de Bordeaux, Pessac.

Pinède, N., Reymond, D., Le Blanc, B., Lespinet-Najib, V. (2011). Terminologie hypertexte. Dynamique temporelle d'une taxonomie. In *14ème colloque international sur le Document Electronique CIDE*. Rabat, 98–110.

Rastier, F. (2001). Glossaire-index des notions. In *Arts et sciences du texte*, Rastier, F. (ed.). Presses Universitaires de France, Paris.

Souchier, E. (1998). L'image du texte pour une théorie de l'énonciation éditoriale. *Les cahiers de médiologie*, 2(6), 137–145.

Souchier, E., Jeanneret, Y., Le Marec, J. (eds) (2003). *Lire, écrire, récrire. Objets, signes et pratiques des médias informatisés*. Bibliothèque publique d'information, Paris.

Stockinger, P. (2005). *Les sites web. Conception, description et évaluation*. Hermès-Lavoisier, Paris.

Warner, A.J. (2004). Information architecture and vocabularies for "browse" and "search". In *Information Architecture: Designing Information Environments for Purpose*, Gilchrist, A., Mahon, B. (eds). Facet Publishing, London.

Wilkinson, D., Harries, G., Thelwall, M., Price, L. (2003). Motivations for academic web site interlinking: Evidence for the Web as a novel source of information on informal scholarly communication. *Journal of Information Science*, 29(1), 49–56.

9

The Documediality of Cross-border Organizations

Marie-Hélène HERMAND

MICA, Université Bordeaux Montaigne, Pessac, France

9.1. Introduction

This chapter is focused on the valorization of hybrid organizations on the Web, specifically organizations that bring together people and entities located in border regions and grouped together for the purpose of cooperation. These organizations – which can be institutional, economic, educational or associative – create spaces for meeting, interaction and where tensions or competition can even sometimes occur. Particularly in the areas of strategies and mechanisms of mutual influence, they build specific semantic universes around major issues that are shared on both sides of national borders (such as education, health and tourism) or that cannot be envisioned at a strictly national scale (such as cross-border labor, environmental issues, mobility and migration).

Cross-border organizations embody a major contemporary paradox: in a globalized world, border dynamics (movement, openness, control, closure) are at the heart of all crises (security dynamics during attacks, repressive dynamics during the migration crisis, selective dynamics during health emergencies). That is why the border territories and the entities that allow them to operate are at the heart of the concerns of many researchers in the humanities and social sciences (Considère and Perrin 2017; Bazin and Perron 2018) and, more generally, of various social actors (political, economic, scientific, citizens) involved at the cross-border level (Borders Forum, 2020).

Analyzing Websites,
coordinated by Luc MASSOU, Patrick MPONDO-DICKA and Nathalie PINÈDE.
© ISTE Ltd 2023.

Structuring the communicational analysis of these hybrid organizations is both necessary and particularly interesting, as this involves not only continuing to delve into the interconnected relations between territories and the media (Raoul 2020) but also addresses the concept of the intermediate public space (Cottereau 1992) so as to better understand the transitions, overlaps, or transformations of collective representations that are thoroughly anchored in the collective imaginary.

The concept of public space makes it possible to describe the collective imaginary of Europe (as this concept was socio-historically located and created there), but also – potentially and proceeding carefully – other imaginaries in recomposition, such as in Africa (Fofana 2015) or in Asia (Gaubatz 2019). As spaces of proximity transition into public space, intermediate public spaces are likely to be populated by public debate and politics. For them to exist, there must be a shared interest in the conditions of "living together", combined with an intervention in the course of the state of affairs in order to guarantee acceptable conditions for coexistence (Quéré and Cottereau 2003, pp. 366–374). What we are trying to understand here are the modalities of how this particular imaginary is created outside the standard framework.

By observing the communication of cross-border organizations, our interest is focused on a diverse array of interstitial spaces that are given a specific role, according to contexts and eras. This concern echoes the current state of areal studies (Cherfaoui 2017; Ehrhardt 2017) and more particularly the *Cross-Regional Studies* (Ahram et al. 2018) which seek to identify portable concepts and methods to gain new insights on the social processes and practices at work in different areas of the world. This will involve broadening the analytical horizon beyond our immediate Western-centered concerns, allowing us to observe the areas that resist standardization and how new localities are being built in a globalized world.

Though cross-border organizations maintain a strong link with territory and spatiality (national borders are real things), it is the affiliations (linguistic, administrative, cultural and others) that take multiple forms in representations, imaginaries and perceptions. These organizations, which can be seen as both "imagined communities" (Anderson 2016 [1983]) on the borders of legitimate national territories and "affective communities" (Appadurai 2015 [1996]) arising from idealized territories, give rise to a mixed field and are part of the processes of reordering the world.

Our main hypothesis is that no objective or technical definition of cross-border organizations exists, but that there are different conceptions and manifestations of them, which have been developed to varying degrees. In seeking to model the communication processes of these organizations, we are concerned with describing new semantic universes. Because they offer different types of regulating spaces than those we are used to, cross-border entities must first re-define territories. We therefore consider them as historical and symbolic productions, dynamic and flexible, with an eye toward tracing the genealogies allowing us to better understand their communicational positions. This approach, which stems from an archeology of knowledge, requires increased attention to memory clues, because they are likely to help unravel the skein of narratives offered to the public.

9.2. Theoretical and methodological anchoring in semiotics applied to the media

Within the digital ecosystem, the website is a non-material place where the stories and aspirations of cross-border organizations are projected in detail. It provides a privileged – but not unique – observation place to observe the communication of these emerging organizations. It is also an ideal way for initially separate groups (rooted on one side of a border) to present themselves as united (cross-border), insofar as the pursuit of common objectives brings them together.

The semiotics applied to the media, and more specifically to websites, will be used here to analyze the websites of cross-border organizations. Such a perspective requires considering the website as a social actor rather than as a technical object (Stockinger 2005). Considered as a potential place for the creation of organizations, the website also remains "the main means of communication for organizations to get in touch with the public" (Yates and Arbour 2013) and to facilitate "access to international communication" (Rouquette 2017, p. 9). Here, the website will be considered as the dual manifestation of a human intention and an articulation between players, norms, symbolic and socio-technical resources that are significant in a given context.

More precisely, a semiotic expertise with websites of cross-border organizations seeks to produce an applied analysis of the meanings conveyed by identifying both the invariant elements that constitute and reinforce the cross-border message, and in addition, the variations that draw on different representations [and meanings], depending on the contextual anchors considered. We will pay particular attention to the triggering elements of the websites, the needs they meet or the gaps they fill. These questions aim to "interpret the value (cognitive, utilitarian, aesthetic, hedonic, etc.) of a website – or a particular aspect of a website – according to its role for the participants in a given communication ecosystem" (Stockinger 2017, p. 135).

In order to forge this semiotic approach, we will use the conceptual framework of documentality proposed by the Italian philosopher of language Ferraris (2014). The strong hypothesis of the semiotic theory of documentality consists of considering an historical need for documentary recording even before the need for communication and social interaction. In addition to this need for registration to emerge, Ferraris emphasizes the intensification of documentary recording actions in the form of traces that engage and mobilize individuals. These traces, which can be explained to a certain extent in digital media, are evidence of a "documedial revolution"[1] in the sense of the fusion between the media dimension (now largely individualized by social media) and the dimension of documentality (the historical documentary layer at the base of the construction of a social reality).

To observe this fusion between the historical documentary and the media components of the website, we have developed a four-step methodology:

– (Step 1) we choose three models of cross-border organizations with a geopolitical aim – the Euroregions within Europe, the Euroregions on the borders of Europe, the ecoregions in Southern Africa – and we explain why these models can be read using the theory of documentality. This step, which makes the dialog between the ICS and history readily available, consists of identifying the documentary materials produced prior to and necessary for the emergence and publicization of the cross-border organizational models considered.

– (Step 2) we delineate a corpus of three websites from the three cross-border organizational models: the websites of the Austro-Italian Tyrol Alto Adige Trentino Euroregion, the Romanian-Serbo-Hungarian Danube-Criş-Mureş-Tisa Euroregion and the Kavango-Zambezi ecoregion in Southern Africa. This step, which is part of the engineering of the corpus, aims to constitute a set of data that is heterogeneous but structured according to our objective of modeling the communications of cross-border organizations.

– (Step 3) we analyze the documediality of these websites by focusing on the identification of memory clues. This step, which forms part of the semiotic expertise applied to digital media, consists of analyzing the process of thematic expansion (Greimas and Courtès 1993, p. 139) and showing how the cross-border theme is enriched on websites, in particular by the lexicon and visuals.

– (Step 4) we propose a modeling of the results that emphasizes the explanatory importance of organizational contexts. To present a synthesis of the organizational changes in the regularity of cross-border communication, we drew inspiration from

1 See: *Documentality: Web, new media and new perspectives in ontology*. FMSH project directed by M. Ferraris [Online]. Available at: www.fmsh.fr/fr/college-etudesmondiales/27995 [Accessed June 9, 2021].

the "MSDO and MDSO designs" (most similar different outcome/most different same outcome) defined as:

> [The] operationalization of the systematic measurement of similarities and differences of complex systems with regard to the respective research question ("outcome"), whereby "most similar" and "most different" systems designs (MSDO and MDSO) can control for important influencing factors and direct the focus on the remaining areas. (Berg-Schlosser 2018, p. 34)

This qualitative comparative method, proven to analyze complex public policy situations (De Meur et al. 2006), makes it possible to consider cases whose number is too small to fall under the scope of statistics but which concentrate a great diversity and complexity of qualitative observations.

9.3. First step: create a reading of three cross-border organizational models through the lens of documentality

9.3.1. *Within the European Union (EU): the documentality of the fluid Euroregions*

The Euroregions, a portmanteau created by the fusion of the terms 'Europe' and 'region', have been part of the history of European integration since the end of the Second World War. They are diplomatic tools for post-war reconciliation that were legalized in 1980 by the Madrid Charter,[2] and then financed by the European Commission since the 1990s. The Euroregions have been proliferating since the mid-2000s and are developing multilingual communications, mainly accessible on the Web. After an analysis of multilingual discourses, we have proposed to define them in ICS as "a social manifestation based on a shared historical experience, and that is capable of catalyzing complex identities by creating a community of feelings and values" (Hermand 2020, p. 208).

An initial argument makes it possible to consider Euroregional organizations as markers of European documentality. The social object of the "Euroregion" essentially depends on written acts whose application can be broad, from the simple declaration of intent (such as the Alpes-Méditerranée Euroregion, between France and Italy, which has no legal status but still produces discourse) to the legal status most adapted to the objective of cross-border cooperation (such as the Lille-

---

2 European Framework Convention on cross-border cooperation, adopted by the Council of Europe.

Kortrijk-Tournai Eurometropolis, between France and Belgium, which has been endowed with the status of European grouping of territorial cooperation since January 2008).

The second argument is with regard to symbolic construction. In his chapter "Documentalità, o Europa", Ferraris (2014, pp. 286–287) recalls that the EU is a unique case of a "continent unified by documents", and that the spirit of European unification arises from the beautiful story told to its peoples: unity actually comes from a network of norms and bureaucratic acts, from the attribution of Roman citizenship by the Edict of Caracalla to that of European citizenship given by the Maastricht Treaty in 1992. The Euroregions, which refer to two poorly defined pre-existing entities (Europe, whose physical borders are blurred, and the "region", whose names and definitions vary according to national contexts), are for their part the subject of institutionalizations[3], delimitations and denominations[4] which are constantly shifting and evolving. Whether or not they are documented in a completed legal form, they embody the economic, social and territorial cohesion policy – better known as European regional policy – established by the Lisbon Treaty in 2007. Thus, the Euroregional communication challenge consists of evaluating an imprecise political project that transcends national divides by focusing on shared symbolic elements that have the possibility to create meaning.

The third argument comes from the relationship between documentality and governmentality. For Ferraris (2014, pp. 293–295), documentality appears as the foundation of governmentality in the sense that it is a form of sophistication of the bureaucratic apparatus. We know that Europe, which does not follow any geographical or spiritual necessity, results from a progression of written documents and norms that largely prevail over geographical considerations. As far as the Euroregions are concerned, the geographical argument is of crucial importance since it reflects the reality of the proximity of borders that allows these entities to be built on the basis of a call for "erasing borders". But this geographical argument is systematically supplemented by the historical argument which presents borders as obstacles to the continuation of a long shared history between border regions (Hermand 2014, p. 79). Geography is not enough to create cross-border unity: historical traces are needed that prove the pre-existence of links and justify the cross-border configuration of these "fluid Euroregions" within the EU, characterized by various coherent elements (social ties, landscapes, customs) but partitioned by

---

3 The Association of European Border Regions (AEBR) proposes different legal and functional definitions.
4 For example, the Aquitaine-Euskadi Euroregion (2011, France-Spain) was enlarged when France joined it in 2016, and was renamed "New Aquitaine-Euskadi-Navarre" in 2017.

borders whose placement is not always done appropriately (due to linguistic, administrative or fiscal issues).

9.3.2. On the borders of the EU: the documentality of the Euroregion buffers

To consider the Euroregions located on the borders of the EU, Wassenberg (2010) adds an adjective to them that highlights their diplomatic specificity and their strategic or sensitive character: they become "geopolitical" or "multilateral". This adjective allows us to consider the Euroregions located on the borders of the EU as party organizations to which the European regionalization process pays special attention due to the old ideological divide between communism in the East and liberalism in the West.

Geopolitical Euroregions refer to the documentality of the European Neighborhood policy (ENP) launched in 2004 by the EU with 16 countries in Eastern and Southern Europe. These form an expression of this approach, which attempts to promote stability, security and prosperity in the regions directly adjacent to Europe. This neighborhood policy is marked by a less strict documentality than that which governs the procedures for accession to the EU because it is a question of approximation, and not of compliance, with the acquis communitaire (EU body of law). The neighborhood Euroregions can therefore be considered as gateways or stepping stones for participation in the EU internal market. Unlike Western Euroregions where the geographical argument is overtaken by the historical argument, geography retains primacy here, since it is the way in which adjacency to the EU is understood that determines the tensions between actors located inside or outside the European circle of friends. Another aspect of neighborhood documentality is that it is partially hidden since the disclosure of all its issues could, in the words of the General Secretariat of the Council of the EU, "damage relations between the EU and its new neighbours" (in 2005).

From a symbolic point of view, the narrative underlying the establishment of Euroregions along the borders of the EU is less idyllic than that of reconciliation and unification to which the western Euroregions refer. The aim is to strengthen relations of trust in order to contain new threats to democratic stability produced or accentuated by the collapse of the communist regime. In this so-called "securitization" narrative (Balzacq 2007)[5], cross-border flows are associated with

---

5 Balzacq defines securitization as a set of interrelated practices explaining the production, broadcasting, reception, and/or translation of a threat.

coastal ecological risks, communicable diseases, illegal immigration, trafficking, organized crime or terrorist networks.

Approached in communicational terms, the issue of the EU's borders involves the visibility of cross-border initiatives with countries whose geographical location is vague (e.g. Cyprus, on the borders of southern and Eastern Europe) or with a controversial political regime (such as the Central and Eastern European Countries [CEEC], or Turkey). It is necessary to ask whether the communication of these "buffer Euroregions" – an expression that we propose with reference to the term used in urban planning to designate any interstitial space maintained or urgently established to ensure an interception and mitigation function – is concerned with problems considered specific to the borders of the EU such as migration policy, democratic challenges, ecological challenges, economic challenges or the risk of instability, and if so, how this is handled in the digital ecosystem, a space that is considered devoid of immediate physical risks a priori.

9.3.3. *In Southern Africa: the documentality of ecoregions*

The cross-border organizational model of ecoregions developed in Southern Africa makes it possible to take a decentralized approach to Europe's immediate interests and paves the way for other acceptances of the border to be taken into account. Ecoregions are defined by the World Wide Fund for Nature (WWF) as "a large unit of land or water containing a geographically distinct assemblage of species, natural communities, and environmental conditions" and whose boundaries "are not fixed and sharp, but rather encompass an area within which important ecological and evolutionary processes most strongly interact".

In Southern Africa, ecoregions are used more specifically to designate "transfrontier conservation areas (TFCA)" observable in the form of the transfrontier parks known as *Transfrontier Peace Parks*. These parks join together pre-existing natural parks on both sides of national borders. According to the International Union for the Conservation of Nature (IUCN 1994), the *Transfrontier Peace Parks* are "transboundary protected areas that are formally dedicated to the protection and maintenance of biological diversity, and of natural and associated cultural resources, and to the promotion of peace and cooperation".

The geographer Guyot (2006) explains that this political ecology originates from the British colonization that occurred at the end of the 19th century before becoming a component of the white nationalist project in South Africa during the interwar period, then turning into a war zone during the apartheid era of the 1950s–1970s. During the 1990s, a post-modern use for these transfrontier *Peace Parks* began, located "between the logic of cooperation and the logic of domination". Stemming from messages of pacification joined with programmatic speeches on environmental policy, these parks developed in a post-apartheid context and were tasked with contributing to redefining the concept of "living together". They were thus called upon to fulfill a first order geopolitical function (Guyot 2006; Belaidi 2016).

The *Peace Parks* are seen as pioneering areas of nature conservation, in line with international discourses on sustainable development. By addressing crucial issues both on the environmental and on the human level, they offer an opportunity to observe two defining features of transfrontier communication: the staging of common values granted to nature, and the staging of a shared goal of pacification. Whether they are intrinsic to nature, recognized by governments or granted by people, these values must be spread in order to establish the credibility of the ecoregional enterprise.

9.4. Step two: build a corpus of websites from the three cross-border organizational models considered

9.4.1. *The website of the Tyrol Alto Adige Trentino Euroregion*

The Tyrol Alto Adige Trentino region, which includes border regions of Austria and Italy, is a model of cross-border organization in Europe in many areas (such as politics, law, institutions, language and education). Legally structured in 2011 in the form of a European grouping for territorial cooperation (EGTC), it covers an area of 26,254 km^2 and brings together a population of more than 2.4 million inhabitants.

The institutional website (www.europaregion.info) is multilingual and acts as a mosaic of content accessible in four languages (German, Italian, Ladin and English) and in different formats (text, sound, audiovisual). With rich editorial content and regular updates, it provides content dedicated to all areas of cross-border life: politics, administration, the economy, mobility, education and research, tourism and leisure (Figure 9.1).

Among the most salient editorial content, we can note the presence of an interactive bilingual map in Italian and German (maps.europaregion.info) which lets users locate all administrations and institutions, and provides resources for mobility, energy and healthcare within the Euroregion. This map provides a gateway to collections of content presenting nearly encyclopedic listings on various themes, demonstrating a significant multilingual editorial investment.

Figure 9.1. *Upper part of the home page from the Euroregion website, Italian version[6]. For a color version of this figure, see www.iste.co.uk/massou/analyzing.zip*

9.4.2. *The website of the Danube-Criş-Mureş-Tisa Euroregion*

Observing the website of the Danube-Criş-Mureş-Tisa Euroregion (DKMT), we note "the change in the historical horizon since the fall of the Berlin Wall by

---

6 Available at: www.europaregion.info/en/default.asp.

highlighting the presence within the EU of at least two cultural areas defined by Fernand Braudel, Western Europe and Middle Europe, with divergent interests" (Nowicki 2008, p. 110, author's translation). The DKMT Euroregion, which includes border regions of Hungary, Romania and Serbia, was founded in 1997, long before the enlargement process[7]. It covers an area of 71,867 km² and brings together a population of more than 5.3 million inhabitants. Critescu (2003) mentions that the experiments and projects undertaken in this Euroregion had the ambition to "serve as a model for the establishment of other Euroregions in Central and Eastern Europe, as well as a basis for reflection for the policies of European bodies" (author's translation).

The institutional website (www.dkmt.net) is multilingual, with content accessible in Hungarian, Romanian, Serbian and English. It offers textual content that is descriptive (presentation of the Euroregion and its executive board), programmatic (current programs) and documentary (gallery, publications) in nature. There are also three editing areas on the home page that link to noteworthy related content, such as the quadrilingual (in Hungarian, Romanian, Serbian and English) Euroregional Information Centre of DKMT, the quadrilingual site (in this case Hungarian, Romanian, English and German) entitled Borderless routes and adventures in the DKMT Euroregion, and the "Security without borders" page, which presents a program co-financed by the European Commission to maintain border security (Figure 9.2).

Despite its antiquity, this site offers an archetype of cross-border documediality in Central Europe. Though it is currently dormant, as can be observed on the dates of the last updates, it is still accessible and functional. It is located in a digital ecosystem where the reference to cross-border cooperation around the Danube, the centerpiece of the connection between eastern and western Europe (Boulineau 2018), is now embodied by websites entirely in English, such as Danube Region Strategy (danube-region.eu) or Danube Macro Region Business Week 2021 (www.dmrbw.net). This linguistic observation confirms that the documediality here is less strict than that observed in the fluid Euroregions of Western Europe: where the fluid Euroregion offers multilingualism in accordance with the official languages in its cross-border area, the buffer Euroregion now tends to favor English.

---

7 Hungary entered the EU on May 1st, 2004. Romania entered it on the January 1st, 2007. Serbia has had the status of a candidate for entry into the EU since March 1st 2012.

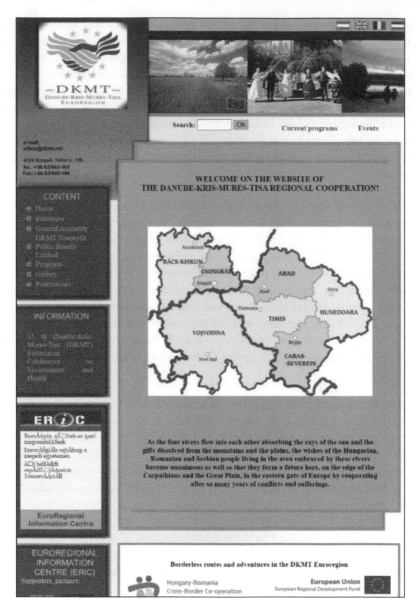

Figure 9.2. *Upper part of the home page from the Euroregion website, English version[8].*
For a color version of this figure, see www.iste.co.uk/massou/analyzing.zip

---

8 Available at: www.dkmt.net/en.

9.4.3. *The website of Kavango-Zambezi Transfrontier Conservation Area*

The Kavango-Zambezi Transfrontier Conservation Area (KaZa TFCA) ecoregion includes natural parks located between Angola, Botswana, Namibia, Zambia and Zimbabwe, and covers an area of 519,912 km². Between 2003 and 2006, the Southern African Development Community made this ecoregion one of its official projects, seeking to create the largest transfrontier terrestrial conservation area on the planet. The park has officially existed since March 15, 2012.

Figure 9.3. *Upper part of the home page from the ecoregion website, English version[9]. For a color version of this figure, see www.iste.co.uk/massou/analyzing.zip*

Accessible from the website for the 10 African *Transfrontier Peace Parks*[10] (www.peaceparks.org), the website of the KaZa TFCA ecoregion (kavangozambezi. org) is bilingual in Portuguese and English. It is broken down into textual content that seeks to give an overview of the ecoregion (partner countries, donors,

9 Available at: www.kavangozambezi.org/en.
10 There are 18 such parks throughout Southern Africa.

stakeholders, important milestones), inform the public (about the park and its news, nature and wildlife, tourist visas, travel conditions, health and safety) and promote scientific research projects implemented in the park. In addition to these textual elements, a photo gallery of the natural features of the park (such as mammals, landscapes, and birds) and interactive maps are some of its prominent visual content (Figure 9.3).

The inclusion of a long list of hyperlinks also provides a large network of partner websites linking to a variety of non-governmental organizations, foundations, research institutes, ministries and companies that share an interest in cross-border affairs. This is done in order to form a group of stakeholders working toward the broad common theme of the preservation of transfrontier natural heritage and to show the many possible variations on this theme: shared water management (The Permanent Okavango River Basin Water Commission), animal protection (Elephants Without Borders), the development of sustainable tourism (Boundless Southern Africa), etc.

9.5. Stage three: identify the memory processes to unravel the skein of cross-border narratives presented to audiences

9.5.1. *Call for a shared memory: anchoring within a territory-symbol*

9.5.1.1. *The revitalization of a legendary territory*

The first type of inscription within memory relates to the anchoring within a fantastical and legendary territory. The institutional website of the Tyrol-Alto Adige Trentino Euroregion is peppered with references to the "soul" of the Dolomites through the naming of many paths of legends, translated into the four languages of the site. The Dolomites are lands filled with popular legends that feature fantastical characters (elves, fairies and gnomes) passed down from generation to generation. A "cultural courier" (Cooper-Richet et al. 2005) of these legends appears in the form of a local self-taught intellectual: Karl Felix Wolf (1879–1966), a journalist-writer-anthropologist born to an Austrian father and an Italian mother, and author of the best-known collection of sagas dedicated to the soul of the Dolomites.

The recurring references to the figure and works of this cultural courier, well known to the local populations, allow the Euroregion to register on two levels: that of a legitimate reception in the narrow circle of the academic world because of the collections of the archive fund kept at the University of Innsbruck, and that of a reception by diversion in a wider cultural milieu on the occasion of events dedicated to the author.

Figure 9.4. *Revitalization of the legendary Dolomitic territory through the valuation from the literary archives of a cultural courier, German version[11]. For a color version of this figure, see www.iste.co.uk/massou/analyzing.zip*

The mention of this cultural courier thus contributes to revitalizing a heritage that is all too often forgotten and to anchoring the Euroregion in a territory with

11 Available at: www.europaregion.info/de/news.asp.

naturalistic, touristic and ethnographic uses. By providing the Euroregion with support by an author from the beginning of the 20th century inspired by the tradition of the brothers Grimm, the website proposes a vision of the Alpine world presented as a "conservatory of wonders" (Hertz, cited by Dunoyer (2019)) according to a native or nearby anthropological approach marked by ecological concerns. It can therefore be said that here the use of literary archives contributes to "the recognition of a certain territorial identity, beyond political borders" (Paris 2015) (Figure 9.4).

9.5.1.2. *The reconstruction of an historical territory*

A second type of memorial inscription relates to the reconstruction of an historical territory. The official website of the Romanian-Serbian-Hungarian Euroregion DKMT is working to re-found the image of an historical reference territory well known to local populations (the Banat) and to consolidate that of a contemporary geographical invention (the Euroregion), which brings together three vast border entities. At the origin of the DKMT Euroregion, the elected officials also pursued the objective of recomposing a territorial structure backed by the identity of the Banat[12].

The Euroregional model supported by these elected representatives is based on the multicultural nature of the Banat inherited from the former Austro-Hungarian Empire. To provide the backdrop for this defining trait, one firmly anchored in the collective imagination, the website develops two characteristic *topoi* of the historical Banat – viticulture and gastronomy, both resulting from cultural mixtures – by proposing cross-border discovery routes (Borderless routes and adventures in the DKMT Euroregion). Periodically broken up since ancient times by crises and revivals, today oenologists have declared that the Banatean wine culture is seeing the beginnings of international success[13]. Similarly, the Banat gastronomic culture, as the heir to a mixture of culinary traditions, supports the multicultural image of the DKMT Euroregion.

In this archetype of cross-border communication of an organization located in central Europe, it is impossible to speak of a complex sensory staging, as Badulescu (2015) was able to observe in his analysis of the digital communication of the Romanian wines of Cotnari and Murtfatlar. The stage built

---

12 The historical region of Banat was a border-region of the former Kingdom of Hungary, governed by a "ban". Located in the southeast of Europe, and whose historical capital is Timişoara, it is today divided between the Romanian, Serbian and Hungarian Banat. In the High Middle Ages, a border-march was a fief created in a border area, either after a conquest or by the detachment of another territory, and to which the sovereign assigns a special function of defense against neighboring territories.

13 Blog "Vins du monde, le goût des vins d'ailleurs" ("Wines of the world, the taste of wines from other places"), see: www.vinsdumonde.blog/la-surprise-des-vins-roumains.

here conceals too few multimodal connections to create a sophisticated imagination, but it announces an ability to represent taste and smell through the provision of geographical maps mentioning wine and gastronomic points of interest. The verbal statements that accompany these suggested places is limited to factual information relating to the equipment, the grape varieties, the volumes produced and the history of the factories or the vineyards. Lacking an exclusively commercial objective, the symbolic communication of Banat wine and gastronomy has been reactivated to essentially assume a geographical value. First though, this would involve putting the wine and gastronomy of the DKMT Euroregion on a map to make them known by means of an implicit reminder of the historical Banat territory (Figure 9.5).

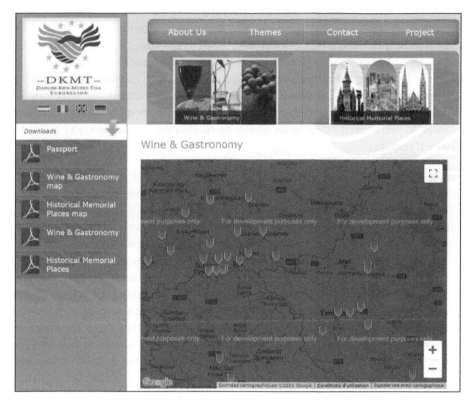

Figure 9.5. *Reactivation of the historic Banatean territory through the mapping of wine and dining, English version[14]. For a color version of this figure, see www.iste.co.uk/massou/analyzing.zip*

---

14 See: www.borderless.dkmt.eu/Thematics_wine.

9.5.1.3. *The idealization of a wild territory*

A third type of memorial inscription relates to the idealization of a wild and free natural landscape. *The KaZa Dream* is the title of an important portion of the editorial work found on the homepage of the official website of the African park, Kavango-Zambezi Transfrontier Conservation Area. This time, the works center around an idealized natural territory by presenting the delimited conservation area (Area Conservation), partners and stakeholders in the management of the park (Partners & Stakeholders), the important stages of its development (Milestones) and the discovery of a "tourism without boundaries" (Tourism without Boundaries).

The main semiotic process consists of emphasizing the extreme richness of bio-diversity by means of photographic galleries that stage the profusion and majesty of intact landscapes: thundering waterfalls, wide expanses, a diverse array of landscapes and plant species, and endangered animal species. The natural setting of the rivers is represented in each image (Chobe, Okavango, Zambezi), while man's participation as a tourist-explorer is never visually represented but only briefly evoked ("these moments and many others are available to the Kavango-Zambezi explorer"). The overall effect is an idyllic representation of the park and a call to explore it responsibly.

The separation of man and nature echoes the concept of nature or wilderness. This concept, which began in the United States in the 19th century in reaction to the devastation of the Great Plains, refers to "the earth and its community of life are untrammeled by man, where man himself is a visitor who does not remain" (Wilderness Act 1964). The transfrontier scale of nature appears very coherent here, since it is the transfrontier basins of the rivers that give relevance to the suggested area. This visual association of the wilderness with Transboundary Peace Parks is used for the defense of a common good (this is the initial objective of the "conservation area"), for its aesthetic values (grandiose landscapes) and for the economic support provided to the tourist industry (which willingly uses the image of sweeping virgin landscapes). The scientific and pedagogical values, which are less prominent, are not, however, absent, since research programs in biodiversity and environment are also presented.

9.5.2. *Call for a shared history: anchoring within a legitimate quest*

9.5.2.1. *The quest for freedom*

The founding myth of the quest for freedom is recurrent in the institutional site of the Tyrol Alto Adige Trentino Euroregion. It is represented by the figure of a charismatic leader who is both a hero and a martyr. The South Tyrolean Andreas

Hofer, known for having supported the first armed insurrection in Innsbruck in 1809 against the Napoleonic and Bavarian dominions, is regularly mentioned through announcements of cultural events, commemorative ceremonies and associative or commercial activities. Captured, tried and executed in 1810 in Mantua after taking refuge in his native mountains, this charismatic leader embodies the political symbol of the peasant revolt following the cession of Tyrol to Bavaria by the Austrian Empire (Cole 1994).

9.5.2.2. *The quest for security*

On the website of the Romanian-Serbian-Hungarian Euroregion DKMT, a set of documents is dedicated to the topic of security, which as we have seen, constitutes the anchor of cross-border documentality in Central Europe. The category *Security without borders* seeks to demonstrate that a border can be secure without being closed. The *leitmotiv* of this buffer Euroregion is therefore to "open the borders" rather than "erase the borders", the watchword of the fluid western Euroregions.

The lexicon used shows that the Euroregion of Central Europe plays a strategic role ("it is one of the determinant areas of Europe on the way of unification"). It refers to the founding role attributed to geopolitical Euroregions ("to contribute to the democratization, the stabilization, the integration in Europe") and to the fact that this role is now recognized ("Nations recognized that more effective defense can be provided in cooperation"). The myth of security therefore provides a fixed response to the multiple risks that have been known for a long time in the region ("natural disasters", "cross border attacks", "dangerous substances", "industrial accidents and epidemiology").

The registration of the DKMT Euroregion in the historical sphere is done here through the faithful transposition onto the website of the documentality that grants security functions to the borders of Europe. The Euroregion assumes the role of a model to be followed, which makes it possible to formulate recommendations ("to provide a basis for future development of cross-border and international cooperation"). By acting as a sort of "coating" around the core areas of Europe, it gains a symbolic status that surpasses, embodies and gives a location to the many fears associated with the borders of Europe.

9.5.2.3. *The quest for peace*

The invitation to visit the Kavango-Zambezi transboundary African park is based on a recollection of the process of pacification of this conflict zone during the apartheid era. The argument is both political (about allowing people to live together) and ecological (about inviting people to discover nature while protecting it).

The first method used for appealing to a shared history is the association with messages of pacification. Implicitly backed by a post-apartheid message on peace, the website promotes the transfrontier park within a framework of idealized geopolitical cooperation. This concept of an ideal world of peace is constructed before the general website for the *Peace Parks*, where we find 83 occurrences of the name Nelson Mandela[15]. As co-founder of the Peace Parks Foundation, a common framework offered to African transfrontier parks, Mandela appears as an identifiable historical figure. Having been awarded prizes and featured in events organized in his honor, this spiritual figure – a pioneer, sage, and influencer – allows for a link to be made between reducing inequalities and improving the environment.

A second process, which in this case can be observed directly within the website for Kavango-Zambezi Park, involves promoting the legal or regulatory devices that are essential to the organization of effective cooperation between neighboring Southern African states. The category of Tourism without Boundaries displays cross-border tourism as an essential socioeconomic pillar of the region, but one that is subject to strong constraints. To meet the requirement for tourists to obtain country-specific visas, the detailed description of the KaZa UniVisa pilot project (launched in 2014) highlights the political will that exists to facilitate tourists' travel between the two countries participating in the project (Zambia and Zimbabwe). The promise behind this initiative refers to the strong economic growth of tourism that is expected. Without hiding the delicate period when this temporary visa was suspended in 2016, the central message remains that of hard work and long-term perseverance to incorporate all partner states in this initiative to develop mobility to support cross-border tourism.

9.5.3. *The call for a shared heritage: an anchoring in shared living*

9.5.3.1. *The scientific mediation of a military heritage*

Within the institutional site of the Tyrol Alto Adige Trentino Euroregion, the recent subdomain (2019) historegio.europaregion.info is dedicated to the Historegio project, which focuses on providing an account for lay people of the scientific history between Austria and Italy. Historegio, bilingual in Italian and German, is supported by an archive on the First World War and the history of the school during the conflict.

The scientific mediation of the military heritage is supported by a viewpoint formed through archival materials like postcards and period publications, historical

---

15 Available at: www.peaceparks.org/ (request made on June 9, 2021).

notices, timelines, encyclopedic notices provided and commented by researchers from the universities of Bolzano and Innsbruck. The paradigms specific to the military heritage are utilized in the interactive mapping of collective, utilitarian and functional technical spaces (cemeteries, lookouts, forts, barracks). The restitution of these historically and spatially located scenes of life takes place through the presentation of war routes (defense lines, shelters, caves, smuggling passages, artillery positions, etc.).

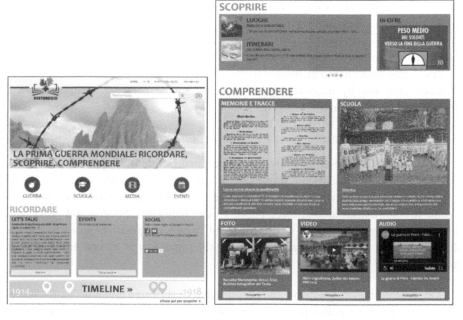

Figure 9.6. *Scientific mediation of the military heritage of the Euroregion, Italian version[16]. For a color version of this figure, see www.iste.co.uk/massou/analyzing.zip*

The adopted bias does not erase the traces of the lives led by the armies and the populations. The approach of scientific mediation is intended to be as artificial as possible: the section "Memorie e tracce/Erinnerungen und Spuren" (Memories and traces) gives visibility to objects of daily life during the war. These objects serve as discursive bases. They appear on posters (about the shortage of coffee, about the ingenuity needed to produce objects in short supply) and provide illustrative testimonies about food production practices in wartime (which food products were scarce and which were available, daily combat strategies for food) or about

16 Available at: www.historegio.europaregion.info/it/14-18.asp.

schooling during the war (how children were used, directives governing school life, compensation for the lack of teachers' manpower, requisitions of buildings, the organizing of isolated childcare centers, etc.).

Another column, published weekly and entitled "100 anni fa/Vor 100 Jahren" (100 years ago), focuses on the living conditions of the civilian population and explains the impact of the conflict on the trapped populations. It communicates a sensitive vision of war and articulates purely scientific missions with an unprecedented mission of *cittadinanza Euroregionale* (Euroregional citizenship). Such a scientific media enterprise of historical archives develops the Euroregion's ability to tell its own story and to "create a common heritage" for the people who live there. Its goal is to develop a shared narritive on multiple media and with many voices. It also seeks not to be limited to the institutional and scientific spheres, but to enhance civil life by encouraging citizens to provide personal archives from a contributory perspective (Figure 9.6).

9.5.3.2. *The cultural mediation of an architectural and religious heritage*

Located at the same distance from Budapest and Belgrade, Sofia and Vienna, the DKMT Euroregion makes the argument on its website that the centrality of its geographical location will allow it to become a hub for international relations once again. It is organized around three major cities: Timişoara, Szeged and Novi Sad. These cities form a network at the heart of which cooperative projects for the development of infrastructure and tourism or the protection of natural environments take place.

On the Euroregion's website, the presentation of different urban heritages serves as a source for cross-pollination. For example, the site draws attention to the city of Timişoara with an interactive geographical map that lists its points of interest. Among these points of interest is the Banat Museum, located inside the Huniade Castle, which is particularly significant for this blending of historical backgrounds. Its eclectic facade bears witness to the memory of eras from its construction by Italian masters in the beginning of the 14th century, to that of the Ottoman occupation of the 16th to the 18th century, and then the reconstruction work carried out after the siege of the Hungarian revolutionaries in 1849.

More broadly, the entire city of Timişoara is emblematic of the historical blending: once known as "Little Vienna", and despite the radical transformations of the city over the centuries (Buzilà 1984), it has preserved various buildings in baroque and classical, art nouveau, neo-Romanesque and neo-Baroque styles. By promoting its religious buildings from different eras and cultures (such as its Catholic and Serbian Orthodox cathedrals), the website becomes a record of and the conduit for these many different religious beliefs inherited through its pluralistic past.

In addition to the urban architecture files and photographs, the city of Timişoara, the capital of culture in 2021, is highlighted on the site through photographs that offer a strong symbolism of this mixing effect because of influential minorities (such as Germans, Swabians, Hungarians, Serbs, Roma, Italians, Bulgarians, Croats, Czechs and Slovaks). Rather than positioning itself as a peripheral Euroregion, the DKMT buffer Euroregion, because of the urban and human elements highlighted on its website, can be read as the memory and foreshadowing of a certain Europeanness of cultural, religious and social cross-pollination (Figure 9.7).

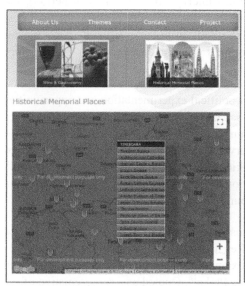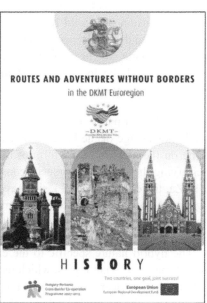

Figure 9.7. *Cultural mediation of the architectural and religious heritage from the Euroregion, English version[17]. For a color version of this figure, see www.iste.co.uk/massou/analyzing.zip*

9.5.3.3. *The commercial mediation of a natural heritage*

While the site of the Kavango-Zambezi transboundary park shows images of unspoiled natural scenes free from any human interventions, in reality it places the

---

17 Available at: www/historegio.europaregion.info/it/14-18.asp.

highest value on ecotourism. This mobilization of the nature of the parks is the result of a long history (Giraut et al. 2005). During apartheid, the border parks were used for military purposes, while after apartheid, the parks – which came to extend across national borders - have become the centerpiece of arguments that they reduce inequalities and increase incomes, two conditions presented as necessary for living together in harmony.

Incentives for travel or discovery give rise to the portrayal of an environment where animals and plants are considered both leisure objects (which tourists can come to discover) and marketable resources (tourists will pay to discover them). Tourism is emerging as a priority economic objective, and the hybrid image of cross-border parks is that of a codified place where different visions of nature are given: the vision of a wild natural setting (inherited from the British period), the vision of a land to be shaped (inherited from the Afrikaner period), the vision of natural heritage to be conserved (inherited from international development discourses) and the local vision stemming from the discourses on participatory resource management.

Cross-border parks are both places of political experimentation and opportunities to take advantage of the benefits of globalization. This territorial engineering takes shape on the website in the form of a number of different indicators: a lexicon for identifying the objective pursued (conservation area), appeals to tourists ("Let's go to KaZa, travelling in KaZa"), signs evoking tourist information points (the "point i" logo) or a slogan referring to the definition of border as a demarcation line between regions rather than between countries (tourism without boundaries).

The hybrid nature specific to the cross-border park thus results from a tangled web of many different logics, which makes it possible to recycle figures or speeches that are already clearly understood. For example, Anton Rupert's name is mentioned 106 times in the portal dedicated to Peace Parks[18]. Quoted as a representative of the WWF, Rupert is also a symbol of the Afrikaner businessman, as the former CEO of the tobacco company Rembrandt and Rothmans International. Another example is provided by the discourse built around the cultural villages, places where everyday life is at the service of tourists (the explorer) hosted by a mediator (the park ranger) for commercial purposes.

---

18 Available at: www.peaceparks.org/ (request made on June 9, 2021).

9.6. Step four: qualitatively comparing the results

The MSDO design (most similar) is often more exploratory in nature than the MDSO (most different) (Berg-Schlosser 2018, p. 38). Each variable must be dichotomized (coded as 0 or 1) to give a simplified version of reality. Though this is necessarily very reductive, this approach here has the sole objective of unveiling what truly matters in terms of causing the desired results (in this case, a cross-border organization website) to happen. The previous stages of the analysis make it possible to identify several variations: documentality, multilingualism, trauma, intentionality, heritage, authority figures, professional networks and multi-media staging are all conditions shared by cross-border organizations to varying degrees.

Cross-border organizational models	Cross-border models exploited for geopolitical purposes		
	Fluid Euroregions	Buffer Euroregions	Ecoregions
Observed cases (websites)	Europaregion Tirol Südtirol Trentino	Danube-Criș-Mureș-Tisa Euroregion (DKMT)	Kavango-Zambezi Transfrontier Conservation Area
Conditions of realization			
Strict documentality	1	0	1
Multilingual practices	1	1	1
Traumatic memories	1	1	1
Initial intentionality	1	1	1
Common heritage	1	1	1
Authority figures	1	1	1
Professional networks	1	1	1
Multimedia sophistication	1	0	1

Table 9.1. *General conditions for the creation of a cross-border organization website (inspired by MSDO design)*

Table 9.1 lists these variables and clarifies those that are the most conducive (code 1) or the least conducive (code 0) to their publicization for each cross-border model. We can see that the documentality does not have to be absolutely strict (i.e. identified, explained and accessible) to guarantee visibility on a website. It can sometimes be hidden and unknown due to reasons such as political motives, as we have seen in the case of buffer Euroregions. Similarly, the multi-media sophistication (i.e. the connections between recent technical functionalities on various media) can be very low, as we have seen in the case of the DKMT buffer Euroregion. On the other hand, the presence of elements such as multilingual content, a traumatic memory, an initial intentionality, a common heritage, authority figures and professional networks are a more obvious and more successful condition for the three models (Table 9.1).

The MDSO design is located at a more in-depth level of analysis. Focusing on documentality, the following table specifies the historical documentary traces that vary systematically according to the cross-border model and that precede the creation of the websites for cross-border organizations (Table 9.2).

Cross-border organizational models	Fluid Euroregions	Buffer Euroregions	Ecoregions
Documediality	Traces of historical documentary recording		
(1) Triggering traumatic event	World War II	Communist regime	Apartheid
(2) Human intentionality	Reconciliation	Adhesion	Pacification
(3) Constituent discourse	European policy of cohesion	European neighborhood policy	International development policy
(4) Founding narrative	Cooperation	Securitization	Conservation
(5) Argumentation	Politico-economic	Politico-diplomatic	Politico-ecological
(6) *Leitmotiv*	Erasing borders	Opening borders	Pacifying borders

Table 9.2. *Historical documentary records specified according to cross-border organizational models (inspiration from MDSO design)*

These traces refer to the recording in the historical sphere:

– (Lines 1 and 2) of a traumatic event and a consequent human intentionality: the western fluid Euroregions were created after World War II with an intent of reconciliation; the buffer Euroregions of central Europe proliferated after the end of the communist regime with the intent of access to the EU; the eco-regions of Southern Africa were favored at the end of Apartheid with an intent of pacification.

– (Lines 3 and 4) of a constituent speech[19] conveying a founding narrative: fluid Euroregions refer to the sophisticated discourse of European cohesion policy and the narrative of cooperation; buffer Euroregions refer to the discourse of European neighbourhood policy and the narrative of securitization; southern African ecoregions refer to international development discourses and the narrative of conservation of protected areas.

– (Lines 5 and 6) of an argument backed by a *leitmotiv*: The fluid Euroregions develop a politico-economic argument backed by the *leitmotiv* of the abolition of borders to facilitate trade; the buffer Euroregions develop a politico-diplomatic argument backed by the *leitmotiv* of the opening of borders to demonstrate their ability to ensure security along the edges of the EU; the ecoregions of Southern Africa develop a political-ecological argument backed by the *leitmotiv* of the pacification of borders to promote the entry of tourists.

Table 9.3, this time focused on the documediality, specifies the traces of the a priori historical elements that surface and vary in the websites analyzed.

These historical elements a priori take the form of:

– (Lines 1 and 2) appeals to the past and recourse to universal values: the revitalization of a legendary territory associated with freedom (the website of the Austro-Italian Euroregion); the reconstitution of an historical territory guaranteeing security along the borders of the EU (the website of the DKMT Euroregion); the idealization of a pacified wild territory (the website of the Kavango-Zambezi ecoregion).

– (Line 3) mediation of a shared heritage, whether military, architectural, religious or natural.

---

19 Constituent discourses refer to higher sources on which institutional discourses can base their existence: they provide absolute legitimation through one or more texts and have come to found a new order (of thought, of the world, of institutions, of social relations (Maingueneau, D. and Cossutta, F. (1995). L'analyse des discours constituants. *Langages*, 117, "Les analyses du discours en France". Larousse, Paris).

– (Line 4) references to legitimizing authorities: the connection with the EU, States and regions (in the case of Euroregions); the articulation of IUCN, WWF, States and regions (in the case of ecoregions).

– (Line 5) human figures: the local cultural courier (Karl Felix Wolf), the charismatic hero and martyred leader (Andreas Hofer), the inhabitants (of a mixed-race town, of a *cultural village*), the tourist-explorer, the ranger/mediator.

– (Line 6) landscapes, animal or plant figures (fantastic mountains, majestic rivers, vineyards and food crops, wildlife roaming free under supervision).

– (Line 7) professional and commercial networks (related to wine, dining, tourism, the environment).

Observed cases (websites)	Tyrol Alto Adige Trentino Euroregion	Danube-Criș-Mureș-Tisa Euroregion (DKMT)	Kavango-Zambezi Transfrontier Conservation Area (KaZa TFCA)
Documediality	Traces of historical data a priori that are displayed on websites		
(1) Appeals to the past	Revitalization of a legendary territory	Reconstitution of a historic territory	Idealization of a wild territory
(2) Universal values	Freedom	Securitization	Peace
(3) Mediation of heritage	Military heritage	Architectural and religious heritage	Natural heritage
(4) Institutional authorities	EU, States, regions	EU, States, regions	IUCN, WWF, States, regions
(5) Human figures	Cultural courier, charismatic leader	City residents	Village residents tourist-explorer, ranger/mediator
(6) Natural elements	Mountains	Rivers, vineyards	Rivers, fauna, flora
(7) Professional networks	All economic sectors	Wine, gastronomy	Environment, tourism

Table 9.3. *A priori historical, specified according to the websites of the cross-border organizations analyzed (inspired by MDSO design)*

9.7. Conclusion

We have worked on a corpus of three websites considered to be specific cases and significant forms of three cross-border organizational models, located in Western Europe, Central Europe and Southern Africa, respectively. The notion of cross-border organizations was a logical choice for studying the mediatization of hybrid entities responsible for embodying intermediate public spaces. The website stood out as a layer of media where historical data a priori from a pre-existing documentary layer in this medium can be brought to the fore. In order to model the connections between the documentary layer and the media layer, we have developed a methodology that allowed us to:

– (Step 1) understand what motivates the emerging communications of cross-border organizations, by considering the online editorial activities in the light of documentary records prior to the act of communication.

– (Step 2) show the role played by websites in enriching cross-border issues, whether they are archetypal, unsophisticated web interfaces or contributing contemporary interfaces.

– (Step 3) highlight the importance of the traces of memory spread through websites and their ability to legitimize organizations on an unprecedented scale of representation.

– (Step 4) specify the results according to the contexts, taking inspiration from a qualitative method of comparing public policies and adapting it to our objectives of communication.

The investment in time and in a disciplinary openness to history, to bring up to date the a priori historic occurrences, led us to show how websites can be reconnected to the objectives, needs and practices of communities of emerging actors. This approach, which can be described as an archaeology of knowledge updated in the light of documediality, confirms the crucial importance of context, history and archives to understand the communication of emerging organizations. This makes it possible to validate our hypothesis of a diversity of conceptions underlying the communication of cross-border organizations and, above all, to specify the different conceptions of cross-border issues at work within the websites.

We are also able to specify the online editorial goals of the cross-border organizational models considered. Three types of valuation are favored: diplomatic (valuation of institutional and economic cooperation), memorial (valuation of reconfigured ancient territories) and ethnographic (valuation of a shared experience).

The analyzed websites thus contribute to forging cross-border communication in several ways:

– they allow for cross-border topics to be expanded, not only because of the structured addition of specialized content or technical features, but also because of the different language versions that amplify the meaning and reception of cross-border organizations;

– they contradict linear narratives (at the national or regional level) and come with a potentially critical dimension, since they confirm the evolutionary character of geopolitical configurations (from national to transnational), give visibility to an interstitial scale of power (the cross-border scale) and thus redistribute a share of power;

– they propose new territorial configurations by transforming old physical objects (postcards, posters, engravings, copies) into immaterial traces (photos, sounds, videos, interactive maps) and by encouraging audiences to confront authentic traces in parallel (mountains, rivers, wildlife, cities, villages);

– they offer a particularly useful plasticity to materialize intermediate public spaces with scalable size and components.

Caught up in a complex network of professional communications (diplomatic, scientific, tourist, environmental) where each stakeholder contributes to building the cross-border reference material, websites are also backed by idealized representations that partially veil the pursued interests, immutable rivalries and potential conflicts, or even a whole collection of the traumatic memories at the origin of cross-border organizations (war, communism, segregation).

Our work, which raises the question of new territorial representations built by a priori historical elements publicized in digital media (in this case, websites), is part of a broader enterprise of modeling the cross-border discursive universe in various global areas. This universe of meaning is envisioned as a powerful revealer of emerging organizations and a laboratory of intermediate public spaces (e.g. spaces of solidarity or tense neighborhoods, ignored or speculative, plural or problematic belonging, intensification or disruption of flows). The modeling of this universe of meaning, which largely involves the study of websites in terms of their editorial richness, will have to be extended by examining how collective values are negotiated with a view to creating communities of cross-border understanding or border disputes.

9.8. References

Ahram, A.I., Köllner, P., Sil, R. (2018). *Comparative Area Studies: Methodological Rationales and Cross-Regional Applications*. Oxford University Press, New York.

Anderson, B. (2006). *L'imaginaire national. Réflexions sur l'origine et l'essor du nationalisme*. La Découverte, Paris.

Appadurai, A. (2015). *Après le colonialisme : les conséquences culturelles de la globalisation*. Payot, Paris.

Badulescu, C. (2015). La communication numérique en terrain sensible. Le cas des vins Cotnari et Murfatlar. *Questions de communication*, 28, 81–100.

Balzacq, T. (2007). La politique européenne de voisinage, un complexe de sécurité à géométrie variable. *Cultures & Conflits*, 66, 31–59.

Bazin, A. and Perron, C. (eds) (2018). *How to Address the Loss? Forced Migrations, Lost Territories and the Politics of History. A Comparative Approach in Europe and at its Margins in the XXth Century*. Peter Lang, Bern.

Belaidi, N. (2016). La paix par la coopération environnementale, un nouveau modèle de conservation ? *Afrique contemporaine*, 257(1), 129–143.

Berg-Schlosser, D. (2018). Comparative area studies. The golden mean between area studies and universalist approaches? In *Comparative Area Studies. Methodological Rationales & Cross-Regional Applications*, Ahram A.I., Köllner P., Sil, R. (eds). Oxford University Press, New York.

Borders Forum (2020). 1st Borders Forum. Cross-border territories on the front line. November 2020 [Online]. Available at: https://bordersforum.eu/elementor-2382/ [Accessed June 9, 2021].

Boulineau, E. (2018). La macrorégion du Danube portée par l'Union européenne : quelques enjeux d'européanité pour l'Europe médiane. In *L'européanité en Europe médiane*, Dessberg F., Cattaruzza, A. (eds). Bruylant, Brussels.

Buzilà, A. (1984). Un ensemble de monuments baroques à Timisoara. *Baroque*, 11 [Online]. Available at: https://journals.openedition.org/baroque/563 [Accessed February 2, 2021].

Cherfaoui, A. (2017). Reconfigurer la recherche sur les aires culturelles : le comparatisme, une voie revisitée. *Diogène*, 258–259–260(2), 197–208.

Cole, L. (1994). Andreas Hofer: The social and cultural construction of a national myth in Tirol, 1809–1909. Working document, European University Institute, Florence.

Considère, S. and Perrin, T. (eds) (2017). *Frontières et représentations sociales. Questions et perspectives méthodologiques*. L'Harmattan, Paris.

Cooper-Richet, D., Mollier, J.-Y., Silem, A. (eds) (2005). *Passeurs culturels dans le monde des médias et de l'édition en Europe (XIXe et XXe siècles)*. Presses de l'ENSSIB, Lyon.

Cottereau, A. (1992). "Esprit public" et capacité de juger : la stabilisation d'un espace public en France aux lendemains de la Révolution. In *Pouvoir et légitimité, figures de l'espace public*, Cottereau, A., Ladrière, P. (eds). Éditions de l'EHESS, Paris.

Cristescu, J. (2003). Coopérations en Europe du Sud-Est. *Le Courrier des pays de l'Est*, 1039(9), 17–30.

De Meur, G., Bursens, P., Gottcheiner, A. (2006). MSDO/MDSO revisited for public policy analysis. In *Innovative Comparative Methods for Policy Analysis*, Rihoux, B., Grimm, H. Springer, Boston.

Delivré, É. (2015). Bâtir une histoire régionale, un pari inédit. L'enseignement de l'histoire dans la région du Trentin-Haut-Adige. *Revue internationale d'éducation de Sèvres*, 69, 115–121.

Dunoyer, C. (2019). "Monde alpin". *Anthropen.org* [Online]. Available at: https://www.anthropen.org/voir/Monde%20alpin [Accessed February 2, 2021].

Ehrhardt, D. (2017). Après l'élargissement des transferts culturels : les Transfer Studies comme renouvellement des études aréales. *Diogène*, 2, 209–220.

Ferraris, M. (2014). *Documentalità. Perché è necessario lasciar tracce*. Laterza, Roma-Bari.

Fofana, H. (2015). "L'espace public" : un concept opératoire en contexte africain ? *Participations*, 12(2), 245–256.

Gaubatz, P. (2019). New China square: Chinese public space in developmental, environmental and social contexts. *Journal of Urban Affairs*, 50(2), 1235–1262.

Giraut, F., Guyot, S., Houssay-Holzschuch, M. (2005). La nature, les territoires et le politique en Afrique du Sud. *Annales. Histoire, Sciences Sociales*, 4, 695–717.

Goirand, C. (2015). Rituels démocratiques et mise en scène de la participation populaire dans les assemblées du budget participatif à Recife (Brésil). *Participations*, 11(1), 53–85.

Goujon, A. (2005). L'Europe élargie en quête d'identité. *Politique européenne*, 15(1), 137–163.

Greimas, A.J. and Courtès, J. (1993). *Sémiotique. Dictionnaire raisonné de la théorie du langage*. Hachette, Paris.

Guyot, S. (2006). Géopolitique des parcs (trans)frontaliers en Afrique australe. Les Cahiers d'Outre-Mer. *Revue de géographie de Bordeaux*, 59(234), 215–232.

Hermand, M.-H. (2014). Le discours eurorégional. Indices convergents de légitimation d'un espace institutionnel. *Mots. Les langages du politique*, 106, 71–85.

Hermand, M.-H. (2020). *Eurorégions. L'éclosion de la communication transfrontalière*. Éditions de l'Université de Bruxelles, Brussels.

Nowicki, J. (2008). La diversité culturelle comme élément d'identité nationale : le cas de l'europe médiane. *Hermès, La revue*, 51, 101–105.

Quéré, L. and Cottereau, A. (2003). Postface. In *Le public en action*, Barril, C., Carrel, M., Guerrero, J.-C., Marquez, A. (eds). L'Harmattan, Paris.

Raoul, B. (2020). *Le territoire à l'épreuve de la communication. Mutations, imaginaires, discours.* Presses Universitaires du Septentrion, Lille.

Rouquette, J. (2017). La stratégie d'un site internet, un exercice nécessaire. In *Site internet : audit et stratégie*, Rouquette, S. (ed.). De Boeck, Brussels.

Stockinger, P. (2005). *Les sites web : description, conception et évaluation.* Hermès-Lavoisier, Paris.

Stockinger, P. (ed.) (2017). Éléments théoriques et méthodologiques pour une expertise de sites web. In *Site internet : audit et stratégie*. De Boeck, Brussels.

Wassenberg, B. (2010). Le voisinage de proximité : les eurorégions "géopolitiques" aux frontières externes de l'UE (1993-2009). *Matériaux pour l'histoire de notre temps*, 97–98(1), 45–49.

Yates, S. and Arbur, M. (2013). L'usage des médias socionumériques par les organismes publics : le cas du Québec. *Communiquer*, 9, 55–76.

10

"Tell Us Your Data", Between Euphemization, Standardization, and Digital Poetics

Camille RONDOT

GRIPIC, Sorbonne Université, Paris, France

10.1. Introduction

This contribution originates from our pedagogical experience in managing an M2 training course named Media and Digital Materials, anchored in the information and communication sciences. It is part of a reflexive approach which seeks to combine teaching experience and research experience by questioning courses given by professionals and the skills targeted in this training. In this chapter, we propose providing a critical perspective on course units that we did not know well before and which questioned us, in particular how they have come to be referred to in English: social data listening or also data storytelling. We intend to develop a reflection on the orientation of professions related to digital technology and innovation as well as on how to deal with market expectations, with the intent to reflect on the professional integration of students at the end of their studies. To accomplish this, this work analyzes both the establishment of a professional rhetoric as well as its semiotization on specialized sites.

In this work, the questioning of what we will refer to here as "new professional skills" dedicated to Web analysis will form part of an exploratory logic. This will

Analyzing Websites,
coordinated by Luc MASSOU, Patrick MPONDO-DICKA and Nathalie PINÈDE.
© ISTE Ltd 2023.

allow us more specifically to highlight the emergence of professional practices that testify to particular representations of the public, and the "traces" they leave on the Web. These expressions refer to tools developed by professionals to show the change as well as the adaptation of companies to problems such as big data. To analyze these issues, we have chosen here to select a single expression of "social data listening" and to study the professional communications produced by participants to justify, sell and build their expertise.

Thus, at the origin of this work, we question the role of discourses and their implementation in dedicated spaces to legitimize a professional posture and inscribe skills in a specific context of innovation related to Web professions. As such, there are several questions that emerge: are these discourses specific to social data listening or are they part of a broader rhetoric? What representations and imaginations of the Web and the public do they use as a basis? At the crossroads of these two questions, the starting point of our reflection is anchored in the analysis of the storytelling carried out in these skill sets. The rhetoric employed, from the very utterance of the expression "social media listening", implies both a personification and a euphemization of strategic processes. Finally, this implies that what is being implemented here is a simple "listening" process, from which it would be possible to create a narrative around the "traces" left by Internet users.

To analyze these tensions and understand the processes of storytelling, we used a two-stage process. For our first step, we have compiled an initial corpus based on the selection of three sites for agencies or consultants stating that they have experience with the issue[1]. This allowed us to identify the existence of a *Livre blanc* written in 2016 named *Social media listening: du bruit au signal. Manifeste pour une refondation des études sur les médias sociaux*[2] ("Social media listening: from noise to signal. A manifesto for a reformation of social media studies") in which we found several of the key figures linked to the sites mentioned above[3]. These figures were also found in the reports of events of a professional association, Social Media Talk, with the organization of several thematic conferences around the issue, in particular:

---

1 We selected the following agencies: The Metrics Factory, which describes itself as "a communication and digital marketing consulting agency with a core of expertise based on the analysis of social data" (site: www.themetricsfactory.com); Opinion Way, which develops expertise in "social media research" (site: www.opinion-way.com/fr/nos-solutions/social-media-research-smr.html); and Research & Web Conseil, whose founder describes herself as a specialist in social data listening (site: www.rwc.fr/agence).

2 Available at: www.visionarymarketing.com/wp-content/uploads/2016/09/v2.pdf.

3 The authors of the publication include the founder of Research & Web Council; the *Livre blanc* can be downloaded from the page cited in note 1 of Opinion Way, and the founder of The Metrics Factory was interviewed in the *Livre blanc*.

"Tous plateformisés #4" Quel avenir pour la social data ? ("Everything is platformed #4" What is the future for social data?) [4] or *Social data : où en est la méthodologie ?* (Social data: where is the methodology?)[5]. In the second step, we proceeded to analyze the articles in French that were included in the first five pages of Google, with the last update of the list made on July 7, 2020.

To analyze these articles, we rely on a semiodiscursive approach for digital devices, utilizing both Roland Barthes' project to propose a semioclasty (Barthes 1957) as well as the work carried out in discourse analysis, in particular those of Krieg-Planque (2009), and more particularly, on the notion of formulas and discursive "freezing". With Roland Barthes, we ask ourselves how the discourses around social data listening are part of a system of signs that can be disassembled. This system connotes to a set of values that are both professional and related to a socio-technical context, which we are seeking to understand in this work. To analyze them, we carried out a semiological analysis of expressions by identifying all the terms associated with the expression social data listening: between lexical fields and context. In addition to this, we also analyzed the illustration images mobilized to see how they came to embody professional skills and postures. With Alice Krieg-Planque, as an underlying goal of this work, we seek to analyze the circulation of the expression social data listening, to observe how, due to its use in several professional spaces on the Web, it has finally become naturalized. Thus, without debate entering the common vocabulary.

At the crossroads of these approaches, between semiology and discourse analysis, this work analyzes a communicational pretension, that is to say, in this case a project aimed at creating a conception of communication, a new profession (Jeanneret 2014). Starting on the basis of Yves Jeanneret's work, in this work, we seek to deconstruct the discourses that surround it in order to see how they construct a euphemized, standardized and poeticized representation of the use of "data" on digital social networks. In our opinion, this is based on issues of triviality and polychresis, as understood by Yves Jeanneret. It involves questioning the social data listening and the rhetoric related to the use of plurality of its meanings and possible

---

4 Available at: www.socialmediaclub.fr/2019/04/24/session-tous-plateformises-4-quel-avenir-pour-l a-social-data/. Presentation of a conference entitled *"Tous plate-formisés, quel avenir pour la social data ?"* where two of the presenters worked for agencies in our corpus: one is a member of The Metrics Factory and the other of Opinion Way.

5 Available   at: www.socialmediaclub.fr/2018/07/02/social-data-ou-en-est-la-methodologie/. Presentation of a conference called *"Social data : où en est la méthodologie"* with two facilitators from the agencies of our corpus: one member of The Metrics Factory and another from Research & Web Opinion.

appropriations as a measuring stick, all of which extends beyond expression in a wider professional field related to communication and innovation on the Web.

To understand the way in which the expression social data listening circulates on the Web and to understand its semiological and discursive specificities, we will proceed in two stages. First, we will analyze "listening to social media" as a semantic-discursive construction in the service of professional expertise. Second, we will show that it is part of a poetics of the visible and the audible, all of which is very much related to the semantic field of listening, which is present in the expression we analyze.

10.2. Epistemological and methodological issues

Social data listening is often reduced in the articles of our corpus to the shortened form: social listening.

Though it is used much less often in the case presented here, it nevertheless constitutes a fundamental semantic tool for explaining the expression. This makes it possible to understand how it constitutes a communicational claim in and of itself (Rondot 2015), which, beyond this claim to act on communication, comes to constitute a foundation to be shared in order to form a posture of professional expertise. This is translated through several semiodiscursive processes. It is translated first through the implementation of an embodied reading of social networks, then by the demonstration of a panoply (Labelle 2007) of skills that have been put in place, and finally by highlighting the value of social data that would be insufficiently utilized within the logic of big data.

The underlying point here is to highlight the way in which the expressions and the documents forming our corpus contribute to defining and founding a form of "discipline". This is in the sense that this involves both the creation of standards related to a profession – in the making – while providing itself with principles – the role of the *Livre blanc* – and its own set of tools.

10.2.1. *Performance, notoriety and visibility: a disruptive discourse*

As is the case for the *Livre blanc*, the articles in our corpus, or the professional websites that we have analyzed, a constant comes up when dealing with social data listening. This relatively new concept (depending on the date of the elements of our corpus, it was created between 2016 and 2020) would constitute an innovative approach, breaking with the field of studies (quantitative and qualitative).

Source	Quote analyzed
Livre blanc *social media listening : du bruit au signal. Manifeste pour une refondation des études sur les médias sociaux*, 2016	"Companies, encouraged in this by the 'pure players' research institutes and the desertion of the subject by the classical institutes, have embarked on a race for technology and quantitative measurements on social media. Committed to this race, they have missed out on the tremendous potential allowed by these types of studies to dialogue with their customers and prospects, to innovate, reinvent their products, and be in touch with the weak signals that are essential for allowing brands to progress".
Website of the Agency RWC	"Research & Web Conseil is an agency with a new approach: we facilitate the integration and deployment of social listening in your existing consumer listening devices".
Opinion Way website	"From now on, we no longer just measure your brand's voice shares on the Web, or thematically classify transcripts".
Digital Intelligence consulting firm, article entitled: "[Interview] Reflections around *social listening* with Laurent Geffroy, Social Data Director of Orange".	"Social listening is no longer a novelty for brands. They have understood the importance of social media, monitoring, and listening for marketing, communication, or commercial purposes. But monitoring on its own is no longer enough. It is necessary to create intelligence, help with decision-making, and promote the implementation of actions. Social data has an important role to play, because it is able to initiate, challenge, or identify opportunities. Especially since social data is the most extensive and information-rich form of external data".

Table 10.1. *Quotes from the corpus showing the need break away*

This innovative and disruptive nature, countering classical studies, is embodied in particular in the deployment of a vocabulary and more particularly in the proposal of an embodied reading of digital social networks, from passive listening to active listening: "In the field, we have observed that the desire to measure everything, out of intellectual naivete or a fear of malicious attacks, has no meaning and does not replace active listening" (Livre blanc, p. 13)[6]. The focus is not so much on the collection of "social data" as it is on the interpretation of this data. In this perspective, the ability of a certain number of experts to know how to set up these tools becomes a decisive criterion in how they are deployed. Moreover, it is a

---

6 The citations extracted from the corpus and presented in the body of our text are presented in italics to differentiate them from research article citations.

testament to the "scientific" nature of this professional methodology; the *Livre blanc* once again presents a serious attitude and questions a professional field:

> We Must Stop this Mad Rush to Produce Results. In a context of collecting a gigantic volume of data, and in an execution of the analysis delivered to the client in record time, methodological vagueness benefits far too often from a very high tolerance and a certain silence. (Livre blanc, p. 28)[7]

By claiming to seek to establish "a refoundation of studies on social media", the *Livre blanc* frames social data listening from a critical perspective, thus claiming to take a step back on a field from which it emanates and on which it depends. This comes in a context where the "data" amassed from the Web are a strategic challenge for many companies.

The first phase of this rhetoric that is deployed allows for a set of players to position themselves, while justifying and legitimizing the expertise deployed around these "new-professional skills". Here, they rely both on technical promises, as the technical solution is fundamental to social data listening, and on an "economy of promise", as was used and analyzed by Vincent Bullich in his article "*Big Data : stratégies industrielles et économie de la promesse*" ("Big Data: industrial strategies and the economy of promise"): "The challenge is therefore to produce communications capable of giving their promoters a position in the public and social space that favors 'mobilization, circulation, and the accumulation of resources' (Joly 2010, p. 205)" (Bullich 2016, p. 11). What gives value to these famous "social data" here is the ability of experts to build a research strategy adapted to the demands of the market and the client concerned.

The use of examples is particularly effective to demonstrate this: whether to justify the interest of the method supported here or to show the aberrant nature of certain studies. Thus, from the second page of the *Livre blanc*, a case presented as the foundation of social media studies is shown and then picked apart in order to reveal its limits, ultimately concluding with the following sentence:

> Since then, studies on social media seem to have settled into a recurring routine that never fully commits to either illusory completeness or picturesque anecdotes that are not particularly interesting. However, great unrealized potential is possible using these

---

7 Available at: www.visionarymarketing.com/wp-content/uploads/2016/09/v2.pdf.

tools, as long as we make sense of their use and interpretation. (Livre blanc, p. 12)[8]

Thus, faced with the multiple studies about digital social networks and the issues raised by "big data", social data listening provides a solution: to enable companies to make effective decisions by bringing into view what would otherwise not be visible.

Citations from the *Livre blanc*, semantic field of vision
This "infobesity" is too often the tree that hides the forest and does not allow innovation to emerge". (p. 5)
"The lack of memory and understanding of the true mechanisms of reputation and the reality behind the fictional stories of the media have resulted in a short-sightedness among brands that have contributed to accumulating bad practices [...]". (p. 11)
"More transparency in our tool kits so that they are not as opaque as the algorithms that make them up". (p. 15)
"Because as a result of striving for exhaustive listening on these grounds, we certainly collect a lot of volume, but we end up creating 'magnifying glass effects' on a small number of contributors". (p. 23)
"At the expense of rewards, in particular through giving visibility to the judgment of these ambassadors, it almost puts them at the level of 'professional experts'". (p. 23)
"However, the amounts of content accessible in each of these categories can be so disproportionate that a single type of content can overwhelm and obscure all the others". (p. 26)

Table 10.2. *Quotes from the Livre blanc social media listening: du bruit au signal. Manifeste pour une refondation des études sur les médias sociaux (2016)[9], semantic field of vision*

Finally, beyond the issues of visibility, the players involved are tasked with providing clarity in two different areas: bringing new things to light while fortifying the rationality of decision-makers to allow them to make the right strategic choices. This discursive scheme is reinforced by the establishment of an authorizing narrative reflected in the *Livre blanc* in which the argumentative and rhetorical dimension is fundamental.

---

8 Available at: www.visionarymarketing.com/wp-content/uploads/2016/09/v2.pdf.

9 Available at: www.visionarymarketing.com/wp-content/uploads/2016/09/v2.pdf.

Citations from the *Livre blanc*, semantic field of vision	Proposed analysis
"When the noise jammed the signal"	This involves starting from an observation while pointing out that there is no satisfactory solution, then explaining that we must be reasonable and abandon the illusion that it would be possible to analyze and collect everything.
"Moving 'from noise to signal"	Next, the actors propose building a new solution by asking the right questions and knowing how to mobilize the right players.
"'Hybridizing' to better understand the world"	Finally, the solution is proposed to "retransform the studies": a hybridization of methods.

Table 10.3. *Analysis of the narrative of the Livre blanc social media listening: du bruit au signal. Manifeste pour une refondation des études sur les médias sociaux (2016)*

From the construction of common references to the deployment of a common rhetoric, the circulation of expression social data listening clearly shows the way in which conceptions of communication, translated into a communicational intent, can lead to – or call for – the creation of professions (Jeanneret 2014).

10.2.2. *Empowered skills: a discourse on the method as a foundational basis*

These discourses do not consist solely of the participants signifying the disruption caused by social data listening. The adoption of this technique also contributes to founding what we have referred to as a discipline with a methodological reflection. Beginning with the foreword of the *Livre blanc*, the authors of the document start from an observation, a problem to be solved:

So, which data, anyway? The opaque nature of the methodologies, both at the level of data collection and their study, does not make the approach very intelligible, nor does it serve the company's interest. We can make the numbers say pretty much whatever we want, but we still have to keep in mind that they are not neutral, and that they are the result of several different filters. And we can't forget that "the raw materials are already transformed data"! (Livre blanc 2016, p. 5)

This discourse on the method is particularly heuristic for the authors to justify and legitimize their approach: they offer an expert look at a professional domain. This expertise takes on multiple features, as described by Roser Cusso and Corrine Gobin about political discourse in an issue of the journal *Mots*, which is dedicated to expert discourses (Cusso and Gobin 2008).

> One of the first characteristics of this register of discourse is that it is produced by organizations that base a good part of their legislation precisely on the capacity of expertise that is attributed to them. Bernard Maris makes a useful distinction in this regard between the scholarly discourse, which maintains its legitimacy through scientific confrontation and debate between peers and the expert discourse which imposes its legitimacy through the special relationship that has been established between these experts, the political powers, and public opinion. (Cusso and Gobin 2008, p. 6)

At the crossroads of these two types of expertise, the discourses used by the drafters of the *Livre blanc* represent a very specific attribution circuit of this expertise. This is done through professional associations such as Social Media Talk, which has organized round tables devoted to questions such as "Social data: where is the methodology?", and has made use of a technical discourse borrowing from the scholarly discourse. Though there is no question for the actors to claim to be scientific, which would be more in the register of research, the links with the latter are discussed: "It is a question of finding more synergies with the research" (Livre blanc 2016, expert opinion, p. 33). The second trait described by the authors regarding expertise is a relative neutrality: "The strength of this expert discourse is indeed that it gives itself the appearance of a simple correspondence to the proper state of affairs" (Cusso and Gobin 2008, p. 7). In this case, the program put forward by the participants is to regain a form of neutrality in the studies by overhauling a set of methodologies and by being more "transparent" about the underlying biases and issues. The last two features discussed are more related to the semantic field deployed to build the field of expertise, using catchall words and a certain standardization of the discourse.

What is at stake here with the implementation of a professional expertise strategy involves legitimizing a posture and the formation of a common professional culture. In this context, discursive and semantic choices take on their full meaning and constitute a fundamental rhetorical matrix around three types of processes: the use of oppositional pairs to determine a decisive and motivating project (moving from passive listening to active listening), the mobilization of a specific vocabulary leading to "measuring noise" or "listening to the signal", which will ultimately intervene within the communications by "listening to whispers" while having the ability to "minimize interference".

This rhetoric of professional expertise is also based on the presentation of a panoply[10], centered around a core of technical tools. In this way, social data listening is presented as a tool that should be implemented, thus giving it a fundamental technical dimension[11]. Some articles have even sought to help their readers find the most effective software tools currently available: "*Social listening : explication, importance et dix exemples d'outils*" (Newberry 2019) ("Social listening: explanation, why it is important, and ten examples of software tools") and "*Social Listening: Outils et bonnes pratiques pour vous lancer* (Valat 2020)" ("Social Listening: software tools and best practices to get you started"). In this way, beyond the methodological tools (the type of study to be deployed), the choice is also at the level of the technical solutions developed. These tools are also linked to companies that monetize these technical solutions and bring them into a competitive logic. In this way, in an article from *Siècle Digital* entitled "*Quel avenir pour le social listening ?*" ("What is the future for social listening?") (Charbit 2019), we learn that the year 2018 would be a year of "profound changes" with a series of buyouts[12].

Therefore, the frequent use of the terms software or IT tools, and therefore the promotion of the technical dimension of these "new professional skills", operates in two ways: on the one hand, it neutralizes a set of issues (it is no longer a question of "making the right choice" among a panel of tools), while on the other hand, resorting to one solution or another means adopting an approach led by a company or a conglomerate of companies. With this idea in mind, several articles in our corpus advocate for solutions filed in a competitive system primarily centered around selling one specific product rather than another (Rochand 2018), revealing forms of de-publicization (Patrin-Leclère et al. 2014). In this case, the rankings are

---

10 Here, we borrow the expression from Sarah Labelle (2007, p. 21): "The term 'panoply' appears interesting in several respects. Etymologically, a 'panoplia' refers to all weapons given to the infantrymen who go into battle. This qualification makes it possible to highlight a series of devices that are both heterogeneous and convergent".

11 In our corpus of articles, we have identified about a hundred occurrences of this term.

12 "In 2018, Social Listening entered a new phase, concentrating the market even more. Several of the players have changed their ownership status: Mention was bought by the Swedish firm Mynewdesk, Talkwalker came under the control of American owners, and Synthesio joined Ipsos. Two important mergers can be noted: Meltwater and Sysomos that joined forces, and in particular Crimson, which joined Brandwatch. Finally, Cision purchased Falcon.io, and Linkfluence scoop.it in Charbit, J. (January 22, 2019). Quel avenir pour le Social Listening ?. *Siècle digital* [Online]. Available at: www.siecledigital.fr/2019/01/22/quel-avenir-pour-le-social-listening/ [Accessed on July 7, 2020].

intended to negate that the nature of these contributions is fundamentally related to advertising and marketing. At the center point between discourses, the panoply is thus both proof of the mastery of an expertise while being at the crossroads of economic issues.

10.2.3. *From social data to consumer knowledge: information rhetoric*

This panoply originates from a necessity: the need to know how to locate, collect and exploit data. Thus, we find this term at the core of the professional rhetoric on social data listening, which comes to describe the material to be exploited but also a potential source of wealth, if we know how to use it properly. An analysis of the various documents in our corpus has allowed us to see the frequent use of the term (approximately 30 occurrences for our entire corpus of articles, and about 50 for the *Livre blanc*).

Source	Quotes extracted from the corpus of articles from the Web
Newberry, C. (July 11, 2019). Social Listening: explanation, importance and 10 examples of tools. *Hootsuite Blog.*	Brandwatch allows you to monitor the tone and impact of a conversation from among 95 million data sources.
Netino (September 8, 2019). 6 conseils pour mieux exploiter votre social data. *Netino.*	Speaking of Twitter, monthly number of active users: 336 million.
Valat, P. (March 10, 2020). Social Listening : Outils et bonnes pratiques pour vous lancer. *Meltwater.*	In practice, social listening allows users to listen to a much broader panel than consumer meetings will ever be able to match, by surveying databases of several million people which are constantly growing.
	Chinese social media has an ocean of data to offer marketers.

Table 10.4. *Examples of demonstrating the amount of social "data" accessible because of social data listening*

Described as the origin of social data listening, it is sometimes referred to as "social", later using the term "social data" because as it is derived from social networks. This qualifier gives new life to these data, and voices an intent. According to this idea, everything that is produced by the users of social networks should be determined by a specific character: its sociability. Thus, as we will see in the next part, the exploitation of these data and the related professional skills go hand in hand with their own message, one that proposes "listening to conversations" and "measuring feelings", all from an economic and strategic perspective.

To do this, the actors deploy their panoply around issues that echo the images of the Web, from the same perspective as those deployed within the context of the processing and collection of big data. Indeed, what is highlighted here is not the creation of "social data", it is how accessible they are: social data listening is the solution for access "millions of data points". These data are often characterized by their volume (see section 10.3).

10.3. A poetics of the visible and the audible

To talk about the poetics of the visible and the audible requires questioning the creative dimension of communication and its forms. In this second section, we will primarily seek to analyze how social data listening is embodied in semiotic and discursive forms anchored in a very particular rhetoric which was given a preliminary outline in the first section of this chapter. If the raw material processed and constructed by the actors is data, here it is put forward as "social data", which are itself derived from the analysis of online "conversations". As we have noted in our investigations, the experts in social data listening wish to encourage people to hold conversations that they would consider to be ordinary, thus revealing a rhetorical connection between the visible and invisible. This is carried out in several ways, which we will address in this section. First of all, for the participants, it is an action of revealing the visible, that is to say, to propose an exploitation of "social data" that is already present on digital social networks, but is rarely exploited or not exploited enough, due to a lack of suitable methodologies. As we will see here, if the rhetoric used is based on a euphemization of messages, leading people to talk about their feelings and conversations, it is also fundamentally rooted in a logic of surveillance that appears as totally naturalized, or even neutralized.

10.3.1. Revealing the visible and making ordinary conversations speak

In the discourse of professionals on social data listening, the term "conversation" is ubiquitous. They propose implementing tools for listening to conversations on digital social networks. This use of the conversation model is not new and has been analyzed in particular in an issue of the journal *Communication & Langages* entitled "La communication revisitée par la conversation" ("Communication revisited by conversation") directed by Valérie Patrin-Leclère in 2011. With Caroline Marti

(De Montety), the journal highlights the promises of such a vocabulary in the field of communication, and more particularly, in marketing:

> Behind this reactivation of the original model of non-mediated exchange between individuals is the promise of a "natural" communication: the conversation acts as a return to the sources of human exchange, definitively replacing the distorted, artificial, and surprisingly archaic communication strategies developed "before" today. Conversations have existed throughout human history, but this is a complete conversion: the conversation is now a communication freed from strategy, washed clean of the idea of professional instrumentation and instrumentalization, and purified of the suspicion of manipulation. The novelty lies in this idealized return to early communication: when a "communication" was neither conceived nor thought out; when communicating was as natural as breathing. (De Montety and Patrin-Leclère 2011)

We highlighted this rhetoric of methodological rupture in the first section of this chapter in which there is indeed a before and an after, in which a conversion to a more "social" approach to communication processes, and here more particularly to data, is initiated. This is reflected through the implementation of a humanized and oral vocabulary of "data", which is above all written (see Table 10.5): it is not a question of producing a reading but of listening to what is being said, of identifying murmurs and even of being able or refusing to interfere in a conversation. Through this vocabulary converted to oral form, the emerging idea is that it is possible to identify "natural conversations".

This rhetoric of orality and authenticity translated through the use of the term conversation (social or natural) mobilizes imaginaries suggesting that writings on digital social networks allow brands and companies to enter the intimacy of users – potential customers – to have access to what they think. In this scheme, the use of a vocabulary related to orality denotes above all a negation of the scriptural materiality of the devices, and brings us back to the imaginaries and promises of digital social networks: places where everyone expresses themselves, free from any influence – be it social or technosemiotic. And if each digital social network can be accurately examined to identify its assets, and most importantly the potentially accessible "mass of data", the editorial constraints and the frameworks of digital expression are neutralized.

Source
Quotes extracted from the corpus of articles from the Web

Website of Opinion Way, on the page entitled "Social Media Intelligence"	Opinion Way identifies the natural conversations that take place on the Web about your brand and your products and services.
Website of The Metrics Factory, from the page "Data for action"	Audience Profiling. Create a detailed portrait of your audiences to target them better.
Website of Research & Web Conseil	After several years in different agencies, she joined Linkfluence in 2010 where she deals with strategies for listening to social Web conversations for large international groups.
Corpus of articles from the Web	
Brandwatch. (May 15, 2017). 10 applications pratiques du social listening. *Emarketing.fr*	Social data can help you identify conversations about your product categories and specific products.
	Social listening allows you to identify these opportunities for you to take part in the conversation.
Newberry, C. (July 11, 2019). Social Listening: explanation, importance and 10 examples of tools. *Hootsuite Blog*	Social listening is a listening activity: you will be able to follow, analyze and respond to conversations about your brand and your company directly online.
	The university also uses social listening to discover relevant conversations.
	Very often, interrupting a conversation and trying to sell a product is not a wise choice.
	Brandwatch allows you to monitor the tone and impact of a conversation from among 95 million data sources. You will be able to receive email alerts so that you know when an important conversation is taking place.
Valat, P. (March 10, 2020). Social Listening : Outils et bonnes pratiques pour vous lancer. *Meltwater*	They are established from the observation and analysis of social conversations about a brand, a need or a problem.
	"Like figures, conversations can be processed and analyzed to be able to obtain insights and anticipate buying intentions and recommendations".

Table 10.5. *Examples of quotations from the corpus including the term "conversation"*

Beyond listening to conversations and knowing how to use and take advantage of them to arrive at strategic decisions, the discourses we have analyzed seek to go beyond the representations related to the analysis of the big data:

On the contrary, social data listening is no longer concerned with numbers, but instead analyzes the feelings behind the publications on social networks. It's no longer just about listing the number of times your brand is mentioned: social listening allows you to understand what people may feel and think about you and your competitors. (Newberry 2017)

Rejecting quantitative and numerical elements feeds the communicational pretension that we have identified through the expression social data listening: between the metaphor of listening and the identification of feelings, the discourses we have analyzed are based on an opposition between quantitative studies and qualitative studies. In doing so, they put forward the issue of affect at the heart of their approach, echoing a set of professional proposals/means of deployment, such as "emotional marketing".

Resorting to the semantic field of emotion when it comes to identifying what consumers – or potential consumers – think about a brand or an enterprise also puts aside a reflection in terms of opinion or reputation. And if, as Camille Alloing notes, referring to the work of Nicole D'Almeida, "in the field of information and communication sciences, reputation is presented as a phenomenon that interrogates in equal measure the question of the visibility of an entity (to be seen) and the judgments that result from or allow this visibility (to be judged)" (Alloing 2016, p. 6), the placement of listening to feelings instead serves as a particularly efficient euphemization process in terms of masking the underlying issues.

10.3.2. Revealing what is visible through surveillance: between euphemized discourse and the desire to create a panopticon

At the heart of these discourses, a series of power-related issues emerge in a more or less visible way, often euphemistically. There are a multitude of these issues, yet they are reflected particularly in the frequent use of several expressions whose operativeness is singular in this case: here, a neutralization and smoothing-over of speeches is being carried out. The processes involved echo the work done by Alice Krieg-Planque on the concept of the "formula", first about the formula of "ethnic purification" and then in particular that of "sustainable development"[13]. We utilize these works within the framework of a semiodiscursive approach to discourses, which at their core consider the issues related to the circulation of discourses, and here more particularly expression *social data listening*. In addition to following its circulation – which we have done earlier – this last section of our chapter seeks to examine the semantic and semiotic ecosystem of expressions, and its effects of connotation. Indeed, the term listening, beyond allowing a form of visualization of massive data corpora while echoing the "qualitative" dimension of studies associated with other expressions, can lead to the reversal of the analysis. Through an association with the terms of surveillance and weak signals, which are found recurrently in all the documents in our corpus, "social media listening" thus takes on a negative connotation, connected with the imaginary of intelligence operations. The concept thus ceases to be about "entering into a conversation" with potential customers or actual customers, instead having to do with "spying" on them, or rather observing them without their knowledge.

> *Companies, encouraged in this by the "pure players" research institutes and the desertion of the subject by the classical institutes, have embarked on a race for technology and quantitative measurements on social media. Committed to this race, they have missed out on the tremendous potential allowed by these types of studies to dialogue with their customers and prospects, to innovate, reinvent their products, and be in touch with the weak signals that are essential for allowing brands to progress.*

Figure 10.1. *Translated quote from the cover of the Livre blanc social media listening: du bruit au signal. Manifeste pour une refondation des études sur les médias sociaux (2016). See: www.visionarymarketing.com/wp-content/uploads/2016/09/v2.pdf [Accessed June 8, 2020]*

From the first page of the *Livre blanc*, the semantic field of intelligence is made presented through the use of an expression: "weak signals". Though this might seem trivial, Camille Alloing and Nicolas Moinet show that it is quite the opposite:

> As Bilel Benbouzid (2016) notes about Predpol: "the marketing techniques used reduce discussions to persuasion". The myth of the weak signal would then seems to be soluble within the new conventions concerning predictive algorithms. These conventions associate both the self-fulfilling nature of certain approaches in

---

13 In other words, a set of formulations which, because of their use at a given moment and in a given public space, crystallize political and social issues that these expressions at the same time help to build (Krieg-Planque 2009, p. 7).

foresight, the sometimes well-entrenched practices of governance through statistics, and the often prophetic discourses of the dominant actors of the Web. (Alloing and Moinet 2016)

In addition to its reference to espionage, the expression "weak signals" also echoes the theoretical schemes of communications which could be described reductively as seeking to identify signals passing through channels. Moreover, the *Livre blanc* indicates that one of the issues of social data listening is to "go from noise to signal" (2016, p. 15)[14]. In this idea, the signal, considered as a physical quantity to be measured, is reduced to its technical dimension while at the same time seeking to identify a way to measure it and ultimately to translate it, so as to obtain potentially strategic information. The technicalization of discourses once again denies its mediatized component, or at least reduces it to a discourse of specialists for specialists.

> However, these tools have been designed to meet the needs of the monitoring of subjects in current events. Their credo is to allow you to monitor subjects and brands in real time. And they quietly participate in the overvaluing of this content produced instantaneously. They are therefore not software tools designed and customized to respond to questions from marketing studies.

Figure 10.2. *Page 16 (translated) from Livre blanc social media listening: du bruit au signal. Manifeste pour une refondation des études sur les médias sociaux (2016). See: www.visionarymarketing.com/wp-content/uploads/2016/09/v2.pdf [Accessed June 8, 2020]. For a color version of this figure, see www.iste.co.uk/massou/analyzing. zip*

Therefore, the use of the expression "weak signals" invokes a mixture of different contexts: that of intelligence, and that of the technical abilities necessary to "decipher the information". In this rhetoric of the visible and the readable, the skills related to social data listening become essential, also bearing witness to the fact that the collection and identification of the elements in question is not obvious. Reducing the collection of information to that of "weak signals" also helps to sidestep a number of ethical or legal issues, which, although they appear in some articles in our

---

14 Available at: www.visionarymarketing.com/wp-content/uploads/2016/09/v2.pdf.

corpus, are not predominant. In this perspective, the interconnection between conversational rhetoric and the analysis of "weak signals" reveals the existence of dissonances within the discourses that are analyzed; while this is not the case we limit ourselves to a type of discourse in a text unit such as an article, it is true in the sum of the elements of our corpus. A poetics of figures works in the service of neutralizing the collected data and the collection processes, not by concealing the prefabricated nature of the operations, but by subordinating it to the role of expertise, and therefore to a group of insiders.

Additionally, after informing us not to miss the "weak signals", the *Livre blanc* also calls on us to respond to the "monitoring needs" of professionals. Here too, surveillance is based on a process of euphemization: it is not individuals who are being monitored, but subjects. The dimensions of control and authority, which are fundamentally associated with the concept of surveillance, are thus set aside because they are diluted in the non-direct nature of the surveillance process.

In this idea, it is interesting to see that if social data listening promises direct access to "masses of data", because of listening to devices often presented in the form of lists, the listening is never that of individuals – it is always that of conversations, trendy topics, or in the end, the digital social networks themselves. And if digital social networks here constitute a way of reaching ways of making society through community imaginaries, they form representations of the world reduced to its simplest device: individuals conversing in a natural way in a form of digital public space. In this perspective, there is a truly panoptic dimension in the proposed device, in the Foucaultian sense of the term: digital social networks come to constitute a global place of discipline, where everything can be seen by those who know how to see the right way. Or, to apply it to our present case: where everything can be heard for those who know how to listen the right way.

This conception is totally opposed to the euphemized and naturalized character of the term surveillance, the use of which does not seem to pose any issue, setting aside the question of the authority of the device, and finally echoing issues which are much more general than social data listening.

Thus, the analyzed discourses lead us to question the intersection of a set of power issues both specific to the Web, specific to digital social networks, or even specific to the formation of "new professional skills". They cause the poetics of figures to intersect, which are now narrated and no longer simply calculated through statistical logic, euphemization of speeches, and standardization. This places us at a crossroads of multiple issues: legitimization processes – related to professional issues – the establishment of self-fulfilling discourses, and also the construction of markets. Indeed, what is at play here is also linked to a competitive logic: the articles we have analyzed and the players we have identified do not all use the same technical solutions, which form a software market parallel to the market for talent.

10.4. Conclusion

The analysis of speeches and the signification of the expression social data listening have allowed us to highlight the way in which a legitimizing professional rhetoric is established. This is based on a series of semantic and discursive markers that can be found both on the sites of professionals claiming these types of skills and on specialized sites that address the subject. Behind this expression, we have identified the existence and implementation of a true promise: to "tell the data" of Internet users so that they can be given usability, and ultimately value. These discourses occur within an economic ecosystem that has been claimed between professional associations, agency websites, professional websites or blogs.

If the strategic dimension of the exploitation of these data is not denied, the discourses related to them act as a euphemization of a series of issues through the use of a very specific vocabulary. It involves "listening to conversations" considered to be "ordinary", in order to then turn them into decision-making tools. In this context, the euphemization is based on the negation of connotations related to surveillance issues in particular. Also, the strong mobilization of "numerical data" makes these courses based on a poetics of the figure, without hiding the prefabricated nature of the use of these data but instead by further reducing these elements as under the control of the expertise of the professionals who take part.

Indeed, at the heart of this contribution is the analysis of the constitution of a professional expertise, with the underlying issues of professionalization and institutionalization of specific functions, such as the "social data expert".

More broadly, at the heart of the emergence of these discourses is a form of "industrialization of meaning" (Sire 2018) anchored in an "economy of promises" (Bullich 2016). Social data listening as a communicational claim is intended to act on communication by giving access to "millions of data" which we do not know how to use, backed by a promise of value, that of making the right strategic choices to work for the good economic health of brands and companies together. The expression thus goes beyond a field of talents to echo the current problems related to the analysis of the Web and the data produced.

If this contribution opens up a set of perspectives, it is in particular because it presents a number of limitations that could be investigated in the context of further research. First, as the choice of the corpus is non-exhaustive, it cannot be considered representative of all the discourses around the syntax questioned here. What guided us in our choice was the discovery of a series of linkages between actors, and in particular a professional association.

Our corpus thus represents an iterative research process which is itself based on a form of storytelling, made readable and visible in this section. Therefore, originating from pedagogical interactions and the meetings held between a series of figures specializing in these issues – whether through student internships or courses – we approached the issue through the lens of professionalization. We started from the observation of the development and deployment of a set of new professional skills that future digital communication professionals could and should be able to master.

In addition, our work was carried out within the context of France and French speakers. In the same way, the rhetoric analyzed here around this syntax could benefit from being compared with other related current phrases such as "data storytelling" or other older ones which also fit into a context of laying claiming to something novel. As such, the prominent nature of the *Livre blanc* is not specific to this syntax or to skills related to the Web and innovation: it is also omnipresent in marketing and communication. The use of other Livre blancs would thus make it possible to integrate and specify the rhetoric analyzed here.

This work could also benefit from being extended through introducing other works along the same lines, as well as by using other methodological approaches which are complementary to those of semiodiscursive analysis. First, it could be compared with other research works in the same perspective. This brings to mind the doctoral research of Jérémy Lucas Boursier, who examines the discourses of communication agencies. In an article published in 2019, he proposes to see "design thinking" as a "discursive motive for a singular professional legitimation" (Lucas-Boursier 2019). In addition, it could also be the subject of a field study, as carried out by Olivia Foli, Sophie Corbillé and Julien Tassel on the use of digital tools by recruiters (Corbillé et al. 2018). From the first perspective, this would be a question of seeing if the standardization and euphemization of discourses identified here are specific to our object, or if it is more transversal. In the second perspective, this time it would be a question of seeing whether and how the participants concerned make use of these "new professional methodologies" to build their activity and their professional identities. There are many different avenues that show it is necessary to deploy a field of Web analysis in a longer perspective to fully understand its evolutions and possible transformations.

10.5. References

Alloing, C. (2016). La fabrique des réputations selon google. *Communication & langages*, 188, 101–122.

Alloing, C. and Moinet, N. (2016). Les signaux faibles : du mythe à la mystification. *Hermès, La Revue*, 76(3), 86–92.

Barthes, R. (1957). *Mythologies*. Le Seuil, Paris.

Bullich, V. (2016). Big Data : stratégies industrielles et économie de la promesse. In *La comunicazione multipla. Media, piattaforme digitali, Over the Top, Big Data*, Pilati, A. (ed.). Magna Carta Edizioni, Rome.

Bullich, V. and Clavier, V. (2018). Production des données, "production de la société". Les big data et algorithmes au regard des sciences de l'information et de la communication. *Les Enjeux de l'information et de la communication*, 19/2.

Charbit, J. (2019). Quel avenir pour le Social Listening ? *Siècle digital* [Online]. Available at: www.siecledigital.fr/2019/01/22/quel-avenir-pour-le-social-listening/ [Accessed 6 December 2022].

Corbillé, S., Foli, O., Tassel, J. (2018). Ce que les recruteurs font des outils numériques : pratiques, enjeux et paradoxes. *Communication & Organisation*, 53, 19–38.

Cussó, R. and Gobin, C. (2008). Du discours politique au discours expert : le changement politique mis hors débat ? *Mots. Les langages du politique*, 88, 5–11.

De Montety, C. and Patrin-Leclère, V. (2011). La conversion à la conversation : le succès d'un succédané. *Communication & langages*, 169(3), 23–37.

Jeanneret, Y. (2014). *Critique de la trivialité*. Éditions Non Standard, Paris.

Krieg-Planque, A. (2009). *La notion de "formule" en analyse du discours. Cadre théorique et méthodologique*. Presses Universitaires de Franche-Comté, Besançon.

Labelle, S. (2007). La ville inscrite dans "la société de l'information" : formes d'investissement d'un objet symbolique. PhD Thesis, Université Paris 4, Paris.

Lucas-Boursier, J. (2019). Le design thinking, motif discursif d'une légitimation professionnelle singulière. *Design et fonction communication*, 8.

Newberry, C. (2019). Social Listening: Explanation, importance, and 10 examples of tools. *Hootsuite Blog* [Online]. Available at: www.blog.hootsuite.com/fr/social-listening/ [Accessed July 7, 2020].

Patrin-Leclère, V., Marti de Montety, C., Berthelot-Guiet, K. (2014). *La fin de la publicité ? Tours et contours de la dépublicitarisation*. Le Bord de l'eau, Lormont.

Rochand, A. (2018). State of the art of Social Listening with Albane Flamant (Talkwalker). *Social media Opatimization* [Online]. Available at: www.socialmediaoptimization.en/state-of-the-art-of-social-listening-with-albane-flamant-talkwalker/ [Accessed on June 8, 2020].

Rondot, C. (2015). Représenter et incarner une organisation internationale : analyse d'une pratique communicationnelle sur le site de l'UNESCO. PhD Thesis, Université Paris 4, Paris.

Sire, G. (2018). Web Sémantique : les politiques du sens et la rhétorique des données. *Les Enjeux de l'information et de la communication*, 19(2), 147–160.

Valat, P. (2020). Social Listening : outils et bonnes pratiques pour vous lancer. *Meltwater* [Online]. Available at: www.meltwater.com/fr/blog/guide-social-listening [Accessed July 7, 2020].

List of Authors

Camille ALLOING
LabFluens
Université du Québec à Montréal
Montreal
Canada

Christine BARATS
CERLIS
Université Paris Descartes
France

Julia BONACCORSI
ELICO
Université Lumière Lyon 2
France

Pergia GKOUSKOU
GRIPIC
Université Clermont Auvergne
Vichy
France

Marie-Hélène HERMAND
MICA
Université Bordeaux Montaigne
Pessac
France

Luc MASSOU
CREM
Université de Lorraine
Metz
France

Patrick MPONDO-DICKA
LERASS
Université Toulouse – Jean Jaurès
France

Nicole PIGNIER
EHIC
Université de Limoges
France

Nathalie PINÈDE
MICA
Université Bordeaux Montaigne
Pessac
France

Camille RONDOT
GRIPIC
Sorbonne Université
Paris
France

Sébastien ROUQUETTE
Communication et Sociétés
Université Clermont Auvergne
Clermont-Ferrand
France

Alexandra SAEMMER
CEMTI
Université Paris 8 Vincennes-Saint-Denis
France

Justine SIMON
ELLIADD
Université de Franche-Comté
Besançon
France

Nolwenn TRÉHONDART
CREM
Université de Lorraine
Metz
France

Index

Printed and bound by CPI Group (UK) Ltd, Croydon, CR0 4YY

27/10/2024

14580248-0002